THE COMPLETE IDIOT'S GUIDE® TO

D0472878

Vegan Baking

by Donna Diegel

ALPHA

A member of Penguin Group (USA) Inc.

To God be the glory, great things He has done.

ALPHA BOOKS

Published by the Penguin Group

Penguin Group (USA) Inc., 375 Hudson Street, New York, New York 10014, USA

Penguin Group (Canada), 90 Eglinton Avenue East, Suite 700, Toronto, Ontario M4P 2Y3, Canada (a division of Pearson Penguin Canada Inc.)

Penguin Books Ltd., 80 Strand, London WC2R 0RL, England

Penguin Ireland, 25 St. Stephen's Green, Dublin 2, Ireland (a division of Penguin Books Ltd.)

Penguin Group (Australia), 250 Camberwell Road, Camberwell, Victoria 3124, Australia (a division of Pearson Australia Group Pty. Ltd.)

Penguin Books India Pvt. Ltd., 11 Community Centre, Panchsheel Park, New Delhi—110 017, India

Penguin Group (NZ), 67 Apollo Drive, Rosedale, North Shore, Auckland 1311, New Zealand (a division of Pearson New Zealand Ltd.)

Penguin Books (South Africa) (Pty.) Ltd., 24 Sturdee Avenue, Rosebank, Johannesburg 2196, South Africa

Penguin Books Ltd., Registered Offices: 80 Strand, London WC2R 0RL, England

Copyright © 2011 by Donna Diegel

International Standard Book Number: 978-1-61564-057-7
Library of Congress Catalog Card Number: 2010913761

13   12   11   8   7   6   5   4   3   2   1

Interpretation of the printing code: The rightmost number of the first series of numbers is the year of the book's printing; the rightmost number of the second series of numbers is the number of the book's printing. For example, a printing code of 11-1 shows that the first printing occurred in 2011.

Printed in the United States of America

Note: This publication contains the opinions and ideas of its author. It is intended to provide helpful and informative material on the subject matter covered. It is sold with the understanding that the author and publisher are not engaged in rendering professional services in the book. If the reader requires personal assistance or advice, a competent professional should be consulted.

The author and publisher specifically disclaim any responsibility for any liability, loss, or risk, personal or otherwise, which is incurred as a consequence, directly or indirectly, of the use and application of any of the contents of this book.

Most Alpha books are available at special quantity discounts for bulk purchases for sales promotions, premiums, fund-raising, or educational use. Special books, or book excerpts, can also be created to fit specific needs.

For details, write: Special Markets, Alpha Books, 375 Hudson Street, New York, NY 10014.

Publisher: *Marie Butler-Knight*
Associate Publisher: *Mike Sanders*
Senior Managing Editor: *Billy Fields*
Senior Acquisitions Editor: *Paul Dinas*
Senior Development Editor: *Christy Wagner*
Production Editor: *Kayla Dugger*

Copy Editor: *Emily Garner*
Cover Designer: *Kurt Owens*
Book Designers: *William Thomas, Rebecca Batchelor*
Indexer: *Angie Bess Martin*
Layout: *Ayanna Lacey*
Proofreader: *Laura Caddell*

Contents

Introduction

Maybe you're new to the vegan lifestyle and are searching for ways to veganize your favorite baked goods you've been missing out on. Or are you an accomplished baker looking to add healthful recipes to your collection? Whatever your reason for wanting to dive into vegan baking, you've come to the right place!

This book contains something for everyone. Muffins, cakes, cupcakes, pies, crisps, buckles, quick breads, yeast breads, and so much more, I've included over 150 recipes for you to try—all 100 percent vegan, all 100 percent delicious!

If you're just starting out on your vegan journey, you might have to change your modus operandi a bit. One thing is constant in vegan eating: no animal products or by-products should cross your lips. This also goes for honey and any food products produced with animal products. Don't worry though; it's not difficult, just a different way of doing things.

Once you get the hang of using alternative ingredients and baking vegan, you'll soon be a baking wiz, whipping up gourmet cupcakes and ultra-creamy cheesecakes. Your family and friends will be amazed they're all vegan!

You *can* have your vegan cake, and eat—and most importantly, *enjoy*—it, too! *Bon appétit!*

How to Use This Book

Each of the six parts in this book digs deep into specific areas of delicious vegan desserts and baked goods, with plenty of tips, ideas, and recipes for new or experienced vegan bakers.

Part 1, Vegan Baking Made Delicious, answers the question, "Why vegan baking?" I explain how vegan baking is different from "regular" baking, and what you need to make the most delicious vegan baked goods. I also discuss a few special tips and techniques, gizmos, and gadgets that will help make your time in your vegan kitchen a little easier and enjoyable. You also learn how to veganize your favorite recipes with easy substitutes.

Part 2, Muffins, Coffee Cakes, and Pastries, starts off with muffins, muffins, and more muffins. With so many muffin choices and variations, you'll be busy for weeks trying them all. Buckles and coffee cakes follow with not only the traditional offerings, but unique recipes as well. Try the Chocolate-Chip and Coffee Coffee Cake, or the Cherry Carob Coffee Cake for those of you who can't have chocolate. And of course, they're all vegan. Who doesn't love breakfast pastries? I've included a selection of easy-to-make Danish, scones, and turnovers, too!

Part 3, Breads, Rolls, and Flatbreads, opens the bakery doors to the wonderful world of quick breads, yeast breads, rolls and sticky buns, flatbreads, and crackers. First up are quick breads, including everyone's favorites—Banana Nut Bread and Gingerbread. Yeast breads are next, with a short primer to help you choose the best yeast to use and instructions on how to use it, with another quick chat on hand-kneading yeast bread versus kneading dough with a mixer. Next, we go on to the sweet bread portion of the book with ooey, gooey Maple Sticky Buns and Cinnamon Rolls. Finally, we get to flatbread and cracker recipes, focaccia, homemade pita pockets, and pizza dough.

Part 4, Cookies, Brownies, and Bars, features every kid's dream—cookies! Whether you're a vegan or not, one taste of these cookies, and you'll be back for more. Classic Chocolate-Chip Cookies, Snickerdoodles, or Oatmeal Raisin Cookies—each one will bring out your inner child. With specialty cookies for holiday platters and vegan Crispy Rice Treats with peanut butter, no matter how old you are—8 or 80—getting caught with your hand in the cookie jar never felt so good! Fudgy brownies and fruit bars are next, with yummy vegan handheld treats just right for sharing. Mmmmm … pass the plate!

Part 5, Classic Pies and Desserts, begins by showing you how to make and roll a perfect Flaky Piecrust for a variety of awesome pies. I explain in detail how to make crusts, including fluting, lattice piecrusts, and double-crusted pies. Fruit and nut pie recipes follow, along with rustic free-form tarts, with directions for freezing baked and unbaked pies. The classic dessert section tempts you with luscious fruit cobblers and crisps, a variety of vegan bread puddings, brown Betties, and clafoutis.

Part 6, Cakes and Cupcakes, is perhaps the sweetest part of the book, with vegan recipes for chocolate, vanilla, carrot, coconut, and spice cakes—and the yummiest vegan frostings to top your masterpieces! These chapters will prove to you that vegan baked goods really do taste terrific! And if that's not enough to tempt you, I include the creamiest, best-tasting "cheesecakes" this side of vegan heaven!

And last, but certainly not least, I've included a glossary of terms and further resources at the back of the book to make your adventure into vegan baking a little easier.

Extras

Sprinkled throughout *The Complete Idiot's Guide to Vegan Baking*, you'll see little sidebars full of important information, tasty tips, vegan definitions, and potential pitfalls you might want to know before you put on your apron. Familiarize yourself with these sidebars—they'll help you navigate these delicious pages:

VEGAN VOCAB

These sidebars explain vegan and nonvegan baking terms you might not be familiar with.

BATTER UP!

Check these sidebars for interesting information about a recipe, ingredients, or just fun trivia.

BAKER'S BONUS

You'll find time- and money-saving tips and tricks for vegan baking in these sidebars.

DOUGH-NOTS

These sidebars alert you to possible baking boo-boos or common mistakes you'll want to avoid.

Acknowledgments

No book would be complete without a note of thanks to all those who helped along the way. My appreciation goes to Allen O'Shea Literary Agency's Marilyn Allen who had faith in me and e-mailed me with a brilliant idea; to Senior Acquisitions Editor Paul Dinas, who oozed patience beyond measure; and to Senior Development Editor Christy Wagner, who put the book in good order and oohed and aahed over all my photos.

I'd also like to thank my husband and best friend, John, for sticking with me through this project, during the late nights baking and writing; and for tasting all my successes and failures throughout our many years together. They've all been worth it babe!

My son, Brad, gets special kudos, as he baked every recipe I threw at him during the writing of this book. Thanks, dude, you did a great job!

To the rest of my family, Kerri, Erika, and John, for their love and support—diving cold turkey into a vegan lifestyle years ago. We always said, "a family that bakes together, stays together." Thanks to my mother-in-law, and my late Mom and Grandma, who each had their own culinary specialties and taught me how to cook and bake. Thanks to all my guinea pig friends who tried all my recipes—now you have to buy them!

And finally, heartfelt thanks to my Dad, who—since I was 6 years old, has done everything from licking the mixing bowl and eating everything, good or bad, that came out of the tiny pink Easy-Bake Oven, to tirelessly washing all the pots and pans at the bakery, to being my present day vegan taste-tester—has been my hero.

Special Thanks to the Technical Reviewer

The Complete Idiot's Guide to Vegan Baking was reviewed by an expert who double-checked the accuracy of what you'll learn here, to help us ensure that this book gives you everything you need to know about baking delicious vegan breads, cakes, cookies, and more. Special thanks are extended to Leslie Bilderback, CMB.

A Certified Master Baker and culinary instructor, Chef Bilderback has written six *Complete Idiot's Guides* on cooking, as well as a monthly column in a local Los Angeles magazine, *The Arroyo*. She teaches baking and pastry at Ecole de Cuisine in Pasadena, travels through the LA Unified School District teaching nutrition to kids, and trains chefs for the U.S. Navy.

Trademarks

All terms mentioned in this book that are known to be or are suspected of being trademarks or service marks have been appropriately capitalized. Alpha Books and Penguin Group (USA) Inc. cannot attest to the accuracy of this information. Use of a term in this book should not be regarded as affecting the validity of any trademark or service mark.

Vegan Baking Made Delicious

Baking is a science that relies on exact ingredient amounts prescribed in a recipe. With the exception of adding philosophy and lifestyle to the recipes, vegan baking is very similar science. Whether you've been practicing veganism for years, or are just beginning your journey, you'll need to know what you can and cannot use in your vegan baking. As with all vegan recipes, animal products of any kind—even honey— are a definite no-no.

Part 1 begins with the reasons for being vegan. Are you searching for good health? Perhaps you're eating vegan to oppose animal cruelty, or maybe it's for spiritual reasons. Whatever your reason, the outcome is pretty much the same as far as vegan food goes. The chapters in Part 1 show you the tricks of the trade, including how to set up your vegan pantry with animal-free ingredients and any special tools or equipment you might find useful to make vegan baking enjoyable and delicious. I also cover substitutions for dairy, eggs, and other miscellaneous animal products that make vegan baking so scrumptious you'll be back for second helpings.

Ready to begin your vegan culinary adventure? Then roll up your sleeves and become one with the dough. With this cookbook in your collection, you can have your vegan cake and eat it, too!

Getting Started with Vegan Baking

In This Chapter

- Why vegan?
- What's different about vegan baking?
- Shopping for your vegan pantry
- Setting up your vegan kitchen

If you're reading this, you're probably already interested in vegan baking and most likely vegan eating, or maybe still just thinking about eating vegan or some variation thereof. And perhaps you also know that in the past, vegan baked goods and desserts have received a bad rap for tasting … well, like cardboard. To some, the words *healthy* and *baked goods* don't belong in the same sentence.

But things have changed in the last two decades as health-conscious consumers have demanded better-tasting products and manufacturers have responded in kind. Problem is, the price tag seems to go up as soon as the words *healthy, diet, vegetarian,* or *vegan* are added to the label.

As a vegan, you probably have a tough time finding healthful baked goods in the supermarket. When you do, it's even harder to find something that tastes halfway decent and doesn't cost two or three times the price you want to pay. Health food stores are finally catching on, realizing that vegan baked goods are a cash cow just waiting to be milked (pun intended). But most of the products still taste like sawdust. Why not make your own, save some money, and enjoy great-tasting vegan baked goods at home? With this book, you can!

The Benefits of Being Vegan

The biggest offenders in nonvegan baking are dairy products (butter, cream, cheese, yogurt, buttermilk, sour cream, cream cheese, dried milk products, etc.), animal and animal by-products (eggs, honey, lard, fat, gelatin, whey, casein, rennet, etc.), and bone char (used to refine sugar and sweeteners). In vegan baking, you have none of that—and, therefore, you have none of the animal fats, proteins, and cholesterol that come along with those things.

As a vegan, you'll most likely be asked, "Where do you get your protein?" Well, where do animals get their protein? Where do the beasts of burden—the ox, elephant, horse, goat, camel, and llama—get their protein? They get all the protein they need to grow strong from plant matter, and so can you. With it, you can be strong and healthy, just like they are.

As a vegan living in a society that strongly encourages the consumption of animal products, you'll feel better about your health, the animals, even the environment while eating a plant-based diet that includes grains, fiber, and nutritious baked goods.

How Is Vegan Baking Different?

What does all this mean to you, the vegan baker? It means all animal products are out. But it does *not* mean all baked goods and desserts are out!

Although most baked goods can be veganized by swapping out a few essential ingredients, like dairy and eggs, with good success, not all desserts can make the transformation and retain the same texture, taste, and appearance. For example, classic lemon meringue pie, angel food cake, and traditional custards are difficult to replicate because they rely so heavily on eggs to produce height and texture. With some desserts, you'll have to face the cruel fact that the meringue pie you loved so much will likely be only a pleasant memory.

Don't despair! You don't have to kiss all your beloved baked goods good-bye. You'll eventually adapt and learn how to veganize your favorite recipes with plant-based ingredients and substitutions that will imitate and transform just about anything you set your heart on.

If you keep in mind that some vegan baked goods might look and taste a little differ-ent from what you've been used to eating, you're sure to enjoy experimenting with the recipes in this book. If you've been a vegan forever, the only difference you'll notice is that *wow!* these baked goods are fantastic!

Tricks of the Trade

Organization and preparation are nine-tenths of a recipe, and your key to vegan baking success, so the first steps to becoming a successful vegan baker are to organize and stock your kitchen. Besides having a recipe totally flop on you, there's nothing more discouraging than to get halfway through the recipe, only to find you're missing a few key ingredients. This tragedy can be avoided by organizing yourself, your recipes, your kitchen, and your pantry.

Organizing your kitchen can be as simple as keeping all your baking ingredients in one designated place. This is especially important if not everyone in the family is eating vegan. Because most of your vegan ingredients will replace dairy products and eggs, this may be easier than you think.

BAKER'S BONUS

When you're setting up your vegan kitchen, be sure to label everything, especially if you transfer the ingredients from one package to another. Baking soda looks an awful lot like baking powder and arrowroot. If you're in a hurry, salt can look amazingly like sugar. Yuck!

Organize your recipes in a separate folder or recipe box, or keep all your vegan and healthful cookbooks in the same area near the kitchen. Refer to them often in the beginning of your vegan baking adventure. Read the recipe a few times, and go shopping if necessary, for all the ingredients you need. Assemble all ingredients on the counter before you turn on the oven.

Check the recipe for any special instructions. It may call for certain ingredients to be chilled or softened at room temperature beforehand, which would alter your timing. Check the recipe for any small appliances you may need, too. The recipe may call for a small hand blender, a grinder, or perhaps a food processor. Check the pan size needed, and make adjustments if your pantry is missing a special springform pan for a particular cheesecake recipe. You'll want to have everything at the ready.

Okay, you're ready to crank up the oven and start baking. Be sure your oven is keeping the correct temperature. Many household ovens can be off by 25°F to 50°F, which would totally spoil what you're baking. Get a small oven thermometer, and check the temperature every now and then. Adjust the temperature as necessary.

Recipes generally go in order of ingredients added, which basically means start at the top and methodically work your way down, taking special note if any extra steps are indicated in the recipe. Sometimes, as in yeast breads, multiple steps must be accomplished in order to advance to the next step.

When hot pans of muffins are coming out of the oven, you need to have somewhere to put them—and fast. Be sure to have good, thick oven mitts or potholders next to the oven. Have a heat-proof counter or workspace ready and waiting with cooling racks or hot pads. Proper cooling is essential to some baked goods. Taking the cheesecake out of the pan too early may result in a California-size fissure down the middle of your prized dessert.

And last but not least, storing your baked goods properly will make them last longer, save you money, and also reward you next week when you pull those yummy cupcakes out of the freezer for a last-minute treat.

Stocking Your Vegan Pantry

A well-stocked pantry makes vegan baking much quicker and easier. But what should you keep on hand? Walking down the aisles of a health food store can be overwhelming, whether you're just starting down the path of vegan baking or have been vegan for years, with all the different and strange-sounding products. Some of these items will come in handy; others you might not need to stock but can purchase on an as-needed basis. In the following paragraphs, I offer some suggestions on items you might want to keep in your vegan pantry.

Many recipes in this cookbook call for *tofu*. Mori-Nu, as well as other brands, makes soft silken tofu that's good as an egg replacer or thickener in many baked goods. It has virtually no taste, so you won't even know it's in there. Some brands come in aseptic packaging that doesn't need to be refrigerated until opened, making it a great pantry staple.

Carob is Mother Nature's chocolate substitute. Technically a legume, carob comes from the ground-up pod of the carob tree. The pods are often roasted before they're ground to give the carob a more "chocolaty" taste. Carob powder is very similar to cocoa powder and can be substituted in most recipes with excellent results. It also contains no caffeine. You can find carob powder at health food stores and some large supermarkets.

Commercial confectioners' and brown sugar, while not technically considered animal products, are often produced and refined with animal bone char–based charcoal, making them unsuitable for vegans. Look for *vegan confectioners' sugar* in the super-market or health food store.

The flour used in these recipes is most often *unbleached all-purpose flour, high-gluten bread flour,* or *pastry flour. Whole-wheat pastry flour* is the secret ingredient in many muffins, coffee cakes, and assorted baked goods because it produces a moist and tender *crumb*. If you can't find pastry flour, consider using cake flour. Double sifting unbleached all-purpose or whole-wheat flour will also help.

VEGAN VOCAB

A tender crumb is something to be desired when baking cakes, muffins, and bread. **Crumb** refers to the internal structure of the baked good. When saying something has a tender crumb, it generally means the item has an even texture, not crumbly or ragged.

Nutritional yeast is very different from the yeast used to leaven bread. It comes in flakes or powder, similar to brewer's yeast, and is used as a condiment or seasoning in vegan cooking. Nutritional yeast's ability to mimic cheese in color and taste makes it very versatile and called for in many recipes and casseroles. High in B vitamins, it's also a good source of protein. Nutritional yeast has a good shelf life, but it's best kept refrigerated in an airtight container. Find it at any health food store in the bulk section.

Some *soy margarines* are nonhydrogenated expeller-pressed natural oil blends (soybean, palm fruit, canola, and olive oils), with soy protein, soy lecithin, and lactic acid derived from sugar beets. Many can be used interchangeably for butter or margarine. Be sure whatever you choose is 100 percent vegan.

Florida Crystals is an unrefined cane sugar that is superior in vegan or healthful baked goods. Made from evaporated cane juice, organic Florida Crystals has no additives and can be used in most recipes calling for granulated sugar. Most commercial brands of granulated cane sugar are processed using bone char from cattle as a whitening filter. Look for organic sugar at the health food store, and read the label to be sure no animal ingredients are used in the processing.

Date sugar is an unprocessed sugar made from dehydrated dates. It's also high in fiber.

Agave syrup is a liquid sweetener derived from the Mexican agave cactus. With a light, delicate flavor sweeter than honey, this syrup can be used in most recipes that call for honey, brown rice syrup, maple syrup, corn syrup, or molasses.

> **BATTER UP!**
>
> Honey is not on the Vegan Society's list of approved vegan ingredients. That said, many vegans still choose to consume honey. Whether you're for honey or against it is a personal choice, but know that I do not include it in the recipes in this book. If you like honey, you can substitute it in most recipes that call for liquid sweeteners such as agave syrup, maple syrup, brown rice syrup, or molasses. Keep in mind, this may alter the taste.

Flaxseeds come in brown or golden, or you can purchase already ground *flaxseed meal*. The whole seeds can be used raw or toasted for a nutty flavor. Ground and mixed with water, this high-fiber seed makes an amazing egg substitute. Whatever version you buy, keep it refrigerated or frozen because it goes rancid quickly.

Egg substitutes such as Ener-G Egg Replacer and Bob's Red Mill, among others, are essential for vegan baking. (See Chapter 2 for more.)

When vegan recipes call for milk, you can use *soy, rice,* or *almond milk.* Buy the plain, unflavored variety for baking.

Soy lecithin, derived from soy beans, is used as an emulsifier and reduces the need for more fat. It also aids in increasing bread volume and stabilizes fermentation. Use either liquid or granular lecithin in bread recipes. A little goes a long way—one bottle of liquid lecithin makes many loaves of bread and lasts a long time. Find it in natural food stores.

Canola oil, vegetable oil, safflower, or *extra-virgin olive oil* are interchangeable. Depending on what recipes you use them in, they may, however, alter the taste.

Vegan marshmallow fluff, a fluffy, sweet, and smooth product made with brown rice syrup, soy protein, natural gums, and flavors, can be used in most recipes that call for marshmallow fluff. It's gluten free and kosher and is often stocked in natural food stores.

Poppy seeds are also handy to have on hand, but be aware that they can go rancid fast. Keep them stored in the freezer in an airtight container.

Hopefully this list eliminates some of the confusion you might face as you stock your vegan pantry. I include a complete list of vegan animal-product substitutions in Chapter 2, so check there for more ingredients you might want to try.

Tools and Equipment You'll Need

You can easily bake healthful breads, desserts, and more when you have the right supplies and ingredients on hand. You may even have some or all of these small appliances, pans, and gadgets already:

- ❏ Heavy-duty high-speed stand mixer and/or a powerful hand mixer with dough hooks, whips, and beater attachments
- ❏ Small electric grinder for grinding flaxseed
- ❏ Food processor for chopping nuts, mixing dough, grating veggies, blending tofu, and more
- ❏ High-speed blender
- ❏ Nonstick or silicone muffin pans, round and square cake pans in different sizes, Pyrex or metal 9×13-inch pans, 8×8-inch pans, regular- and mini-size bread loaf pans, baking and cookie sheets, springform pans, pie pans, etc.
- ❏ Assorted stainless, glass, and other mixing bowls in various sizes
- ❏ Cookie scoops, large and small
- ❏ Rubber or plastic spatulas in various sizes and stiffness
- ❏ Oven thermometer
- ❏ Kitchen scale
- ❏ Vegetable peeler
- ❏ Assorted knives
- ❏ Cutting board
- ❏ Rolling pins
- ❏ Microplane grater/zester or rasp
- ❏ Cherry pitter
- ❏ Pastry brushes
- ❏ *Pastry blender*

VEGAN VOCAB

A **pastry blender** is a gadget you'll use over and over again. Usually made of stainless steel, it has a handle attached to five or six thin, sharp blades that mix the topping ingredients together. A pastry blender duplicates using two knives, and it's quicker and less messy.

❏ Measuring cups and spoons

❏ Wooden and stainless spoons for mixing

❏ Mortar and pestle for pulverizing herbs and spices

❏ Large balloon whisk and assorted others

❏ Parchment paper

❏ Cupcake liners

❏ Pot holders or oven mitts

❏ Wire cooling racks

❏ Zipper-lock bags for storing baked goods

Some of these tools and larger pieces of equipment will simplify your vegan baking, but not all are necessary, and some are merely suggestions. Your budget, workspace, and the amount of baked goods you'll be cranking out of your kitchen will determine which of these tools and gadgets you'll likely have already or need to purchase. Don't go overboard at the beginning. Start slow and build your kitchen one baking pan at a time. Keep it simple, have fun, and make vegan baking a delicious part of your life.

The Least You Need to Know

- Vegan baking means you won't be using any animal products, so you'll need to change the way you shop and the way you bake.
- Health food stores and large supermarkets carry most of the ingredients you need for vegan baking.
- Setting up your vegan kitchen for baking is easier than you think. An oven, mixing bowls, various baking pans, and oven mitts are some of the necessary items you most likely have on hand already.

Quick and Easy Substitutions

In This Chapter

- Easy egg substitutions
- Doing without dairy
- Tofu and other alternative ingredients
- What about honey?

What? Ultra-creamy cheesecake? Without cream cheese or eggs? How is that possible? In this chapter, you discover how easy it is to bake delicious pies, breads, and cookies without butter, milk, and other off-limits dairy products. You also learn how to substitute good-for-you plant ingredients to mimic the all-important egg.

With a little creativity and know-how, you'll be whipping up unbelievably tasty cakes, breads, and other desserts for all your friends—vegan or not.

Excellent Egg Substitutions

In vegan baking, perhaps the hardest thing to do is mimic the job eggs perform. Unlike cooking, where you can always adjust the spices or add another handful of rice to the pot, the art of baking is an exact science. It doesn't always work to throw in an extra teaspoon of this or an additional cup of that. There's no doubt about it: depending on what you're baking, eggs can be a real challenge to replace.

Eggs are used for a variety of reasons. Cakes and cupcakes need the leavening eggs provide. In vegan baking, commercial egg replacers, soft silken tofu, soy yogurt, or baking powder can serve this role. You can also get similar results by re-creating every kid's favorite science project—mixing white or cider vinegar and baking soda to create a powerful chemical reaction that helps baked goods rise.

Vegan-Friendly Egg Replacers

Eggs are also used as binders in muffins, brownies, and pies. For those baked goods, try exchanging Flaxseed Egg Substitute (recipe later in this chapter) or blended tofu. You can also use arrowroot powder, cornstarch, or *agar-agar* powder mixed with water.

When you're not particularly worried about something rising but need just the extra moisture usually supplied by eggs, you can substitute fruit purée like applesauce, mashed banana, juice, or a little nondairy milk.

Here are some common vegan substitutions for 1 large egg:

- $1\frac{1}{2}$ teaspoons *Ener-G Egg Replacer* mixed with 2 tablespoons water

- 1 tablespoon *Bob's Red Mill All-Natural Egg Replacer* mixed with 3 table-spoons water

- $\frac{1}{4}$ cup Flaxseed Egg Substitute (recipe later in this chapter)

- $\frac{1}{4}$ cup tofu blended with a bit of liquid in the recipe

- $\frac{1}{4}$ cup soy yogurt

- $\frac{1}{4}$ cup vegan buttermilk

- $\frac{1}{4}$ cup mashed banana

- $\frac{1}{4}$ cup applesauce

- 1 tablespoon soy flour mixed with 1 tablespoon water

- 1 tablespoon agar-agar mixed with 1 tablespoon water

- 2 tablespoons cornstarch or 2 tablespoons arrowroot powder mixed with 2 tablespoons water

VEGAN VOCAB

Agar-agar, or *agar* or *kanten,* is an odorless and tasteless seaweed derivative used as a vegan alternative to animal-based gelatin. Use it to thicken sauces and in some baked goods.

Ener-G Egg Replacer is an egg substitute made with potato starch, tapioca flour, and leavening agents. Depending on what you add it to, it can have a slightly chalky taste. **Bob's Red Mill All-Natural Egg Replacer** is another good substitute. Unlike Ener-G Egg Replacer, this contains wheat gluten. Therefore, it is *not* suitable for the gluten-intolerant.

- 2 tablespoons all-purpose flour, $\frac{1}{2}$ tablespoon shortening, and $\frac{1}{2}$ teaspoon baking powder mixed with 2 teaspoons water

- 2 tablespoons mashed avocado

Flaxseed Egg Substitute

Flaxseed can be a good egg replacer, as mentioned earlier. But it also serves double-duty as a fiber booster.

Similar to bran, flaxseed is a good source of fiber. We all need fiber to move things through the pipes; however, most people don't get enough through their daily diet. It's recommended you get between 25 and 30 grams fiber per day. You can easily add fiber to your diet by replacing eggs with this flaxseed mixture.

You can find whole brown or golden flaxseeds in a health food store or large super-market and grind them as needed. Store flaxseeds in the refrigerator, or freeze for longer storage, to prevent them from going rancid too quickly. You can use them raw or toasted for a nutty flavor. Toast whole flaxseeds before grinding them.

Flaxseed Egg Substitute

This makes a great egg substitute for many baked goods. It's especially good as a binder in muffins, breads, pies, and dark-colored cookies where the color and "nutty" texture flaxseeds bring won't be as noticeable.

Yield:	Prep time:	Serving size:
1 cup	5 minutes	$\frac{1}{4}$ cup = 1 large egg

$\frac{1}{4}$ cup flaxseeds

$\frac{3}{4}$ cup water

1. In a small grinder, grind flaxseeds until mixture resembles a fine powder.

2. In a blender, combine ground flaxseeds and water, and blend on high speed for 1 or 2 minutes or until thick.

3. Chill for at least 1 hour to set up. It can be used now, but it'll have a more egg-like consistency if allowed to chill. Keep refrigerated for up to 3 days.

BAKER'S BONUS

A small electric coffee grinder comes in handy for grinding flaxseeds to a powder. Large department stores or online sources such as Amazon.com carry Braun, Krups, Hamilton Beach, and other brands of grinders that are perfect for grinding flaxseeds.

Bye-Bye, Butter

Butter is a solid fat used in many traditional nonvegan baked goods. Although it adds flavor, it is an animal product most often made with cow's milk. Butter is used for flavor in sweet dough such as cookies, cake batters, brownies, and other tasty baked goods. It's also used as a tenderizer, to aid browning, and add moisture and texture. In some cases, butter is used as a leavener, too. Cakes and cupcakes, quick breads, and buckles depend on creaming and beating air into the butter and sugar mixture to rise during the baking process.

So what do you use in place of butter? Thankfully, many commercial products are available to take the place of butter.

Some vegetable-based margarines, although not always a healthy choice, can be used with good success. Be sure to read the list of ingredients because some contain whey, or milk products.

Most piecrust recipes rely on solid shortening for flaky dough. For generations, bakers used butter, lard, Crisco shortening, or margarine to make piecrust. For obvious reasons, animal products such as butter and lard are not suitable for vegan diets. Likewise, if you're concerned with unhealthy trans fat, check the label. A good way to tell if the product has trans fat is if it says "partially hydrogenated." However, soy-based nonhydrogenated margarine yields good results in these recipes. And in most cases, you can substitute one part margarine for one part butter.

As a vegan baker, you'll find that soy margarine is a good choice for pie-making. Because it tends to be salted, unlike unsalted butter, it reduces the amount of salt in the recipe by half.

DOUGH-NOT

Thanks to butter's high saturated fat content and its significant amount of cholesterol, it's been suggested to be a major contributor to heart disease and a variety of other ailments.

Earth Balance brand's Vegan Buttery Sticks are made from a nonhydrogenated expeller-pressed natural oil blend (soybean, palm fruit, canola, and olive oils), with soy protein, soy lecithin, and lactic acid derived from sugar beets. It's 100 percent vegan, has no trans fat or dietary cholesterol, is gluten free, and is certified kosher. It comes in handy $1/2$ cup sticks, makes for easy measuring, and can be used interchangeably in most recipes that call for butter or margarine. The buttery color is natural and comes from beta-carotene.

Earth Balance also produces Natural Shortening, which mimics traditional solid shortening but is nonhydrogenated. Also made with an expeller-pressed natural oil blend (palm fruit, soybean, canola, and olive oils), Natural Shortening contains slightly more calories from fat (130 per serving) than Crisco. Spectrum brand also makes good solid vegetable shortenings.

Vegans wishing to substitute other products for butter in their baking can use a variety of vegetable oils such as canola oil, olive oil, and coconut oil, and many others. These oils may do the job, but none will have the buttery taste nonvegans are accustomed to. *When substituting, 1 cup vegan butter or $3/4$ cup vegetable oil = 1 cup butter.*

Fruit purées can also be used as part of or all the butter in certain recipes. Where moisture is desired, you can use prune, plum, pear, peach, pumpkin, or squash purée; applesauce; or fruit butter. Try using half fruit purée for half of the fat in your recipes as a substitute for all butter or nonhydrogenated margarine or oil. You can also use all-natural sugar-free fruit or vegetable baby food purée as part of the fat. This will, however, change the taste of whatever's being baked. *When substituting, $1/3$ cup prune purée = $1/2$ cup butter.*

Mooove Along, Milk

One of the easiest vegan substitutions to make is for animal-based milk. With the great availability of plant-based milk options, there's no need for cow's milk, goat milk, sheep milk, or even buffalo milk. The most popular and readily available commercial nondairy milks are rice milk, soy milk, almond milk, grain milk, and other plant milks.

In this day and age, you can find vegan nondairy milk at just about any supermarket in the natural food aisle. It comes in various flavors, including plain, vanilla, chocolate, and strawberry, and often fat free or "enhanced" with vitamins. Vegan milk is often reasonably priced in aseptic packaging that needs no refrigeration in individual snack sizes, quarts, and half gallons. You can also make it at home for a lot less by soaking and blending ground nuts with water and sweetener.

Use vegan milk in bread puddings, pies, muffins, quick breads, cookies, cakes, cupcakes, and frostings. Keep in mind the consistency may be different from the nonvegan versions. For example, rice milk has a thinner consistency than soy milk and might be more comparable to low-fat or skim milk. Soy milk is generally thicker and goes well in any recipe that calls for whole milk. *When substituting, 1 part vegan milk = 1 part animal milk.*

Coconut cream—the thick portion on the top of full-fat coconut milk—is a close substitute for dairy cream. Chilled coconut cream can be used in your favorite whipped cream recipe by whipping it with an electric mixer fitted with a whisk attachment on high speed. Do not disturb or shake the can before opening. Let the fat float to the top, and scoop off the solid part for your recipes.

Tofu is another nondairy substitute. Extra-firm silken tofu blended with other ingredients produces a medium-thick whipped cream, while soft silken tofu resembles light cream when blended. See Chapter 22 for making your own tofu-based Whipped Topping.

What about *buttermilk?* Traditionally, sour-tasting buttermilk was the liquid left over after churning butter from cream. As you work your way through this book, you'll find recipes calling for "vegan buttermilk." Not to worry: you can easily make it with just two ingredients: lemon juice or vinegar and soy milk. *When substituting, 1 part vegan buttermilk = 1 part cultured buttermilk.*

VEGAN VOCAB

Buttermilk is a fermented dairy product that gets its tartness by either artificially adding lactic acid bacteria to cow's milk, or from naturally occurring bacteria. Cultured buttermilk is generally pasteurized and homogenized for safety reasons, but it's also a thicker product than traditional buttermilk, which makes it appealing to most bakers.

Vegan Buttermilk

Although the buttermilk produced with plant-based milk is slightly different from its animal-based counterpart, the end results should be the same in the finished baked good.

Yield:	Prep time:
1 cup	5 minutes

2 TB. fresh lemon juice, or white or cider vinegar

1 cup plain soy milk

1. In a small cup or jar, combine lemon juice and soy milk.

2. Let stand at least 5 minutes to "curdle."

What About Yogurt?

The addition of vegan yogurt in baked goods adds moisture and yields a tender texture. It can also be used as an egg substitute in many recipes.

You can make your own vegan yogurt using many of the recipes found online and in vegan cookbooks. Making homemade yogurt is easy, provided you have a yogurt maker, thermometer, and agar-agar or other thickening ingredients. For this cookbook, I'm calling for commercially available plant-based soy yogurt to replace animal-based dairy yogurt.

Plain soy yogurt works the best in recipes calling for yogurt. Flavored soy yogurts would do fine as an egg substitute in fruit-based vegan recipes such as Strawberry Muffins (recipe in Chapter 3), Lemon Tea Cake (recipe in Chapter 6), or Blueberry Buckle (recipe in Chapter 4). Just use the appropriate flavor for each recipe. *When substituting, 1 part soy yogurt = 1 part dairy yogurt. 1/4 cup soy yogurt = 1 large egg.*

Subbing for Sour Cream

Many vegan sour creams are commercially available in health food stores or large supermarkets in the natural foods aisle, but it's also easy to save money and make it at home. *When substituting, 1 part vegan sour cream = 1 part dairy sour cream.*

Vegan Sour Cream

This homemade vegan sour "cream" is similar to its dairy cousin. A bit of lemon juice and vinegar gives it its familiar sour tang.

Yield:	Prep time:
1¼ cups	10 minutes

1 cup soft silken tofu	2 tsp. apple cider vinegar
2 TB. fresh lemon juice	½ tsp. agave or brown rice syrup
2 TB. canola or vegetable oil	Pinch salt

1. In a food processor, combine tofu, lemon juice, canola oil, apple cider vinegar, agave syrup, and salt. Pulse for 2 or 3 minutes or until mixture is smooth.

2. Pour into a container, cover, and refrigerate for up to 3 days. The finished sour cream must stay cold to maintain its texture.

Getting Creative with Cheese

If you've recently made the switch from an animal-based diet to eating vegan, cheese will most likely be one of the hardest things to give up, especially if you're a cheese-cake lover! Cream cheese is one of those delicious—and necessary—ingredients when making cheesecake, cheese fillings, and breads. Don't despair! There's no reason to give up the good things in life like cheesecake when there are vegan products that imitate the "cheesy" flavor and texture you're looking for!

Cream Cheese

Although you could make vegan cheesecakes using only tofu, cream cheese makes luscious, extra-creamy vegan cheesecakes taste even better. Moreover, it gives cheesecake a special rich mouthfeel you'll only get when you use cream cheese. If you want to make a vegan version of a New York–style Strawberry Cheesecake (recipe in Chapter 9), try using a commercially produced soy cream cheese.

You can also make your own vegan cream cheese with firm tofu and soy yogurt, or raw cashews. However, the finished product is much softer and is better suited to using in dips and sauces than a firm cream cheese needed to stand up in a rich, creamy cheesecake.

Tofutti brand makes two excellent Better Than Cream Cheese products that make a perfectly rich and extra creamy cheesecake. (Use the plain varieties rather than the flavored.) One is made with partially hydrogenated soybean oil, and another, a nonhydrogenated vegan cream cheese, is made without hydrogenated oils using expeller-processed natural soybean oil blend. These cream cheeses are most often packaged in 8-ounce tubs and can be found in the refrigerated section of health food stores and many large supermarkets. *When substituting, 1 part soy cream cheese = 1 part dairy cream cheese.*

Hard and Semi-Soft Cheeses

I've included a few recipes in this book that call for grated cheese. For example, the Cheesy Rolls (recipe in Chapter 8) calls for vegan cheddar cheese and nutritional yeast flakes. These two ingredients make the Cheesy Rolls … well, "cheesy"!

Unlike bakers' active dry yeast, or compressed cake yeast, nutritional yeast is an inac-tive yeast with a nutty, cheeselike flavor. It contains a wide assortment of minerals and B vitamins and can provide a reliable dietary source of vitamin B_{12}. It comes in a fine powder, suitable for making "cheesy" gravies and sauces, or in small and large flakes, perfect for adding to macaroni and cheese, casseroles, breads, and anything else that needs a cheesy flavor. Follow the recipe for amounts and instructions.

Although most hard and semi-soft vegan cheeses are made of soy or rice, some brands are nut-based, the most common being almond or cashew. Tofutti brand carries vegan American and mozzarella soy-cheese slices.

DOUGH-NOT

Be sure to always check ingredient lists because some soy cheeses contain casein or a milk derivative known as caseinate.

For recipes calling for hard vegan cheese, grate with a cheese grater or put through a food processor with the grater attachment.

Healthful Honey Replacers

The Vegan Society formally defines veganism as "the doctrine that man should live without exploiting animals." Some vegans maintain that honey is an animal product, claiming that honeybees are intelligent, feel pain, and are being exploited and enslaved by man. Many vegans avoid honey for that reason, but consuming honey is a matter of personal choice.

Purists have a number of options when it comes to replacing honey, including barley malt and corn syrup. (These will, however, alter the taste a little.) But let's look at some other healthy alternatives to honey.

Also known as agave nectar, *agave syrup* is a liquid sweetener derived from the Mexican agave cactus. It has a light, delicate flavor sweeter than honey, so you can use 25 percent less in recipes.

Pure maple syrup, a sweetener made from the sap of sugar maple or black maple trees, comes in different grades. Dark Amber and Grade B maple syrups are most often used in baked goods and desserts. Both grades have a stronger maple flavor than the Fancy Grade A maple syrup used for pancakes. When substituting maple syrup for honey, use the same amount. However, be aware that because maple syrup has a strong and distinct flavor, it can alter the finished taste of your baked goods.

Brown rice syrup is a sweetener produced by fermenting brown rice with enzymes to break down the grain's natural starches. The liquid is then strained off and cooked down to a syruplike consistency. *When substituting, $1^1/_4$ cups rice syrup = 1 cup sugar (use $^1/_4$ cup less of another liquid in the recipe, too).*

Molasses or *blackstrap molasses* is a dark, thick, bittersweet syrup that results from the production of sugar. It contains several B vitamins, calcium, magnesium, potassium, iron, copper, and manganese. Because molasses has such a strong and unique flavor, it has limited applications particularly for taste because the substitution is equal parts for equal parts. However, if you're making something with a delicate or mild flavor, it would be better to use rice syrup, agave syrup, or even maple syrup. You could also use half molasses and half agave, or rice syrup so the flavor isn't so strong.

The Least You Need to Know

- Eggs are one of the toughest ingredients to bake without, but with the substitutions in this chapter, you can be egg free and loving it!
- Dairy products are highly overrated. Make yourself a "cheesecake" with a cream cheese alternative, and see how good a dairy-free lifestyle can really be.
- With so many new vegan and healthy items to try at the supermarket, alternatives like tofu and agave syrup are just a few of the many ways to make vegan eating more delicious than ever!
- Not into honey? Don't worry. With so many alternatives to the bees' pride and joy, you'll have no shortage of delicious choices and flavors to pick from.

Muffins, Coffee Cakes, and Pastries

Good morning! This part of the book is all about breakfast goodies. You'll find a wide variety of easy-to-make vegan pastries, muffins, coffee cakes, and buckles in the following pages. Many of these vegan recipes come together quickly and will have you in and out of the kitchen in no time. They can be made ahead and eaten later, so whip up an extra batch now and freeze them for another day.

Part 2 starts off with a large selection of delightful muffins. Their individual serving size makes them perfect for lunch boxes, brunches, and pastry platters. In Chapter 2, I introduced a fiber-rich flaxseed egg substitute. It's time to put that recipe to the test and use it as an egg replacement in Part 2's muffin recipes.

There's no need to skip breakfast with the list of vegan pastries offered here. Assorted coffee cakes and buckles are loaded with fresh berries, nuts, and topped with streusel. There's even a carob coffee cake studded with cherries for those of you who can't have chocolate. From turnovers to Danish, strudel to scones, there's something for everyone here.

And speaking of substitutions, you'll get used to using tofu cream cheese as a substitute for dairy cream cheese, which will come in handy in the "cheesecake" chapter later on.

Just because you're vegan, doesn't mean you can't enjoy scrumptious pastries, so grab your spatula and muffin pans, and start baking!

A Muffin a Day ...

In This Chapter

- Muffin-baking tips
- Freezing suggestions for leftovers
- Fresh-fruit and dried-fruit muffins

Everyone loves muffins. They're the not-so-sweet "cupcake" cousins you can eat every day, guilt free. They're quick and easy, and because they need no yeast, they can be mixed and baked for company in 30 minutes!

In this chapter, I give you muffins for every day of the week, for every reason and every season. With all the choices in this chapter, you truly can have a muffin a day and not get bored!

Muffin-Baking Tips

Making vegan muffins is especially easy because you don't have to fuss with dairy and eggs. Basic muffin recipes lend themselves to creativity, so play around and see what different options you come up with. Use traditional options like the Banana Muffin recipe as a canvas; by throwing a few handfuls of vegan chocolate chips into the batter, you've created a new muffin! Or switch up the dried fruits in the Tooty-Fruity Muffins if you don't like dates and prunes. For an alternate egg substitute suggestion, pick something else from the list in Chapter 2. All these muffin recipes are vegan, so have fun experimenting!

What size muffins should you make? Your choice! Muffin pans come in all sizes, from large, Texas-size muffins; to regular-size muffins, which the recipes in this chapter were calculated for; to little, teeny, mini muffin pans. Nonstick pans work well if you spray them with vegetable spray first, or you can use colorful, themed paper cupcake liners for easy cleanup. Mini loaf pans are also available; approximately 4 muffins equal 1 mini loaf. If you use the loaf pan, increase the baking time accordingly. Generally, you'd add 10 to 15 more minutes or cook until a toothpick inserted in the center comes out clean.

All ovens were not created equal, and baking times may vary from oven to oven. Always preheat your oven, and resist opening the oven door for the first 15 minutes of baking. This can drastically reduce a muffin's height in the end.

Don't worry if you made too many muffins. They freeze really well. Simply layer muffins between waxed paper and paper towels in an airtight container for longer storage, or freeze them in zipper-lock plastic bags for short-term storage. Muffins last up to 3 months in the freezer, so you have plenty of time to eat them. Thaw muffins in the bag on the counter for a few hours, or overnight in the fridge before serving. If you only need one muffin, remove it from the bag, wrap it in a piece of paper towel, and let it thaw on the counter for 20 to 30 minutes.

Apple Cinnamon Streusel Muffins

Spicy and moist with cinnamon, fresh apples, and walnuts, these muffins are hearty enough to take you through the day.

Yield:	Prep time:	Bake time:	Serving size:
15 to 18 muffins	30 to 40 minutes	23 to 26 minutes	1 muffin

⅓ cup light brown sugar, firmly packed

1 tsp. ground cinnamon

3⅓ cups unbleached all-purpose flour

⅓ cup plus ½ cup chopped walnuts (optional)

2 TB. plus ½ cup nonhydrogenated vegan margarine, melted and cooled

4 tsp. aluminum-free baking powder

⅛ tsp. salt

Egg substitute for 2 large eggs

1 cup soy, rice, or almond milk

½ tsp. pure vanilla extract

1 cup unbleached cane sugar

2 large cored, peeled, and grated Cortland, Granny Smith, Empire, Gravenstein, or other hard crisp apples

1. Preheat the oven to 375°F. Line 15 to 18 muffin cups with paper cupcake liners.

2. In a small bowl, and using a wooden spoon, mix together light brown sugar, ½ teaspoon ground cinnamon, ⅓ cup unbleached all-purpose flour, ⅓ cup walnuts (if using), and 2 tablespoons melted vegan margarine until crumbly.

3. Into a large bowl, sift remaining 3 cups flour, aluminum-free baking powder, remaining ½ teaspoon ground cinnamon, and salt, or blend with a wire whisk.

4. In a separate large bowl, and using a large whisk, whip egg substitute, soy milk, vanilla extract, and unbleached cane sugar for 1 or 2 minutes or until well blended. Add remaining ½ cup melted vegan margarine, and whisk again. Using a rubber spatula or wooden spoon, *fold* in apples and remaining ½ cup walnuts (if using).

5. Using a rubber spatula, fold dry ingredients into wet ingredients just until moistened. Do not overmix.

6. Using a ⅓ cup ice cream scoop, fill muffin cups ¾ full. Sprinkle brown sugar–cinnamon streusel mixture on top, equally dividing among muffins. Bake for 23 to 26 minutes or until lightly browned and muffin tops spring back when lightly touched.

7. Remove from the oven, and cool for 5 minutes in the pan on a wire rack. Carefully release muffins from the pan, and cool completely. Store in an airtight container, or freeze in zipper-lock bags.

VEGAN VOCAB

To **fold** is to gently combine a dense and light mixture—in this case the dry ingredients into the wet ingredients—with a circular action from the middle of the bowl.

Strawberry Cheesecake Muffins

If you love strawberry cheesecake, you'll love these moist berry muffins. The strawberry jam and vegan cheesecake batter baked inside the muffins is a nice sweet surprise when you bite into them.

Yield:	Prep time:	Bake time:	Serving size:
10 to 12 muffins	30 to 40 minutes	20 to 25 minutes	1 muffin

2¾ cups unbleached all-purpose flour

1 TB. aluminum-free baking powder

¼ tsp. salt

Egg substitute for 1 large egg

1¼ cups soy, rice, or almond milk

½ cup light brown sugar, firmly packed

⅓ cup nonhydrogenated vegan margarine, melted

½ tsp. grated lemon zest

¼ tsp. pure almond extract

4 oz. vegan cream cheese, softened

½ cup vegan confectioners' sugar

½ cup seedless strawberry jam

¼ cup unbleached cane sugar

1. Preheat the oven to 350°F. Line 10 to 12 muffin cups with paper cupcake liners.

2. Into a large bowl, sift unbleached all-purpose flour, aluminum-free baking powder, and salt, or blend with a wire whisk.

3. In a separate large bowl, and using a large whisk, whip together egg substitute, soy milk, light brown sugar, melted vegan margarine, lemon zest, and almond extract for 1 or 2 minutes or until well blended.

4. Using a large rubber spatula, fold dry ingredients into wet ingredients just until moistened. Do not overmix.

5. In a small bowl, and using a wooden spoon or an electric mixer on medium speed, beat vegan cream cheese and confectioners' sugar until creamy and smooth.

6. Spoon roughly ⅓ cup batter into each prepared muffin cup. Place 1 tablespoonful cream cheese mixture on top of batter, and top with 1 teaspoonful jam. Spoon remaining muffin batter on top to fill cups ¾ full. Sprinkle a little unbleached cane sugar on each muffin. Bake for 20 to 25 minutes or until light golden brown and muffin tops spring back when lightly touched.

7. Remove from the oven, and cool for 5 minutes in the pan on a wire rack. Carefully release muffins from the pan, and cool completely. Store in an airtight container, or freeze in zipper-lock bags.

> **BAKER'S BONUS**
>
> Melting vegan margarine in the microwave is a snap. Just place in a microwave-safe bowl and heat on medium power for 15 to 20 seconds or until liquid. Let cool slightly before adding to the muffin batter.

Carrot Cake Muffins with Lemony Glaze

Loaded with carrots, pineapple, and walnuts, and topped with delicious lemon icing, these spicy vegan muffins are just like moist and yummy baby carrot cakes, but without all the fuss.

Yield:	Prep time:	Bake time:	Serving size:
16 to 20 muffins	30 minutes	23 to 28 minutes	1 muffin

3 cups whole-wheat pastry flour

3½ tsp. aluminum-free baking powder

1 TB. cornstarch

1½ tsp. ground cinnamon

1 tsp. baking soda

¼ tsp. salt

½ cup rolled oats

½ cup soy, rice, or almond milk

½ cup Flaxseed Egg Substitute (recipe in Chapter 2)

½ cup canola oil

½ cup maple, agave, or brown rice syrup

1½ tsp. pure vanilla extract

¾ cup unsweetened crushed pineapple, drained

2 cups grated carrots (about 3 large carrots, peeled)

1 cup chopped walnuts

½ cup vegan confectioners' sugar

1 TB. fresh lemon juice

1. Preheat the oven to 375°F. Line 16 to 20 muffin cups with paper cupcake liners.

2. Into a large bowl, sift whole-wheat pastry flour, aluminum-free baking powder, cornstarch, ground cinnamon, baking soda, and salt, or blend with a wire whisk. Add rolled oats, and mix.

3. In a separate large bowl, and using an electric mixer fitted with a whisk attachment on high speed, beat soy milk, Flaxseed Egg Substitute, canola oil, maple syrup, and vanilla extract for 1 or 2 minutes or until light in texture and color. Add crushed pineapple and grated carrots, and mix again with a rubber spatula, scraping down the sides of the bowl as needed. Add chopped walnuts, and stir in.

4. Using a rubber spatula, fold dry ingredients into wet ingredients just until moistened. Do not overmix.

5. Using a ⅓ cup ice cream scoop, fill muffin cups ¾ full. Bake for 23 to 28 minutes or until muffin tops spring back when lightly touched.

6. Remove from the oven, and cool for 5 minutes in the pan on a wire rack. Carefully release muffins from the pan, and cool completely before icing.

7. While muffins cool, in a small cup, mix confectioners' sugar and lemon juice until smooth. Drizzle glaze over muffins, and let dry. Store in an airtight container, or freeze in zipper-lock bags.

BATTER UP!

You can easily double this recipe and freeze the rest for later. Or you can bake the entire batch of carrot muffin batter in an 8×8-inch baking pan for 35 to 45 minutes or until a knife inserted in the center comes out clean. When it's completely cool, drizzle some lemon icing over it.

Lemon Poppy Seed Muffins

These whole-wheat lemony muffins, featuring fresh lemon zest and crunchy poppy seeds and drizzled with lemon icing, not only taste good, but they're also good for you!

Yield:	Prep time:	Bake time:	Serving size:
16 to 20 muffins	30 minutes	23 to 28 minutes	1 muffin

3½ cups whole-wheat pastry flour	½ cup soy, rice, or almond milk
1 TB. aluminum-free baking powder	½ cup Flaxseed Egg Substitute (recipe in Chapter 2)
1 TB. cornstarch	½ cup canola oil
¾ tsp. baking soda	¾ cup agave or brown rice syrup
¼ tsp. salt	¾ cup plus 1 TB. fresh lemon juice
⅓ cup poppy seeds	4 tsp. pure lemon extract
Zest of 1 lemon	½ cup vegan confectioners' sugar

1. Preheat the oven to 375°F. Line 16 to 20 muffin cups with paper cupcake liners.

2. Into a large bowl, sift whole-wheat pastry flour, aluminum-free baking powder, cornstarch, baking soda, and salt, or blend with a wire whisk. Mix in poppy seeds and lemon zest.

3. In a separate large bowl, and using an electric mixer fitted with a whisk attachment on high speed, beat soy milk, Flaxseed Egg Substitute, canola oil, agave syrup, ¾ cup lemon juice, and lemon extract for 1 or 2 minutes or until light in texture and color.

4. Using a large rubber spatula, fold dry ingredients into wet ingredients just until moistened. Do not overmix.

5. Using a ⅓ cup ice cream scoop, fill muffin cups ¾ full. Bake for 23 to 28 minutes or until muffin tops spring back when lightly touched.

6. Remove from the oven, and cool for 5 minutes in the pan on a wire rack. Carefully release muffins from the pan, and cool completely before icing.

7. While muffins cool, in a small cup, mix confectioners' sugar and remaining 1 tablespoon lemon juice until smooth. Drizzle on muffins, and let dry. Store in an airtight container, or freeze in zipper-lock bags.

Best Blueberry Muffins

Plump, juicy blueberries make these whole-wheat muffins moist and tasty. You won't believe they're vegan!

Yield:	Prep time:	Bake time:	Serving size:
16 to 20 muffins	30 minutes	23 to 25 minutes	1 muffin

3½ cups whole-wheat pastry flour

1 TB. aluminum-free baking powder

1 TB. cornstarch

¾ tsp. baking soda

2 cups soy, rice, or almond milk

½ cup Flaxseed Egg Substitute (recipe in Chapter 2)

½ cup canola oil

¾ cup agave, brown rice, or pure maple syrup

4 tsp. pure vanilla extract

2½ cups fresh or frozen blueberries

¼ cup unbleached cane sugar

1. Preheat the oven to 375°F. Line 16 to 20 muffin tins with paper cupcake liners.

2. Into a large bowl, sift whole-wheat pastry flour, aluminum-free baking powder, cornstarch, and baking soda, or blend with a wire whisk.

3. In a separate large bowl, and using an electric mixer fitted with a whisk attachment on high speed, beat soy milk, Flaxseed Egg Substitute, canola oil, agave syrup, and vanilla extract for 1 or 2 minutes or until light in texture and color.

4. Using a large rubber spatula, fold dry ingredients into wet ingredients just until moistened. Do not overmix. Gently fold in blueberries, scraping down the sides of the bowl with a rubber spatula.

5. Using a ⅓ cup ice cream scoop, fill muffin cups ¾ full. Sprinkle a little unbleached cane sugar on each muffin. Bake for 23 to 25 minutes, or until muffin tops spring back when lightly touched.

6. Remove from the oven, and cool for 5 minutes in the pan on a wire rack. Carefully release muffins from the pan, and cool completely. Store in an airtight container, or freeze in zipper-lock bags.

BAKER'S BONUS

Fresh or frozen blueberries are fine for these muffins. If you do use frozen berries, be sure not to let them thaw.

Peachy Keen Muffins

These delicious muffins are studded with fresh, juicy peaches straight from the orchard. Orange juice and almond extract bring out the sun-kissed flavor of the ripe peaches.

Yield:	Prep time:	Bake time:	Serving size:
16 to 20 muffins	30 minutes	22 to 25 minutes	1 muffin

3¾ cups whole-wheat pastry flour

2¼ tsp. aluminum-free baking powder

1 TB. cornstarch

¾ tsp. baking soda

¼ tsp. salt

1 cup almonds, sliced and toasted lightly

⅔ cup soy, rice, or almond milk

½ cup Flaxseed Egg Substitute (recipe in Chapter 2)

½ cup canola oil

¾ cup agave, maple, or brown rice syrup

½ cup orange juice concentrate, not reconstituted

1½ tsp. pure almond extract

2½ cups fresh or frozen peaches, drained, blotted, and chopped small

¼ cup unbleached cane sugar

1. Preheat the oven to 375°F. Line 16 to 20 muffin cups with paper cupcake liners.

2. Into a large bowl, sift whole-wheat pastry flour, aluminum-free baking powder, cornstarch, baking soda, and salt, or blend with a wire whisk. Add almonds, and mix well.

3. In a separate large bowl, and using an electric mixer fitted with a whisk attachment on high speed, beat soy milk, Flaxseed Egg Substitute, canola oil, agave syrup, orange juice concentrate, and almond extract for 1 or 2 minutes or until light in texture and color.

4. Using a large rubber spatula, fold dry ingredients into wet ingredients just until moistened. Do not overmix. Gently fold in peaches, scraping down the sides of the bowl with a rubber spatula.

5. Using a ⅓ cup ice cream scoop, fill muffin cups ¾ full. Sprinkle a little unbleached cane sugar on each muffin. Bake for 22 to 25 minutes, or until muffin tops spring back when lightly touched.

6. Remove from the oven, and cool for 5 minutes in the pan on a wire rack. Carefully release muffins from the pan, and cool completely. Store in an airtight container, or freeze in zipper-lock bags.

Variation: If you don't have orange juice concentrate, you can substitute regular orange juice. Add 1 teaspoon pure orange extract to the batter as well.

Pumpkin Muffins

Smooth pumpkin, plump raisins, cinnamon, ginger, and nutmeg combine in these muffins that will remind you of fall foliage.

Yield:	Prep time:	Bake time:	Serving size:
20 to 24 muffins	30 minutes	22 to 25 minutes	1 muffin

4 cups whole-wheat pastry flour

1½ TB. aluminum-free baking powder

1 TB. cornstarch

1 tsp. baking soda

1 tsp. ground cinnamon

1 tsp. ground ginger

¾ tsp. ground nutmeg

¼ tsp. salt

3 cups soy, rice, or almond milk

¾ cup Flaxseed Egg Substitute (recipe in Chapter 2)

¾ cup canola oil

1 tsp. pure vanilla extract

1⅓ cups plus ¼ cup Florida Crystals, or unbleached cane sugar

2 cups canned or fresh pumpkin purée (see sidebar)

1 cup raisins

1. Preheat the oven to 375°F. Line 20 to 24 muffin cups with paper cupcake liners.

2. Into a large bowl, sift whole-wheat pastry flour, aluminum-free baking powder, cornstarch, baking soda, ground cinnamon, ground ginger, ground nutmeg, and salt, or blend with a wire whisk.

3. In a separate large bowl, and using an electric mixer fitted with a whisk attachment on high speed, beat soy milk, Flaxseed Egg Substitute, canola oil, vanilla extract, 1⅓ cups Florida Crystals, and pumpkin purée for 1 or 2 minutes or until light in texture and color. Add raisins, and mix well.

4. Using a large rubber spatula, fold dry ingredients into wet ingredients just until moistened. Do not overmix. Scrape down the sides of the bowl with a rubber spatula.

5. Using a ⅓ cup measure, fill muffin cups ¾ full. Sprinkle a little Florida Crystals on each muffin. Bake for 22 to 25 minutes or until muffin tops spring back when lightly touched.

6. Remove from the oven, and cool for 5 minutes in the pan on a wire rack. Carefully release muffins from the pan, and cool completely. Store in an airtight container, or freeze in zipper-lock bags.

> **DOUGH-NOT**
>
> You can also use fresh cooked and puréed pumpkin in these muffins, but be sure the pumpkin isn't full of water and moisture, as watery pumpkin purée can change the consistency of the muffins and they won't come out right. Otherwise, use canned pumpkin for this recipe.

Raisin Bran Muffins

Whole-wheat muffins with flaxseed, *oat bran*, maple syrup, and molasses, and loaded with raisins and walnuts—talk about fiber!

Yield:	Prep time:	Bake time:	Serving size:
16 to 20 muffins	30 minutes	22 to 25 minutes	1 muffin

2 cups whole-wheat pastry flour

1 TB. cornstarch

1¼ TB. aluminum-free baking powder

1 tsp. baking soda

1 tsp. ground cinnamon

¼ tsp. salt

1½ cups oat bran

1 cup soy, rice, or almond milk

½ cup Flaxseed Egg Substitute (recipe in Chapter 2)

½ cup canola oil

¼ cup maple syrup

½ cup molasses

2 cups raisins

1 cup chopped walnuts (optional)

¼ cup unbleached cane sugar

1. Preheat the oven to 375°F. Line 16 to 20 muffin cups with paper cupcake liners.

2. Into a large bowl, sift whole-wheat pastry flour, cornstarch, aluminum-free baking powder, baking soda, ground cinnamon, and salt, or blend with a wire whisk. Add oat bran, and mix well.

3. In a separate large bowl, and using an electric mixer fitted with a whisk attachment on high speed, beat soy milk, Flaxseed Egg Substitute, canola oil, maple syrup, and molasses for 1 or 2 minutes or until light in texture and color. Add raisins and walnuts (if using), and mix.

4. Using a large rubber spatula, fold dry ingredients into wet ingredients just until moistened. Do not overmix. Scrape down the sides of the bowl with a rubber spatula.

5. Using a ⅓ cup ice cream scoop, fill muffin cups ¾ full. Sprinkle a little unbleached cane sugar on each muffin. Bake for 22 to 25 minutes or until muffin top springs back when lightly touched.

6. Remove from the oven, and cool for 5 minutes in the pan on a wire rack. Carefully release muffins from the pan, and cool completely. Store in an airtight container, or freeze in zipper-lock bags.

VEGAN VOCAB

Oat bran is the outer husk of the oat grain. It's loaded with fiber and has a rich, nutty flavor. Find it in the bulk aisle of your local natural food store.

Strawberry Muffins

Make these muffins at the height of strawberry season. Juicy, fresh strawberries are always the best, but these muffins taste good even with frozen strawberries. Add some strawberry extract for extra flavor.

Yield:	Prep time:	Bake time:	Serving size:
16 to 20 muffins	30 minutes	22 to 26 minutes	1 muffin

½ cup nonhydrogenated vegan margarine, melted and cooled

3 cups unbleached all-purpose flour

1 TB. cornstarch

4 tsp. aluminum-free baking powder

¼ tsp. salt

Egg substitute for 2 large eggs

1 cup soy, rice, or almond milk

½ tsp. strawberry extract, or pure orange extract

1 cup plus ¼ cup unbleached cane sugar

1 pt. fresh strawberries, finely chopped

1. Preheat the oven to 375°F. Line 16 to 20 muffin cups with paper cupcake liners.

2. Into a large bowl, sift unbleached all-purpose flour, cornstarch, aluminum-free baking powder, and salt, or blend with a wire whisk.

3. In a separate large bowl, and using a whisk, whip egg substitute, soy milk, strawberry extract, and 1 cup unbleached cane sugar for 1 or 2 minutes or until well blended. Add melted vegan margarine, and whisk again.

4. Using a large rubber spatula, fold dry ingredients into wet ingredients just until moistened. Gently fold in strawberries. Do not overmix.

5. Using a ⅓ cup ice cream scoop, fill muffin cups ¾ full. Sprinkle remaining ¼ cup unbleached cane sugar on each muffin. Bake for 22 to 26 minutes or until lightly browned and muffin tops spring back when lightly touched.

6. Remove from the oven, and cool for 5 minutes in the pan on a wire rack. Carefully release muffins from the pan, and cool completely. Store in an airtight container, or freeze in zipper-lock bags.

BAKER'S BONUS

If you can't find fresh strawberries, frozen strawberries will work in this recipe. Don't let them thaw out though. Chop the strawberries, and use them frozen. They won't bleed as much or turn to mush.

Banana Muffins

A close cousin to the famous banana nut bread, these muffins contain a lot of fiber, thanks to the flaxseed, roasted sunflower seeds, mashed bananas, cinnamon, and nutmeg combination.

Yield:	Prep time:	Bake time:	Serving size:
16 to 20 muffins	30 minutes	22 to 26 minutes	1 muffin

4½ cups whole-wheat pastry flour

2 TB. aluminum-free baking powder

1 TB. cornstarch

1 tsp. baking soda

1 TB. ground cinnamon

¼ tsp. ground ginger

2 tsp. ground nutmeg

¼ tsp. salt

2 cups soy, rice, or almond milk

¾ cup Flaxseed Egg Substitute (recipe in Chapter 2)

¾ cup canola oil

2 tsp. pure vanilla extract

2 tsp. banana extract or pure vanilla extract

1⅓ cups plus ¼ cup Florida Crystals or unbleached cane sugar

2 to 3 extra-ripe bananas, peeled and mashed well (1 cup)

1 cup sunflower seeds, hulled and roasted

1. Preheat the oven to 375°F. Line 16 to 20 muffin cups with paper cupcake liners.

2. Into a large bowl, sift whole-wheat pastry flour, aluminum-free baking powder, cornstarch, baking soda, ground cinnamon, ground ginger, ground nutmeg, and salt, or blend with a wire whisk.

3. In a separate large bowl, and using an electric mixer fitted with a whisk attachment on high speed, beat soy milk, Flaxseed Egg Substitute, canola oil, vanilla extract, banana extract, Florida Crystals, and bananas for 1 or 2 minutes or until light in texture and color. Add sunflower seeds, and mix well.

4. Using a large rubber spatula, fold dry ingredients into wet ingredients just until moistened. Do not overmix. Scrape down the sides of the bowl with a rubber spatula.

5. Using a ⅓ cup ice cream scoop, fill muffin cups ¾ full. Sprinkle a little Florida Crystals on each muffin. Bake for 22 to 26 minutes or until muffin tops spring back when lightly touched.

6. Remove from the oven, and cool for 5 minutes in the pan on a wire rack. Carefully release muffins from the pan, and cool completely. Store in an airtight container, or freeze in zipper-lock bags.

Variation: For **Banana Nut Muffins,** add 1 cup chopped walnuts to the batter along with the sunflower seeds.

Tooty-Fruity Muffins

These muffins contain so much fruit, the dates, raisins, apricots, prunes, and fresh apples spill out of the muffin cups! Add some sunflower seeds for a loaded muffin.

Yield:	Prep time:	Bake time:	Serving size:
16 to 20 muffins	30 to 40 minutes	22 to 26 minutes	1 muffin

½ cup pitted dates

¼ cup dried pitted prunes

½ cup dried apricots

½ cup raisins

3½ cups whole-wheat pastry flour

1½ TB. aluminum-free baking powder

1 TB. cornstarch

1 tsp. baking soda

1½ tsp. ground cinnamon

1½ tsp. ground allspice

1 tsp. ground nutmeg

1 tsp. ground ginger

½ tsp. salt

1 cup sunflower seeds, hulled and roasted

1 cup soy, rice, or almond milk

½ cup Flaxseed Egg Substitute (recipe in Chapter 2)

½ cup canola oil

¾ cup maple syrup, agave, or brown rice syrup

2 tsp. pure vanilla extract

1 medium to large, peeled, cored, and finely chopped Cortland, Granny Smith, Empire, Gravenstein, or other hard crisp apple (1 cup)

¼ cup unbleached cane sugar

1. Preheat the oven to 375°F. Line 16 to 20 muffin cups with paper cupcake liners.

2. In a food processor fitted with a cutting blade, chop dried dates, dried prunes, dried apricots, and raisins until very fine.

3. Into a large bowl, sift whole-wheat flour, aluminum-free baking powder, corn-starch, baking soda, ground cinnamon, ground allspice, ground nutmeg, ground ginger, and salt, or blend with a wire whisk. Add sunflower seeds, and mix well.

4. In a separate large bowl, and using an electric mixer fitted with a whisk attach-ment on high speed, beat soy milk, Flaxseed Egg Substitute, canola oil, maple syrup, and vanilla extract for 1 or 2 minutes or until light in texture and color. Add chopped dried fruit mixture and apples, and mix well, making sure all fruit has broken up in liquid.

5. Using a large rubber spatula, fold dry ingredients into wet ingredients just until moistened. Do not overmix. Scrape down the sides of the bowl with a rubber spatula.

6. Using a ⅓ cup ice cream scoop, fill muffin cups ¾ full. Sprinkle a little un-bleached cane sugar on each muffin. Bake for 22 to 26 minutes or until muffin tops spring back when lightly touched.

7. Remove from the oven, and cool for 5 minutes in the pan on a wire rack. Care-fully release muffins from the pan, and cool completely. Store in an airtight container, or freeze in zipper-lock bags.

BATTER UP!

The dried fruit in this recipe needs to be chopped in a food processor until very, very fine, almost ground into mush, but not quite. If you don't have a food processor, do the job with a chef knife, coating the fruit in either a little oil, sugar, or flour from the recipe to make it less sticky on the knife.

Corn Muffins

This basic humble corn muffin recipe has yellow *cornmeal*, whole-wheat flour, and whole kernel corn in it for a real treat.

Yield:	Prep time:	Bake time:	Serving size:
12 to 16 muffins	15 to 20 minutes	20 to 24 minutes	1 muffin

1 cup unbleached all-purpose flour	Egg substitute for 2 large eggs
1 cup whole-wheat pastry flour	2 cups soy, rice, or almond milk
4 tsp. aluminum-free baking powder	½ cup unbleached cane sugar
¾ tsp. salt	½ cup canola oil
1½ cups cornmeal	1 (15-oz.) can whole kernel corn, drained (optional)

1. Preheat the oven to 375°F. Line 12 to 16 muffin cups with paper cupcake liners.

2. Into a large bowl, sift all-purpose flour, whole-wheat pastry flour, aluminum-free baking powder, and salt, or blend with a wire whisk. Add cornmeal, and mix well with a spoon.

3. In a separate large bowl, and using a whisk, whip egg substitute, soy milk, unbleached cane sugar, and canola oil for 1 or 2 minutes or until well blended. Add corn (if using), and mix well.

4. Using a large rubber spatula, fold dry ingredients into wet ingredients just until moistened. Do not overmix.

5. Using a ⅓ cup measure, fill muffin cups ¾ full. Bake for 20 to 24 minutes or until lightly browned and muffin tops spring back when lightly touched.

6. Remove from the oven, and cool for 5 minutes in the pan on a wire rack. Carefully release muffins from the pan, and cool completely. Store in an airtight container, or freeze in zipper-lock bags.

VEGAN VOCAB

Cornmeal comes in fine, medium, and coarse grind, and yellow, white, and blue colors. Steel-cut yellow cornmeal is ground with almost all the husk and germ removed. Stone-ground cornmeal is a bit nuttier. White cornmeal is most often used in southern cooking for cornbread, and blue cornmeal is a little more rare. Any of these colors can be used, but be sure the cornmeal is a fine grind for this recipe.

Buckles and Coffee Cakes

In This Chapter

- Delicious buckles
- Scrumptious coffee cakes
- Fruit-filled treats
- Chocolate and carob-based coffee cakes

The thought of Mom's crumbly cinnamon coffee cake with brown sugar streusel makes your mouth water. Or maybe Grandma's old-fashioned buckle loaded with blueberries does it for you. Just because you're vegan doesn't mean you have to do without these yummy treats. Whatever you choose—buckle or coffee cake—they're both in this chapter, dairy free and egg free.

Buckles Versus Coffee Cakes

What's the difference between a buckle and a coffee cake? Both buckles and coffee cakes are like quick breads and muffins, which rely on chemical leaveners such as baking powder and baking soda to rise.

A buckle is more like a one-layer cake with a finer texture. Buckles generally have fruit baked in the batter with a streusel topping that gives them a "buckled" look, hence the name. A coffee cake, on the other hand, has a more crumbly texture similar to a muffin, and most often it's adorned with cinnamon streusel topping.

Blueberry Buckle

This vegan buckle, with fresh lemon zest and cinnamon in the batter, is studded with plump blueberries. The finishing touch? The baked buckle is soaked with sweet-tart lemon syrup.

Yield:	Prep time:	Bake time:	Serving size:
1 (9-inch) buckle	30 minutes	45 to 50 minutes	1 slice

1½ cups unbleached all-purpose flour

⅓ cup light brown sugar, firmly packed

½ tsp. plus pinch salt

4 TB. grated lemon zest

⅓ cup plus 6 TB. nonhydrogenated vegan margarine

½ cup whole-wheat flour

1 tsp. cornstarch

1 tsp. aluminum-free baking powder

½ tsp. baking soda

¼ tsp. ground cinnamon

¾ cup plus ⅓ cup unbleached cane sugar

Egg substitute for 2 large eggs

½ cup Vegan Buttermilk (recipe in Chapter 2)

2½ cups fresh or frozen blueberries

¼ cup water

Juice of 1 lemon

1. Preheat the oven to 350°F. Lightly coat a 9-inch square or round baking dish with cooking oil spray.

2. In a medium bowl, and using a wooden spoon, blend ½ cup unbleached all-purpose flour, light brown sugar, pinch salt, and 2 tablespoons lemon zest. Add ⅓ cup vegan margarine, and using a pastry blender, *cut in* until mixture resembles small peas. Set aside for streusel topping.

3. Into a separate medium bowl, sift remaining 1 cup unbleached all-purpose flour, whole-wheat flour, cornstarch, aluminum-free baking powder, baking soda, remaining ½ teaspoon salt, and ground cinnamon, or blend with a wire whisk.

4. In a large bowl, and using an electric mixer fitted with a paddle attachment on high speed, beat remaining 6 tablespoons vegan margarine, ¾ cup unbleached cane sugar, and remaining 2 tablespoons lemon zest for 1 or 2 minutes or until light and fluffy, scraping the bowl as needed with a rubber spatula. Add egg substitute, mix well, and scrape down the bowl.

5. Reduce speed to low, add ½ of dry ingredients to batter, alternating with Vegan Buttermilk, and mix well.

6. Add remaining dry ingredients, and mix only until batter is well blended, scraping down the bowl once more. Using a spatula, fold in ½ of blueberries.

7. Spread batter into the prepared baking dish. Sprinkle remaining blueberries over batter, and sprinkle streusel topping mixture over top. Bake for 45 to 50 minutes or until light golden and slightly puffed.

8. Ten minutes before buckle is done baking, make lemon syrup. In a small saucepan over medium heat, bring remaining ⅓ cup unbleached cane sugar, water, and lemon juice to a boil, stirring constantly. Reduce heat to low, and cook syrup for 8 to 10 minutes or until slightly thickened.

9. Remove buckle from oven, and immediately pour hot lemon syrup over top, being careful not to splatter. Cool on a wire rack for at least 30 minutes before serving. Store in an airtight container, or double-wrap with plastic wrap or foil, and freeze.

Variation: For **Raspberry Buckle,** substitute fresh (not frozen) raspberries for the blueberries.

VEGAN VOCAB

Cut in is a method of incorporating fat into dry ingredients by breaking it into small pieces. With heat, moisture is released from the fat, creating a flaky texture. Much like using two knives cutting the fat into the dry ingredients in a crisscross pattern, it's quicker and less messy with the same results. You can also crumble the ingredients with your fingertips or blend with a fork until crumbly.

Orange Cranberry Buckle

Freshly squeezed orange juice and tangy cranberries make this buckle not only delicious, but pretty enough to serve to company.

Yield:	Prep time:	Bake time:	Serving size:
1 (9-inch) buckle	30 minutes	45 to 50 minutes	1 slice

1½ cups unbleached all-purpose flour

⅓ cup light brown sugar, firmly packed

½ tsp. plus pinch salt

4 TB. grated orange zest

⅓ cup plus 6 TB. nonhydrogenated vegan margarine

½ cup whole-wheat flour

1 tsp. cornstarch

1 tsp. aluminum-free baking powder

½ tsp. baking soda

¼ tsp. ground cinnamon

¾ cup plus ⅓ cup unbleached cane sugar

Egg substitute for 2 large eggs

½ cup Vegan Buttermilk (recipe in Chapter 2)

2½ cups fresh or frozen whole or sliced cranberries

½ cup chopped walnuts (optional)

¼ cup water

Juice of 1 orange

1. Preheat the oven to 350°F. Lightly coat a 9-inch square or round baking dish with cooking oil spray.

2. In a medium bowl, and using a wooden spoon, blend ½ cup unbleached all-purpose flour, light brown sugar, pinch salt, and 2 tablespoons orange zest. Add ⅓ cup vegan margarine, and using a pastry blender, cut in until mixture resembles small peas. Set aside for streusel topping.

3. Into a separate medium bowl, sift remaining 1 cup unbleached all-purpose flour, whole-wheat flour, cornstarch, aluminum-free baking powder, baking soda, remaining ½ teaspoon salt, and ground cinnamon, or blend with a wire whisk.

4. In a large bowl, and using an electric mixer fitted with a paddle attachment on high speed, beat remaining 6 tablespoons vegan margarine, ¾ cup unbleached cane sugar, and remaining 2 tablespoons orange zest for 1 or 2 minutes or until light and fluffy, scraping the bowl as needed with a rubber spatula. Add egg substitute, mix well, and scrape down the bowl.

5. Reduce speed to low, add ½ of dry ingredients to batter, alternating with Vegan Buttermilk, and mix well.

6. Add remaining dry ingredients, and mix only until batter is well blended, scraping down the bowl once more. Using a spatula, fold in ½ of cranberries and walnuts (if using).

7. Spread batter into the prepared baking dish. Sprinkle remaining cranberries and walnuts over batter, and sprinkle streusel topping over top. Bake for 45 to 50 minutes or until light golden and slightly puffed.

8. Ten minutes before buckle is done baking, make orange syrup. In a small saucepan over medium heat, bring remaining ⅓ cup unbleached cane sugar, water, and orange juice to a boil, stirring constantly. Reduce heat to low, and cook syrup for 8 to 10 minutes or until slightly thickened.

9. Remove buckle from oven, and immediately pour hot orange syrup over top, being careful not to splatter. Cool on a wire rack for at least 30 minutes before serving. Store in an airtight container, or double-wrap with plastic wrap or foil, and freeze.

BATTER UP!

Cranberries are not only a delicious addition to many baked goods, the tart berries are also well known for a number of health benefits. Ongoing studies have shown that consuming antioxidant-rich fresh and dried cranberries, along with fresh cranberry juice, may help reduce urinary tract infections. Adding cranberries as part of your daily diet may also help lower the risk of heart disease and certain cancers.

Apple Cinnamon Coffee Cake

This moist breakfast coffee cake, featuring fresh blueberries, apple pie filling, and a yummy brown sugar cinnamon streusel topping, is perfect with a cup of coffee.

Yield:	Prep time:	Bake time:	Serving size:
1 (9×13-inch) cake	30 to 40 minutes	45 to 55 minutes	1 slice

¾ cup light brown sugar, firmly packed

3⅓ cups unbleached all-purpose flour

2 TB. plus ½ cup nonhydrogenated vegan margarine

1 TB. plus 1 tsp. ground cinnamon

½ cup chopped toasted pecans (optional)

1½ TB. aluminum-free baking powder

¼ tsp. salt

Egg substitute for 2 large eggs

1½ cups soy, rice, or almond milk

1½ tsp. pure vanilla extract

1 cup unbleached cane sugar

1½ cups Apple Pie Filling (recipe in Chapter 22), or canned pie filling

¾ cup fresh or frozen blueberries (if frozen, do not thaw)

¼ cup vegan confectioners' sugar

1. Preheat the oven to 350°F. Lightly coat a 9×13-inch baking pan with cooking oil spray.

2. In a small bowl, and using a fork, blend light brown sugar, ⅓ cup unbleached all-purpose flour, 2 tablespoons vegan margarine, and 1 tablespoon ground cinnamon until mixture looks crumbly. Add pecans (if using), and mix well.

3. In a microwavable cup or bowl, melt remaining ½ cup vegan margarine in the microwave for 10 to 15 seconds. Allow to cool slightly.

4. Into a medium bowl, sift remaining 3 cups unbleached all-purpose flour, aluminum-free baking powder, salt, and remaining 1 teaspoon ground cinnamon, or blend with a wire whisk.

5. In a large bowl, whisk together egg substitute, soy milk, and vanilla extract for 1 minute or until frothy. Add unbleached cane sugar, and whisk until well blended. Add melted vegan margarine, and mix well.

6. Using a large rubber spatula, fold dry ingredients into wet ingredients, and mix only until moistened and blended. Do not overmix.

7. Spread ½ of batter into the prepared baking dish. Spread ½ of Apple Pie Filling on top of batter, being careful not to disturb it. Arrange ½ of blueberries on top of filling, and sprinkle ½ of streusel topping over blueberries. Spread remaining batter, remaining Apple Pie Filling, remaining blueberries, and remaining streusel on top.

8. Bake for 45 to 55 minutes or until top springs back when lightly touched or when a knife inserted into the center comes out clean. Cool completely on a wire rack. Sprinkle vegan confectioners' sugar on top of cake before serving.

Variations: For **Cherry** or **Blueberry Coffee Cake,** substitute Cherry or Blueberry Pie Filling (variations in Chapter 22), for the Apple Pie Filling.

BATTER UP!

For unbeatable flavor, roast the pecans first. Place whole or halved pecans on an ungreased lipped baking sheet. Bake in a 350°F oven for 10 to 12 minutes, stirring a few times until light brown and fragrant. You could also toast the pecans on the stovetop in a dry sauté pan over medium heat, stirring until toasted. Let cool and set aside.

Strawberry Cream Cheese Coffee Cake

This luscious almond-flavored coffee cake is layered with vegan cheesecake filling and strawberry preserves and sprinkled with an almond streusel topping.

Yield:	Prep time:	Bake time:	Serving size:
1 (9-inch) cake	30 to 40 minutes	45 to 60 minutes	1 slice

2 cups unbleached all-purpose flour

½ cup whole-wheat pastry flour

¾ cup plus ⅓ cup unbleached cane sugar

¼ cup light brown sugar, firmly packed

¾ cup nonhydrogenated vegan margarine, chilled

¾ tsp. aluminum-free baking powder

½ tsp. baking soda

¼ tsp. salt

½ cup vegan sour cream or yogurt

Egg substitute for 2 large eggs

1⅛ tsp. pure almond extract

1 (8-oz.) pkg. vegan cream cheese, softened

⅔ cup strawberry jam

½ cup sliced toasted almonds

¼ cup vegan confectioners' sugar

1½ tsp. soy, rice, or almond milk

1. Preheat the oven to 350°F. Lightly grease and flour a 9-inch *springform pan* with nonhydrogenated shortening, tapping out excess flour.

2. In a medium bowl, and using an electric mixer fitted with the paddle attachment on medium speed, mix unbleached all-purpose flour, whole-wheat pastry flour, ¾ cup unbleached cane sugar, brown sugar, and chilled vegan margarine for 1 minute or until mixture resembles fine crumbs, being careful not to let it clump up in a ball. Measure out 1 cup streusel, and set aside.

3. In the same bowl, add aluminum-free baking powder, baking soda, salt, and vegan sour cream to remaining streusel mixture. Using a mixer on medium speed, mix for 1 minute or until well blended. Add egg substitute for 1 egg and 1 teaspoon almond extract, and beat only until batter is smooth. Do not overmix.

4. Pour batter into the prepared springform pan and pat batter thickly on the bottom of the pan and ¾ of the way up the sides. Clean the mixing bowl.

5. In the same bowl, and using an electric mixer fitted with the paddle attachment on high speed, beat vegan cream cheese and remaining ⅓ cup unbleached cane sugar. Add remaining substitute for 1 egg, and beat for 1 minute or until light and fluffy. Pour batter into springform pan.

6. Spread jam very gently over batter, being careful not to disturb it.

7. Add almonds to the reserved bowl of streusel, and mix well. Carefully sprinkle over coffee cake, spreading evenly. Bake for 45 to 60 minutes or until middle seems set and no longer jiggly.

8. Cool coffee cake completely before removing springform ring. Carefully slide cooled coffee cake off the bottom and onto a flat cake plate. For best results, chill cake for 2 or 3 hours.

9. Before serving, using a spoon, mix confectioners' sugar, soy milk, and remaining ⅛ teaspoon almond extract until smooth, and drizzle over cooled cake.

Variations: For **Blueberry** or **Raspberry Cream Cheese Coffee Cake,** substitute blueberry or raspberry jam for the strawberry jam.

VEGAN VOCAB

A **springform pan** is useful for delicate baked goods like this coffee cake. The two-piece pan has a removable bottom and sides that spring open with a hinge and latch. The sides are closed and latched when baking and opened after the cake is cool enough to release without it breaking or oozing out. This is also the preferred pan for making cheesecakes.

Chocolate-Chip and Coffee Coffee Cake

This crumbly cocoa coffee cake, filled with real coffee and vegan semisweet chocolate chips and topped with a toasted pecan streusel, makes coffee time even more enjoyable.

Yield:	Prep time:	Bake time:	Serving size:
1 (9×13-inch) cake	30 to 40 minutes	35 to 45 minutes	1 slice

½ cup light brown sugar, firmly packed

½ cup plus 2 cups unbleached all-purpose flour

1 cup nonhydrogenated vegan margarine, softened

¼ cup chopped toasted pecans

½ cup whole-wheat pastry flour

2 TB. natural cocoa powder

2 tsp. aluminum-free baking powder

¾ tsp. baking soda

¼ tsp. salt

1 (8-oz.) pkg. vegan cream cheese, softened

1½ cups unbleached cane sugar

Egg substitute for 2 large eggs

½ cup soy, rice, or almond milk

¼ cup strong coffee

1 tsp. pure vanilla extract

1 cup vegan semisweet chocolate chips

1. Preheat the oven to 350°F. Lightly grease and flour a 9×13-inch baking pan with nonhydrogenated shortening, tapping out excess flour.

2. In a small bowl, and using a fork, blend light brown sugar, ½ cup unbleached all-purpose flour, and ¼ cup vegan margarine until mixture looks crumbly. Add pecans, and mix well. Set aside for streusel topping.

3. Into a large bowl, sift remaining 2 cups unbleached all-purpose flour, whole-wheat pastry flour, natural cocoa powder, aluminum-free baking powder, baking soda, and salt, or blend with a wire whisk.

4. In a separate large bowl, and using an electric mixer fitted with a paddle attachment on high speed, beat vegan cream cheese, remaining ¾ cup vegan margarine, and unbleached cane sugar for 1 or 2 minutes or until light and fluffy, scraping the bowl as needed with a rubber spatula. Add egg substitute, soy milk, coffee, and vanilla extract, and mix for 1 minute, and scrape the bowl once more.

5. Reduce mixer speed to low, add ½ of dry ingredients to batter, and mix to combine. Add remaining dry ingredients, and mix only until ingredients are incorporated. Do not overmix. Using a wooden spoon or rubber spatula, fold in vegan chocolate chips.

6. Spread batter into the prepared pan. Sprinkle streusel mixture over the top, and bake for 35 to 45 minutes or until a toothpick inserted into the center comes out clean. Cool for 30 minutes on a wire rack before serving.

> **BAKER'S BONUS**
>
> For this recipe, use either strong leftover coffee or dissolve 2 teaspoons instant coffee in ¼ cup water.

Cherry Carob Coffee Cake

Carob has a very unique taste, but in this coffee cake, it doubles for cocoa for those who can't have chocolate. Homemade cherry pie filling and sweet carob chips dress up this tasty cake.

Yield:	Prep time:	Bake time:	Serving size:
1 (9×13-inch) cake	20 to 30 minutes	40 to 50 minutes	1 slice

3½ cups whole-wheat pastry flour

½ cup carob powder, sifted

1 TB. aluminum-free baking powder

2 tsp. cornstarch

1 tsp. baking soda

½ tsp. salt

¾ cup soy, rice, or almond milk

¼ cup unsweetened apple juice concentrate, thawed

½ cup canola oil

¾ cup maple syrup

½ (12-oz.) pkg. soft silken tofu, drained

1 TB. pure vanilla extract

1¼ cups shredded unsweetened coconut (optional)

1 cup Cherry Pie Filling (variation in Chapter 22), or canned pie filling

½ cup carob chips (optional)

1. Preheat the oven to 350°F. Lightly *grease and flour* a 9×13-inch baking pan with nonhydrogenated shortening, tapping out excess flour.

2. Into a large bowl, sift whole-wheat pastry flour, carob powder, aluminum-free baking powder, cornstarch, baking soda, and salt, or blend with a wire whisk.

3. In a separate large bowl, and using an electric mixer fitted with a whisk attachment on high speed, beat soy milk, apple juice concentrate, canola oil, maple syrup, soft silken tofu, and vanilla extract for 1 or 2 minutes or until light and fluffy, scraping the bowl as needed with a rubber spatula.

4. Reduce speed to low, add ½ of dry ingredients to batter, and mix to combine. Add remaining dry ingredients, and mix only until ingredients are incorporated. Do not overmix. Using a wooden spoon or rubber spatula, fold in shredded coconut (if using).

5. Spread ½ of batter into the prepared baking dish. Spread or drop dollops of Cherry Pie Filling on top of batter, being careful not to disturb batter. Spread remaining ½ of batter on top, and sprinkle carob chips (if using) evenly on top. Using a sharp knife, gently drag the knife through the coffee cake to swirl. Bake for 40 to 50 minutes or until a toothpick inserted in the center comes out clean.

6. Cool for 30 minutes on a wire rack before serving.

Variation: For **Carob Walnut Coffee Cake,** add 1 cup chopped walnuts to batter before spreading in the pan.

VEGAN VOCAB

The phrase **grease and flour** means to prepare the baking pan with some sort of fat and flour to produce a nonstick surface. In most cases, either nonhydrogenated vegan margarine or a vegan solid shortening such as Crisco is used along with a bit of the flour you're using in the recipe. The easiest way to do this is to apply 1 or 2 teaspoons shortening on a paper towel and wipe the inside surface of the pan. Sprinkle about 1 tablespoon flour on top of the shortening, and tip the pan, rolling it around until the flour completely coats the shortening with a thin film. Tap out any excess flour and discard.

Danish, Scones, and Pastries

In This Chapter

- It's all about the dough
- Delicious Danishes
- Tantalizing turnovers
- Sweet, fruity scones

Imagine going to a fancy brunch and seeing that everything on the pastry tray is loaded with butter, eggs, and cream. So as a vegan, there's nothing at all for you to munch on. Then you spy a separate table full of beautiful Danish, turnovers, strudels, and scones, but you figure it's just like all the others. As you begin to sigh and turn away, you notice the hostess walking up to you. She says, "Ah, I see you found 'your' table! I asked the caterer to make up a bunch of vegan pastries just for you." You smile and consider hugging the hostess because at that moment, you feel like you've died and gone to vegan heaven.

Just about everyone loves pastry, and the dainties in this chapter certainly won't disappoint you. The luscious breakfast and brunch delicacies are here to satisfy your cravings without giving in to the off-limits dairy and eggs.

Danish, Puff Pastry, and Phyllo Dough

The main ingredients in traditional Danish dough and puff pastry dough are butter and, to a lesser degree, eggs. These traditional doughs are laminated. The dough is rolled out, coated with butter, and folded into many layers. It's chilled between rolling so it doesn't get too warm—and, thus, it's easier to handle—and can rest. The process of rolling, buttering, folding, and chilling is necessary to create a flaky dough.

The dough takes hours and hours of time to prepare, with plenty of hands-on action. Phyllo is another dough that takes time to roll and stretch until you get it just right.

These authentic doughs are all very labor-intensive, and unless you have lots of free time on your hands, you'll probably be looking for an easier way to make these tasty pastries at home.

Vegan Pastries

With the following recipes, you can make individual- and family-size pastries at home instead of buying them at the bakery—that is, if you could even find a vegan bakery near you. A braided Danish pastry filled with fruit and vegan cream cheese is a piece of art. Lovely turnovers and tender scones are all very tasty as well as pretty, with their colorful fruits and homemade pie fillings.

I've substituted vegan nonhydrogenated margarine—or vegan butter, if you will—for real dairy butter. And the vegan cream cheese filling tastes just like the real McCoy.

To make things even easier, and still absolutely delicious, I've included a quick Mock Danish Dough to use for a number of pastry recipes. It won't be multi-layered with butter like the nonvegan version, but it will taste awesome—and save you hours of prep time!

You can make the turnovers either with a great store-bought vegan puff pastry or with my Flaky Piecrust (recipe in Chapter 13). Apple Strudel baked in purchased vegan phyllo dough tastes just as good as if you slaved the whole day in the kitchen making it yourself.

And the best part of all? They're vegan, so lick your fingers and enjoy!

Mock Danish Dough

This easy sweet bread dough is rich with vegan butter and nondairy milk. It's soft and tasty with vanilla and cardamom and makes great individual breakfast pastries or long Danish braids.

Yield:	Prep time:
dough for 2 large Danish braids	30 to 60 minutes

1 cup warm soy, rice, or almond milk

2 TB. liquid or granule soy lecithin

¼ cup nonhydrogenated vegan margarine, melted

½ cup unbleached cane sugar

½ tsp. salt

1½ TB. vital wheat gluten

Egg substitute for 2 large eggs

1 TB. pure vanilla extract

¾ tsp. ground cardamom (optional)

3¼ cups bread flour

1½ TB. instant yeast

1. In a large bowl, and using a whisk or an electric mixer fitted with a dough hook attachment on low speed, mix together soy milk, soy lecithin, and melted vegan margarine.

2. Add unbleached cane sugar, salt, vital wheat gluten, egg substitute, vanilla extract, ground cardamom (if using), bread flour, and yeast, and mix until dough forms a ball.

3. Knead by hand, or in a stand mixer on low speed, for about 5 minutes, adding extra flour as needed if dough is too sticky. Stop the mixer, and push down dough if it starts to ride up the hook. Continue kneading 2 to 5 more minutes or until dough comes away from the sides of the bowl and forms a membrane when stretched (like a balloon that doesn't tear).

4. Turn out dough onto a lightly floured surface, knead by hand a few more times, and form into a ball. Cover with a kitchen towel, and let it rest for 15 to 20 minutes.

5. Use dough now, or refrigerate for up to 2 days.

BAKER'S BONUS

It's easy to make extra Mock Danish Dough and freeze it for later. After the dough has finished resting, pat it into a thin round disc, wrap it in plastic wrap, and freeze it for up to 1 month. Thaw overnight in the refrigerator, bring to room temperature, and knead it a few times to make it pliable again. Then simply use as directed in the recipe.

Apple Danish

This large, sweet pastry, chock full of apples, vegan cream cheese, and walnuts and sprinkled with brown sugar streusel, is finished with a drizzle of delicious lemon icing.

Yield:	Prep time:	Bake time:	Serving size:
2 large Danish braids, 10 slices each	30 to 60 minutes	25 to 30 minutes	1 slice

⅓ cup light brown sugar, firmly packed

1½ tsp. ground cinnamon

⅓ cup unbleached all-purpose flour

⅓ cup chopped walnuts (optional)

2 TB. nonhydrogenated vegan margarine, melted

1 batch Mock Danish Dough (recipe earlier in this chapter)

1 cup Apple Pie Filling (recipe in Chapter 22), or canned apple pie filling

1 batch Cream Cheese Filling (recipe in Chapter 22)

2 TB. soy milk

2 tsp. water

2 tsp. agave syrup

½ cup vegan confectioners' sugar

1 TB. fresh lemon juice

1. Line a baking sheet with parchment paper, or spray with vegetable shortening spray.

2. In a small bowl, using a spoon or your fingers, mix together light brown sugar, ½ teaspoon cinnamon, unbleached all-purpose flour, walnuts (if using), and vegan margarine until crumbly.

3. Divide Mock Danish Dough into 2 equal pieces. With a rolling pin, roll out large pieces into 2 (12×18×¼-inch thick) rectangles, trying to get the thickness as even as possible. Carefully place dough on the prepared baking sheet. With a dull butter knife, score a rectangle inside dough, leaving roughly 4½ inches on each of the wide sides and 3 inches on the long sides, being careful not to cut all the way through dough.

4. With a rubber spatula, spread Apple Pie Filling inside the score marks. Sprinkle remaining 1 teaspoon cinnamon evenly over apples. Carefully spoon Cream Cheese Filling onto pie filling and spread evenly on top. Sprinkle streusel mixture over cream cheese filling.

5. With a sharp knife, and starting at the longest edge, cut 1-inch strips on the diagonal from one end to the other, leaving a 1-inch space between filling and the beginning of the cut. Repeat on the opposite side.

6. To braid dough, begin at top of Danish at the small end, and on the right side, fold one strip over filling. Fold another strip, this time from the left side, over filling, overlapping last strip a little. Repeat with another strip on the right and one on the left. Repeat this pattern until you get to bottom of Danish. Pinch, and tuck ends under so filling doesn't leak out. Return to top of Danish, and pinch each strip together with strips that are touching.

7. Lightly cover Danish with plastic wrap and let rise in a warm place until nice and puffy, not quite double in size, being careful not to disturb Danish or expose it to any drafts.

8. Preheat the oven to 350°F.

9. Just before baking, brush Danish lightly with soy milk. Bake for 25 to 35 minutes or until golden brown and pastry feels firm. Allow to cool for 5 minutes, before removing to a wire cooling rack.

10. While Danish cools, in a small bowl, mix water and agave syrup. Using a pastry brush, gently brush agave wash lightly over Danish.

11. In a separate small bowl, mix confectioners' sugar and lemon juice until smooth. When Danish is completely cool, drizzle with icing. Let icing dry before covering lightly with plastic wrap. Eat the same day. Store leftovers in refrigerator. It does not freeze well.

Variation: For individual Danish or pastries, divide dough into 12 to 16 equal-size pieces. With a rolling pin, roll smaller pieces of dough into squares or circles. Continue with the rest of the recipe, omitting the braiding. Reduce baking time to 20 to 25 minutes, or until pastries are firm and golden brown.

BAKER'S BONUS

For variety, you can make this long Danish braid using cherry, lemon, pineapple, peach, raspberry, or strawberry pie filling.

Cheese Danish

These sweet dough pastries, filled with vegan cream cheese and drizzled with vanilla icing, are simply delicious.

Yield:	Prep time:	Bake time:	Serving size:
12 to 16 pastries	30 to 60 minutes	20 to 25 minutes	1 piece

1 batch Mock Danish Dough
 (recipe earlier in this chapter)

1 batch Cream Cheese Filling
 (recipe in Chapter 22)

2 TB. soy milk

2 tsp. water

2 tsp. agave syrup

½ cup vegan confectioners' sugar

1 tsp. pure vanilla extract

1. Line a baking sheet with parchment paper, or spray with vegetable shortening spray.

2. Divide Mock Danish Dough into 12 to 16 equal-size pieces. With a rolling pin, roll pieces of dough into approximately 5×5×¼-inch thick squares. Place roughly 2 tablespoons Cream Cheese Filling in middle of each dough piece. Fold each corner into each other on top of pastry, pinching each to seal, and making a pocket. Place on the prepared baking sheet, leaving enough room for pastry to spread.

3. Lightly cover Danishes with plastic wrap and let rise in a warm place until nice and puffy, not quite double in size, being careful not to disturb Danishes or expose them to any drafts.

4. Preheat the oven to 350°F.

5. Just before baking, brush Danishes lightly with soy milk. Bake for 20 to 25 minutes or until golden brown and pastries feel firm. Allow to cool for 5 minutes.

6. While Danishes cool, in a small bowl, mix water and agave syrup. Using a pastry brush, gently brush agave wash lightly over Danishes.

7. In a separate small bowl, mix confectioners' sugar and vanilla extract until smooth. When Danishes are completely cool, drizzle with icing. Let icing dry before covering lightly with plastic wrap. Filled and iced Danishes are best eaten the same day, and do not lend themselves to freezing. Store leftovers in the refrigerator.

BAKER'S BONUS

Individual unbaked Danishes can be frozen and baked later. Form the individual Danishes, and lay them out on a parchment-lined baking sheet. Do not top them with fillings or brush them with agave syrup or icing before freezing. Freeze solid, layer between parchment or waxed paper, and place in zipper-lock bags. Before baking, place frozen Danishes on prepared baking sheets, and let thaw completely. Allow them to fully rise as directed, top with fillings, and bake according to the recipe. Finish off with agave syrup and icing.

Raspberry Danish

Swirl this sweet Mock Danish Dough into round "snails," bake with a homemade raspberry pie filling, and drizzle with lemon icing for a deliciously easy pastry.

Yield:	Prep time:	Bake time:	Serving size:
12 to 16 pastries	30 to 60 minutes	20 to 25 minutes	1 piece

1 batch Mock Danish Dough
  (recipe earlier in this chapter)

2 TB. soy milk

2 cups Raspberry Pie Filling (recipe in Chapter 22), or canned raspberry pie filling

2 tsp. water

2 tsp. agave syrup

½ cup vegan confectioners' sugar

1 TB. fresh lemon juice

1. Line a baking sheet with parchment paper, or spray with vegetable shortening spray.

2. Divide Mock Danish Dough into 12 to 16 equal-size pieces. With your hands, and on a lightly floured surface, roll dough into a rope about 8 or 9 inches long. With one hand pushing and one hand pulling, twist dough. Pinch one end and hold it down while you spin rope around to make a spiral circle. Pinch tail end under to seal. Repeat with remaining pieces. Place on prepared baking sheet, leaving enough room for pastry to spread.

3. Lightly cover Danishes with plastic wrap and let rise in a warm place until nice and puffy, not quite double in size, being careful not to disturb Danishes or expose them to any drafts.

4. Preheat the oven to 350°F.

5. Just before baking, brush Danishes lightly with soy milk. Gently make a well in the middle of each pastry, being careful not to deflate dough, and spoon approximately 2 tablespoons Raspberry Pie Filling into indentation. Bake for 20 to 25 minutes or until golden brown and pastry feels firm. Allow to cool for 5 minutes.

6. While Danishes cool, in a small bowl, mix water and agave syrup. Using a pastry brush, gently brush agave wash lightly over Danishes.

7. In a separate small bowl, mix confectioners' sugar and lemon juice until smooth. When Danishes are completely cool, drizzle with icing. Let icing dry before covering lightly with plastic wrap. Filled and iced Danishes are best eaten the same day, and do not lend themselves to freezing. Store leftovers in the refrigerator.

Apple Strudel

This classic vegan Apple Strudel is made with raisins, nuts, breadcrumbs, and of course, plenty of apples. The flaky phyllo dough encases it all as it bakes to a beautiful golden brown.

Yield:	Prep time:	Bake time:	Serving size:
1 large strudel, 10 slices	30 to 60 minutes	30 to 40 minutes	1 slice

¾ cup fine breadcrumbs or crushed vanilla cookies	⅓ cup chopped walnuts
3 large Cortland, Granny Smith, Empire, Gravenstein, or other hard crisp apples	1 tsp. ground cinnamon
	½ tsp. ground nutmeg
	8 sheets frozen vegan phyllo dough, thawed
½ cup seedless raisins	½ cup nonhydrogenated vegan margarine, melted and cooled
¼ cup unbleached cane sugar	
¼ cup light brown sugar, firmly packed	¼ cup vegan confectioners' sugar

1. Preheat the oven to 350°F. Line a baking sheet with parchment paper, or spray with vegetable shortening spray.

2. On a lipped baking sheet, spread breadcrumbs in a single layer. Bake for 5 to 10 minutes or until golden brown. Set aside to cool completely.

3. In a large bowl, combine apples, raisins, unbleached cane sugar, light brown sugar, walnuts, ground cinnamon, ground nutmeg, and breadcrumbs. Drain off any liquid that may have collected in the bowl.

4. Place 1 phyllo sheet on the prepared baking sheet, and using a very soft brush or your hand, lightly spread 1 to 1½ tablespoons vegan margarine evenly over top. Add another sheet, and repeat with more vegan margarine. Repeat until all 8 phyllo sheets are stacked.

5. Spoon apple filling on short end of dough, leaving about 2 inches bare on each end. Starting at the edge nearest you, carefully roll strudel to the end, keeping it tight, and tucking in sides as you go along. Place on the prepared baking sheet, and brush with remaining melted vegan margarine.

6. Bake for 30 to 40 minutes or until golden brown and flaky. Cool completely on a wire rack before sprinkling with vegan confectioners' sugar. Wrap with plastic wrap and store any leftovers in the refrigerator. Double-wrapped in plastic wrap, this Apple Strudel can be frozen for longer storage. Do not add confectioners' sugar before freezing. Let thaw completely, and sprinkle with confectioners' sugar before serving.

BATTER UP!

Phyllo dough is made of raw, unleavened dough, rolled in paper-thin sheets. Look for vegan phyllo dough in the freezer section of large supermarkets. Thaw it overnight in the refrigerator, and be sure to keep the phyllo dough covered with a damp cloth while working with it because it dries out very fast.

Apple Turnovers

These traditional bakery turnovers are made with flaky vegan puff pastry dough and apple pie filling and then sprinkled with confectioners' sugar.

Yield:	Prep time:	Bake time:	Serving size:
12 turnovers	30 minutes	22 to 27 minutes	1 turnover

1 (17.25-oz.) pkg. frozen vegan puff pastry dough, thawed

2 cups Apple Pie Filling (recipe found in Chapter 22), or canned apple pie filling

1 or 2 TB. water, at room temperature

½ cup sifted vegan confectioners' sugar

1. Preheat the oven to 375°F. Line a baking sheet with parchment paper, or spray with vegetable shortening spray.

2. Unfold puff pastry and place it on lightly floured surface. If necessary, roll out pastry to a 10×15-inch rectangle. Using a pastry wheel or sharp knife, cut sheets into 6 (5×5-inch) squares.

3. Spoon approximately 2 tablespoons Apple Pie Filling into middle of each puff pastry square. Using a pastry brush, lightly moisten edges of each square with water.

4. Take one corner, and fold it over to the opposite corner to form a triangle. Crimp and seal edges of pastry with the tines of a dinner fork. Using a pair of sharp scissors, clip a small vent hole in middle of turnover. Place on prepared baking sheet, leaving enough room for pastry to spread.

5. Bake for 22 to 27 minutes or until turnovers are puffy and light golden brown. Cool completely on a wire rack before sprinkling with confectioners' sugar. Baked turnovers freeze well. Simply omit the confectioners' sugar before layering between parchment or waxed paper, and freezing in zipper-lock bags. Thaw and sprinkle with confectioners' sugar before serving.

DOUGH-NOT

Most store-bought puff pastry dough is vegan, but homemade puff pastry dough is generally made with butter. Be sure to check the ingredient list for hidden nonvegan ingredients.

Blueberry Turnovers

These old-fashioned blueberry piecrust turnovers are made with homemade Flaky Piecrust and blueberry pie filling and then sprinkled with sugar.

Yield:	Prep time:	Bake time:	Serving size:
12 turnovers	30 minutes	22 to 27 minutes	1 turnover

1 batch Flaky Piecrust (recipe in Chapter 13)

2 cups Blueberry Pie Filling (recipe in Chapter 22), or canned blueberry pie filling

1 or 2 TB. water, at room temperature

2 or 3 TB. soy, rice, or almond milk

¼ cup unbleached cane sugar

1. Preheat the oven to 350°F. Line a baking sheet with parchment paper, or spray with vegetable shortening spray.

2. Divide Flaky Piecrust dough into 3 equal-size pieces. Divide each piece into 4 equal pieces, for a total of 12 pieces. On a well-floured surface, and using a rolling pin, roll each piece of dough into a 5- or 6-inch circle.

3. Spoon 2 tablespoons Blueberry Pie Filling in center of each piecrust. Using a pastry brush, lightly moisten edges of each square with water.

4. Fold piecrust in half, and crimp and seal edges of pastry with the tines of a dinner fork. Using a pair of sharp scissors, clip a small vent hole in middle of turnover. Place on prepared sheet, leaving enough room for pastry to spread. Brush with soy milk, and sprinkle with unbleached cane sugar.

5. Bake for 22 to 27 minutes or until light golden brown. Cool completely on wire racks.

Variation: These turnovers work equally well with any other canned pie filling.

BAKER'S BONUS

Piecrust turnovers freeze great, so make a double batch now, eat half, and freeze the other half for later. Layer unbaked turnovers between waxed paper, and freeze for up to 2 months. Thaw overnight in the refrigerator, and bake the next morning.

Fresh Peach Scones

Make these scrumptious scones when peach season rolls around. Orange juice and orange extract bring out the flavor of the fresh fruit.

Yield:	Prep time:	Bake time:	Serving size:
12 scones	30 minutes	20 to 25 minutes	1 scone

2¼ cups unbleached all-purpose flour

1 TB. aluminum-free baking powder

¼ tsp. baking soda

¼ tsp. salt

¼ cup yellow cornmeal

2 TB. plus ¼ cup unbleached cane sugar

2 TB. light brown sugar, firmly packed

½ cup nonhydrogenated vegan margarine

Egg substitute for 1 large egg

½ cup plus 2 TB. soy milk

¼ cup orange juice

1 tsp. pure orange extract, or ¼ tsp. pure orange oil

¼ cup slivered or sliced almonds (optional)

¾ cup diced fresh or frozen peaches, peeled and blotted dry with paper towels

1. Preheat the oven to 375°F. Line a baking sheet with parchment paper, or spray with vegetable shortening spray.

2. Into a large bowl, sift unbleached flour, aluminum-free baking powder, baking soda, and salt, or blend with a wire whisk. Add cornmeal, 2 tablespoons unbleached cane sugar, and light brown sugar, and blend well. Add vegan margarine, and using a pastry blender, cut in until mixture resembles small peas.

3. In a medium bowl, whisk together egg substitute, soy milk, orange juice, and orange extract. Add to dry ingredients, along with almonds (if using), and mix only until dry ingredients are incorporated. Don't overmix dough. Gently fold in peaches to avoid bruising.

4. Turn out dough onto lightly floured surface, and divide into 2 equal pieces. (You might need more flour if peaches are extra juicy or dough is especially sticky.) Pat dough into round circles about ¾ inch thick.

5. Cut each circle into 6 wedges, and place on the prepared baking sheet, leaving enough room for pastry to spread. Lightly brush scones with remaining 2 tablespoons soy milk, and sprinkle with remaining ¼ cup unbleached cane sugar.

6. Bake for 20 to 25 minutes or until light brown. Cool for 5 minutes, and transfer scones to a wire rack to cool completely.

DOUGH-NOT

Resist the temptation to work too much flour into the dough or to overwork the dough. Scones are meant to be nice and tender, and overworking the dough will make them tough.

Strawberry Scones

Fresh-from-the-garden strawberries, plus strawberry soy yogurt to make them tender, equals a perfect summer treat.

Yield:	Prep time:	Bake time:	Serving size:
12 scones	30 minutes	20 to 25 minutes	1 scone

2¼ cups unbleached all-purpose flour

1 TB. aluminum-free baking powder

¼ tsp. baking soda

¼ tsp. salt

½ cup unbleached cane sugar

¼ cup yellow cornmeal

½ cup nonhydrogenated vegan margarine

Egg substitute for 1 large egg

½ cup strawberry soy yogurt

¼ cup unsweetened apple juice concentrate, not diluted

1 tsp. strawberry extract or pure vanilla extract

1 cup fresh diced strawberries, blotted dry with paper towels

2 TB. soy milk

1. Preheat the oven to 375°F. Line a baking sheet with parchment paper, or spray with vegetable shortening spray.

2. Into a large bowl, sift unbleached all-purpose flour, aluminum-free baking powder, baking soda, and salt, or blend with a wire whisk. Add ¼ cup unbleached cane sugar and cornmeal, and blend well. Add vegan margarine, and using a pastry blender, cut in until mixture resembles small peas.

3. In a medium bowl, whisk together egg substitute, strawberry soy yogurt, apple juice concentrate, and strawberry extract. Add to dry ingredients, and mix only until dry ingredients are incorporated. Don't overmix dough. Gently fold in strawberries to avoid bruising.

4. Turn out dough onto lightly floured surface, and divide into 2 equal pieces. (You might need more flour if strawberries are extra juicy or dough is especially sticky.) Pat dough into round circles about ¾ inch thick. Cut each circle into 6 wedges, and place on prepared baking sheet, leaving enough room for pastry to spread. Lightly brush scones with soy milk, and sprinkle with remaining ¼ cup sugar.

5. Bake for 20 to 25 minutes or until light brown. Cool for 5 minutes, and transfer scones to a wire rack to cool completely.

BATTER UP!

Frozen unsweetened apple juice concentrate gives a big boost of flavor to these scones. Do not dilute the juice, however; use it straight from the can, frozen or thawed. If you don't have the concentrated juice, you can use regular juice in its place.

Apricot Cheddar Scones

Now here's a delightful scone for your recipe collection: delicate vegan buttermilk scones with chopped apricots and vegan cheddar cheese baked into the dough.

Yield:	Prep time:	Bake time:	Serving size:
12 scones	30 minutes	20 to 25 minutes	1 scone

2 cups unbleached all-purpose flour

¼ cup whole-wheat pastry flour

3½ tsp. aluminum-free baking powder

¼ tsp. baking soda

¼ tsp. salt

¼ cup unbleached cane sugar

½ cup nonhydrogenated vegan margarine, chilled

Egg substitute for 1 large egg

½ cup Vegan Buttermilk (recipe in Chapter 2)

¼ cup unsweetened apple juice concentrate, not diluted

½ tsp. pure vanilla extract

1 cup grated vegan rice or soy cheddar cheese

¾ cup finely diced dried apricots

1. Preheat the oven to 375°F. Line a baking sheet with parchment paper, or spray with vegetable shortening spray.

2. Into a large bowl, sift unbleached all-purpose flour, whole-wheat pastry flour, aluminum-free baking powder, baking soda, and salt, or blend with a wire whisk. Add unbleached cane sugar, and blend well. Add vegan margarine, and using a pastry blender, cut in until mixture resembles very small peas.

3. In a medium bowl, whisk together egg substitute, Vegan Buttermilk, apple juice concentrate, and vanilla extract. Add to dry ingredients, and mix only until dry ingredients are incorporated. Don't overmix dough. Gently fold in vegan cheddar cheese and dried apricots.

4. Turn out dough onto a well-floured surface. (You might need more flour if dough is especially sticky.) Using a rolling pin, roll dough to approximately ¾ inch thick. With a 3-inch biscuit cutter, cut out as many scones as possible, and place on prepared baking sheet, leaving enough room for pastry to spread. Gather up any extra dough, roll it or pat it, and cut out remaining scones.

5. Bake for 20 to 25 minutes or until puffy and light brown. Cool for 5 minutes, and transfer scones to a wire rack to cool completely.

> **BAKER'S BONUS**
>
> Hard vegan cheese needs to be grated before adding to this recipe. A simple way to do this is to use a regular cheese grater, or a Microplane grater with larger holes. Vegan cheese can also be grated in a small food processor with the grater attachment.

Breads, Rolls, and Flatbreads

In today's busy world, for most of us, our daily bread consists of basic and everyday sandwich breads, rolls, flatbreads, and crackers. Kind of boring, isn't it? It doesn't have to be!

Making and baking bread has often intimidated some of the most accomplished bakers, but it doesn't have to be the scary, all-day adventure it once was. Before the day of heavy-duty stand mixers and bread machines, a home baker would have to endure standing at the counter to knead the dough for at least 15 minutes until they felt as if their arms would fall off. Things have come a long way since then! You can make great-tasting bread in half the time, and without all the back-breaking, labor-intensive work. Thank goodness for technology and instant yeast!

Bread-making is an intensely personal endeavor. Getting your hands in the flour and kneading the dough can be very therapeutic. It can also be an artistic and creative expression to share with others—make two loaves, give one away.

And this part's quick breads sweetened with fruit and natural flavors are so good, you'll find yourself grabbing a slice and happily smacking your lips, knowing they're totally vegan.

Whatever your reason for making bread, I hope the recipes in Part 3 will become part of your daily bread collection!

Quick Breads

In This Chapter

- Tantalizing quick breads
- Mini loaf and muffin adaptations
- Sweet (and not-so-sweet) quick breads for any occasion
- Succulent cornbread

Quick breads are called "quick" because—you guessed it!—they don't take a long time to make. Quick breads are some of the first baked goods many of us learned to make as grade-school children or by baking with Grandma. These kid-friendly recipes are great for youngsters "playing baker" in the kitchen. With adult supervision, an apron, and a spatula, children can easily learn how to make delicious quick breads.

Usually leavened with baking powder and/or baking soda, these delicious breads take less time and effort than yeast-type breads. Traditional nonvegan quick breads also rely on eggs for binding and texture. However, the vegan quick bread recipes in this chapter get an extra kick from cornstarch, applesauce, and the chemical reaction of vinegar and baking soda.

Banana Nut Bread is probably the most popular quick bread, with the spicy Zucchini Bread coming in a close second. Don't stop there, though! I've given you plenty of varieties in this chapter to keep your taste buds satisfied for a very long time. And when you think you've exhausted this yummy list, get creative and add in your own extra goodies!

Making Mini Loaves and Muffins

There are times when you just don't feel like making a whole loaf of bread. Or maybe you have a brunch to go to and need individual servings. There's a deliciously simple solution: make muffins instead! If you thought quick breads were quick, you'll be amazed at how fast muffins are to whip up. All the bread recipes in this chapter are easy to convert into muffin recipes. Most large quick breads yield 8 to 12 muffins, depending on the size. Muffins usually bake for 22 to 26 minutes or until the tops spring back when lightly touched. Quick breads, on the other hand, can take more than an hour to bake. Lower temperatures ensure even baking and no burnt crust.

Quick breads make great hostess gifts, too. Wrapped in some colored or festive cellophane, and tied with a ribbon and gift tag, these breads are perfect to give away. They also make the cutest mini loaves. One large quick bread yields approximately 3 mini loaves. Follow the recipe, and divide the batter evenly among the greased mini pans you have, filling each ¾ full. Bake for approximately half the specified time, or until a knife inserted in the center comes out clean. Cool completely before wrapping, and hand them out to friends and family!

Cranberry Nut Bread

Full of flavor, this bread is packed with tart cranberries, and sweetened with agave syrup and orange juice. Fresh lemon zest and pure orange extract give this bread pizzazz, while chopped walnuts add extra crunch.

Yield:	Prep time:	Bake time:	Serving size:
2 (8×4-inch) loaves	30 minutes	50 to 65 minutes	1-inch slice

3½ cups whole-wheat pastry flour

2 TB. cornstarch

1 TB. aluminum-free baking powder

1½ tsp. baking soda

¼ tsp. salt

1 TB. lemon zest

⅔ cup soy, rice, or almond milk

¾ cup agave or brown rice syrup

½ cup canola oil

⅓ cup unsweetened orange juice concentrate, thawed

½ (12-oz.) pkg. soft silken tofu

1 TB. pure orange extract

1 cup fresh or frozen cranberries, chopped

½ cup chopped walnuts

1. Preheat the oven to 350°F. Lightly coat 2 (8×4-inch) loaf pans with cooking oil spray.

2. Into a large bowl, sift together whole-wheat pastry flour, cornstarch, aluminum-free baking powder, baking soda, and salt, or blend with a wire whisk. Add lemon zest, and mix well.

3. In a separate large bowl, and using an electric mixer fitted with a whisk attachment on high speed, beat soy milk, agave syrup, canola oil, orange juice concentrate, soft silken tofu, and orange extract for 1 or 2 minutes or until light and foamy. Scrape down the sides of the bowl with a rubber spatula.

4. Reduce speed to low, and with the beater attachment, add ½ of dry ingredients to batter, and mix well, scraping the bowl as needed with a rubber spatula. Add remaining dry ingredients, and mix for 1 or 2 minutes, scraping down the bowl, until batter is nice and smooth. Using a wooden spoon or rubber spatula, fold in cranberries and walnuts.

5. Pour batter into the prepared pans. Bake for 15 minutes, reduce temperature to 325°F, and bake for another 35 to 50 minutes or until a sharp knife inserted into the center comes out clean.

6. Cool loaves for 10 minutes in the pans. Gently remove from the pans, and cool completely on a wire rack before slicing. Wrap leftovers in plastic wrap, or freeze in zipper-lock bags for up to 3 months.

Variations: For **Coconut Cranberry Nut Bread,** add ¾ cup shredded unsweetened coconut to the batter. For **Cranberry White Chocolate Nut Bread,** add 1 cup vegan white chocolate chips to the batter.

BATTER UP!

For an extra burst of orange flavor, this recipe uses frozen unsweetened orange juice concentrate rather than ready-to-drink orange juice.

Apple Cinnamon Bread

Apple juice concentrate is the secret ingredient for extra flavor, and soft silken tofu gives the bread moistness. Add fresh apples and spices, and you have a winning combination!

Yield:	Prep time:	Bake time:	Serving size:
2 (8×4-inch) loaves	30 minutes	45 to 60 minutes	1-inch slice

3½ cups whole-wheat pastry flour

1 TB. cornstarch

1 TB. aluminum-free baking powder

½ tsp. baking soda

¼ tsp. salt

1½ tsp. ground cinnamon

½ tsp. ground nutmeg

⅔ cup soy, rice, or almond milk

¾ cup pure maple or agave syrup

½ cup apple juice concentrate, thawed

¼ cup canola oil

¾ cup soft silken tofu

1 TB. pure vanilla extract

2 large Cortland, Granny Smith, Empire, Gravenstein, or other hard crisp apples, peeled, cored, and finely chopped (2 cups)

1. Preheat the oven to 350°F. Lightly coat 2 (8×4-inch) loaf pans with cooking oil spray.

2. Into a large bowl, sift together whole-wheat pastry flour, cornstarch, aluminum-free baking powder, baking soda, salt, ground cinnamon, and ground nutmeg, or blend with a wire whisk.

3. In a separate large bowl, and using an electric mixer fitted with a whisk attachment on high speed, beat soy milk, maple syrup, apple juice concentrate, canola oil, soft silken tofu, and vanilla extract for 1 or 2 minutes or until light and foamy. Scrape down the sides of the bowl with a rubber spatula.

4. Reduce speed to low, and with the beater attachment, add ½ of dry ingredients to batter, and mix to combine, scraping the bowl as needed with a rubber spatula. Add remaining dry ingredients, and mix for 1 or 2 minutes, scraping down the bowl, or until batter is nice and smooth. Using a wooden spoon or rubber spatula, fold in apples.

5. Pour batter into the prepared pans. Bake for 45 to 60 minutes or until a sharp knife inserted into the center comes out clean.

6. Cool loaves for 10 minutes in the pans. Gently remove from the pans, and cool completely on a wire rack before slicing. Wrap leftovers in plastic wrap, or freeze in zipper-lock bags for up to 3 months.

Variation: For **Apple Cinnamon Nut Bread,** add ½ cup chopped walnuts to the batter.

BATTER UP!

Use hard apples when baking muffins, breads, and pies. Firm apples like Cortland, Granny Smith, Empire, Gravenstein, and other hard local apples stand up to long baking times, whereas soft apples turn to mush at high heat.

Pumpkin Pound Cake

This dense bread is plenty moist, thanks to the pumpkin purée, applesauce, and soy yogurt. Add in loads of spices—allspice, nutmeg, and cinnamon—and it's irresistible.

Yield:	Prep time:	Bake time:	Serving size:
1 (8×4-inch) loaf	30 minutes	45 to 55 minutes	1-inch slice

1¼ cups unbleached all-purpose flour

2 tsp. cornstarch

1¼ tsp. aluminum-free baking powder

½ tsp. baking soda

Pinch salt

⅓ tsp. ground cinnamon

⅓ tsp. ground allspice

⅓ tsp. ground nutmeg

⅓ cup nonhydrogenated vegan margarine, softened

½ cup plus 2 TB. unbleached cane sugar

⅓ cup unsweetened applesauce

⅔ cup canned pumpkin purée (not pumpkin pie mix)

⅓ cup soy yogurt

¾ tsp. pure vanilla extract

1. Preheat the oven to 350°F. Lightly grease and flour 1 (8×4-inch) loaf pan with nonhydrogenated shortening, tapping out excess flour.

2. Into a large bowl, sift together unbleached all-purpose flour, cornstarch, aluminum-free baking powder, baking soda, salt, ground cinnamon, ground allspice, and ground nutmeg, or blend with a wire whisk.

3. In a separate large bowl, and using an electric mixer fitted with a paddle attachment on high speed, beat vegan margarine and unbleached cane sugar for 1 or 2 minutes or until light and fluffy. Scrape down the sides of the bowl with a rubber spatula. Add applesauce, pumpkin purée, soy yogurt, and vanilla extract, and mix for 1 minute, scraping the bowl as needed.

4. Reduce speed to low, add ½ of dry ingredients to batter, and mix to combine. Add remaining dry ingredients, and mix for 1 minute or until batter is nice and smooth with no lumps. Scrape the bowl once more.

5. Pour batter into the prepared pan. Bake for 45 to 55 minutes or until a sharp knife inserted into the center comes out clean.

6. Cool loaf for 10 to 15 minutes in the pans. Gently remove from the pans, and cool completely on a wire rack before slicing. Wrap leftovers in plastic wrap, or freeze in zipper-lock bags for up to 3 months.

Variation: For **Walnut Raisin Pumpkin Pound Cake,** add 1 cup chopped walnuts and 1 cup seedless raisins to the batter.

BAKER'S BONUS

Need hostess gifts to bring to a party? Make mini Pumpkin Pound Cakes and wrap them in pretty cellophane bags. Follow the recipe directions, but prepare 7 to 9 mini loaf pans and bake for 25 to 35 minutes.

Pineapple Bread

Here's something different! This moist and delicious bread, with brown sugar, macadamia nuts, and pineapple, has just the right balance of sweet to tangy.

Yield:	Prep time:	Bake time:	Serving size:
1 (9×5-inch) loaf	30 minutes	50 to 65 minutes	1-inch slice

2 cups unbleached all-purpose flour

2 tsp. cornstarch

1½ tsp. aluminum-free baking powder

½ tsp. baking soda

½ tsp. salt

½ cup nonhydrogenated vegan margarine, softened

¾ cup light brown sugar, lightly packed

Egg substitute for 1 large egg, or ¼ cup unsweetened applesauce

1 (8-oz.) can crushed pineapple, with liquid

¾ tsp. pure vanilla extract

½ cup soy, rice, or almond milk

½ cup chopped macadamia nuts (optional)

1. Preheat the oven to 350°F. Lightly grease and flour 1 (9×5-inch) loaf pan with nonhydrogenated shortening, tapping out excess flour.

2. Into a large bowl, sift together unbleached all-purpose flour, cornstarch, aluminum-free baking powder, baking soda, and salt, or blend with a wire whisk.

3. In a separate large bowl, and using an electric mixer fitted with a paddle attachment on high speed, beat vegan margarine and light brown sugar for 1 or 2 minutes or until light and fluffy. Scrape down the sides of the bowl with a rubber spatula as needed. Add egg substitute, pineapple, and vanilla extract, and mix for 1 minute, scraping the bowl once more.

4. Reduce speed to low, add ½ of dry ingredients to batter, alternating with soy milk, and mix to combine. Add remaining dry ingredients, and mix just until batter is well blended, scraping down the bowl once more. Using a spatula, fold in macadamia nuts (if using).

5. Pour batter into the prepared pan. Bake for 50 to 65 minutes or until a sharp knife inserted into the center comes out clean.

6. Cool for 10 to 15 minutes in the pan. Gently remove from the pan, and cool completely on a wire rack before slicing. Wrap leftovers in plastic wrap, or freeze in zipper-lock bags for up to 3 months.

Variation: For **Pineapple Coconut Bread,** add ½ cup shredded unsweetened coconut to the batter.

Banana Nut Bread

This guilt-free bread gets its flavor from cinnamon, nutmeg, and fresh mashed bananas. Crunchy walnuts give it texture, and vegan chocolate chips … well, that's just over the top perfect!

Yield:	Prep time:	Bake time:	Serving size:
2 (9×5-inch) loaves	30 minutes	50 to 60 minutes	1-inch slice

3 cups unbleached all-purpose flour

1 tsp. ground nutmeg

1 tsp. ground cinnamon

½ tsp. salt

1 cup nonhydrogenated vegan margarine, softened

1 cup Florida Crystals or unbleached cane sugar

Egg substitute for 2 large eggs

3 or 4 bananas, peeled and mashed (2 cups)

1 tsp. pure vanilla extract or banana extract

2 TB. cider vinegar

2 tsp. baking soda

1 cup chopped walnuts (optional)

1. Preheat the oven to 350°F. Lightly coat 2 (9×5-inch) loaf pans with cooking oil spray.

2. Into a large bowl, sift together all-purpose flour, ground nutmeg, ground cinnamon, and salt, or blend with a wire whisk.

3. In a separate large bowl, and using an electric mixer fitted with a paddle attachment on high speed, beat vegan margarine and Florida Crystals for 1 or 2 minutes or until light and fluffy. Scrape down the sides of the bowl with a rubber spatula as needed. Add egg substitute, mashed bananas, and vanilla extract, mix for 1 minute, and scrape the bowl once more.

4. Reduce speed to low, add ½ of dry ingredients to batter, and mix to combine, scraping the bowl as needed with a rubber spatula. Add remaining dry ingredients, and mix for 1 minute, scraping down the bowl, or until batter is well blended.

5. In a small bowl, mix together cider vinegar and baking soda until dissolved. Add to batter, and mix only until well blended. Using a wooden spoon or rubber spatula, fold in walnuts (if using).

6. Pour batter into the prepared pans. Bake for 50 to 60 minutes or until a sharp knife inserted into the center comes out clean.

7. Cool loaves for 10 to 15 minutes in the pans. Gently remove from the pans, and cool completely on a wire rack before slicing. Wrap leftovers in plastic wrap, or freeze in zipper-lock bags for up to 3 months.

Variations: For **Chocolate-Chip Banana Bread,** substitute 1 cup vegan semisweet chocolate chips for walnuts, or add them in addition to walnuts. For **Cinnamon Streusel Banana Bread,** before baking, in a small bowl, mix 2 tablespoons softened nonhydrogenated vegan margarine, 2 tablespoons unbleached all-purpose flour, 2 tablespoons firmly packed brown sugar, and 1 teaspoon ground cinnamon. Sprinkle streusel on top of batter in pans, and bake as directed.

BAKER'S BONUS

To make Banana Nut Muffins instead, scoop the batter into 12 to 16 paper-lined muffin cups ¾ full. Bake for 22 to 25 minutes or until muffin tops spring back when touched. You can also sprinkle the muffins with streusel before baking (see variations).

Lemon Tea Cake

More like a dessert than a quick bread, this delicious tea cake not only has fresh lemon zest in it, it's also soaked in sweet lemony syrup, making it an extra-moist cake.

Yield:	Prep time:	Bake time:	Serving size:
2 (8×4-inch) loaves	40 minutes	50 to 60 minutes	1-inch slice

2½ cups unbleached all-purpose flour

2 TB. cornstarch

2 tsp. aluminum-free baking powder

¼ tsp. salt

2 TB. grated lemon zest

1 cup nonhydrogenated vegan margarine, softened

3½ cups unbleached cane sugar

1 cup soy yogurt, or soft silken tofu

1 cup soy, rice, or almond milk

1 cup fresh lemon juice

1. Preheat the oven to 350°F. Lightly coat 2 (8×4-inch) loaf pans with cooking oil spray.

2. Into a large bowl, sift together unbleached all-purpose flour, cornstarch, aluminum-free baking powder, and salt, or blend with a wire whisk. Add lemon zest, and mix well.

3. In a separate large bowl, and using an electric mixer fitted with a paddle attachment on high speed, beat vegan margarine and 2 cups unbleached cane sugar for 2 or 3 minutes or until light and fluffy. Scrape down the sides of the bowl with a rubber spatula. Add yogurt, and mix for 1 or 2 minutes, scraping the bowl once more.

4. Reduce speed to low, add ½ of dry ingredients to batter, and mix to combine, scraping the bowl as needed. Add remaining dry ingredients, and mix for 1 or 2 minutes. Add soy milk, and mix only enough to blend, being careful not to overmix. Scrape the bowl once more.

5. Divide batter into the prepared pans. Bake for 50 to 60 minutes or until a sharp knife inserted into the center comes out clean.

6. Cool loaves for 5 to 10 minutes in the pans. Gently remove from the pans, and cool slightly on a wire rack while making lemon syrup.

7. In a small saucepan over medium heat, bring remaining 1½ cups unbleached cane sugar and lemon juice to a boil, stirring constantly, until sugar dissolves. Boil for 1 more minute, stirring constantly, or until lemon syrup thickens slightly.

8. Turn off heat, and let cool 5 minutes. Using a fork or a skewer, prick tops of lemon tea cakes all over. Slowly pour hot syrup over lemon tea cakes, making sure to get into all the nooks and crannies. Let cool completely before slicing. Wrap leftovers in plastic wrap, or freeze in zipper-lock bags for up to 3 months.

DOUGH-NOT

The lemon syrup for this recipe should be hot (not boiling) when you pour it onto the Lemon Tea Cakes. As the syrup cools, it thickens, making it difficult to soak into the cakes. Warm the syrup on the stove, or microwave if it gets too cool, and then pour over the cakes immediately.

Zucchini Bread

This dessert bread is deliciously spicy. Add walnuts and vegan chocolate chips to make it really special.

Yield:	Prep time:	Bake time:	Serving size:
2 (9×5-inch) loaves	40 minutes	50 to 65 minutes	1-inch slice

3 cups unbleached all-purpose flour, or ½ all-purpose and ½ whole-wheat

1 TB. ground cinnamon

1 tsp. baking soda

1 tsp. cornstarch

½ tsp. salt

¼ tsp. aluminum-free baking powder

Egg substitute for 3 large eggs

1¾ cups Florida Crystals or unbleached cane sugar

1¾ cups canola oil

2½ tsp. pure vanilla extract

2½ cups finely grated zucchini, skin on and washed

1 cup chopped walnuts or pecans (optional)

1. Preheat the oven to 350°F. Lightly grease and flour 2 (9×5-inch) loaf pans with nonhydrogenated shortening, tapping out excess flour.

2. Into a large bowl, sift together unbleached all-purpose flour, ground cinnamon, baking soda, cornstarch, salt, and aluminum-free baking powder, or blend with a wire whisk.

3. In a separate large bowl, and using an electric mixer fitted with a whisk attachment on high speed, beat egg substitute, Florida Crystals, canola oil, and vanilla extract for 1 or 2 minutes or until light and fluffy. Scrape down the sides of the bowl with a rubber spatula. Add zucchini, and mix for 1 minute, scraping the bowl as needed.

4. Reduce speed to low, and with the beater attachment, add ½ of dry ingredients to batter, and mix to combine. Add remaining dry ingredients, and mix for 1 minute or until batter is well blended. Using a wooden spoon or rubber spatula, fold in walnuts (if using), and scrape the bowl once more.

5. Pour batter into the prepared pans. Bake for 50 to 65 minutes or until a sharp knife inserted into the center comes out clean.

6. Cool loaves for 10 to 15 minutes in the pans. Gently remove from the pans, and cool completely on a wire rack before slicing. Wrap leftovers in plastic wrap, or freeze in zipper-lock bags for up to 3 months.

Variation: For **Zucchini Chocolate-Chip Bread,** add 2 cups vegan semisweet chocolate chips to the batter before baking. Or add the walnuts *and* the chocolate chips!

BAKER'S BONUS

Zucchini Bread is an excellent way to use up all that extra zucchini in the garden—even the oversize zucchinis that are too tough to eat!

Gingerbread

Moist and spicy, this gingerbread cake is made with rich, thick molasses; cinnamon; and ginger. Add some crystallized ginger for a unique taste twist!

Yield:	Prep time:	Bake time:	Serving size:
1 (8×8-inch) cake	20 to 30 minutes	40 to 50 minutes	1 (2½×2½-inch) piece

1¾ cups unbleached all-purpose flour

1 TB. cornstarch

½ tsp. aluminum-free baking powder

¾ tsp. plus ½ tsp. baking soda

½ tsp. salt

1½ tsp. ground ginger

¾ tsp. ground cinnamon

¼ cup nonhydrogenated vegan margarine, softened

¼ cup Florida Crystals or unbleached cane sugar

Egg substitute for 1 large egg

⅔ cup molasses

½ tsp. apple cider vinegar

¼ cup chopped walnuts (optional)

½ cup water, at room temperature

¼ cup crystallized ginger (optional)

1. Preheat the oven to 325°F. Lightly grease and flour a 8×8-inch baking pan with nonhydrogenated shortening, tapping out excess flour.

2. Into a large bowl, sift together all-purpose flour, cornstarch, aluminum-free baking powder, ¾ teaspoon baking soda, salt, ground ginger, and ground cinnamon, or blend with a wire whisk.

3. In a separate large bowl, and using an electric mixer fitted with a paddle attachment on high speed, beat vegan margarine and Florida Crystals for 1 or 2 minutes or until light and fluffy. Scrape down the sides of the bowl with a rubber spatula as needed. Add egg substitute and molasses, mix for 1 minute, and scrape the bowl once more.

4. Reduce speed to low, add ½ of dry ingredients to batter, alternating with water, and mix to combine, scraping the bowl as needed with a rubber spatula. Add remaining dry ingredients, and mix for 1 minute, scraping down the bowl, or until batter is well blended and smooth.

5. In a small bowl, mix vinegar and remaining ½ teaspoon baking soda together until dissolved. Add to batter, and mix only until well blended. Fold in walnuts and crystallized ginger (if using) with a wooden spoon or spatula.

6. Pour batter into the prepared pan. Bake for 40 to 50 minutes or until a toothpick inserted into the center comes out clean.

7. Cool loaf for 15 to 20 minutes in the pan on a wire rack before serving warm. Wrap leftovers in plastic wrap, or freeze in zipper-lock bags for up to 3 months.

BAKER'S BONUS

For Ginger Brandy Whipped Topping, add 1 tablespoon brandy and 1 teaspoon ground ginger to 1 batch Whipped Topping (recipe in Chapter 22). Chill until thick. Before serving, top Gingerbread with a dollop of Ginger Brandy Whipped Topping.

Cornbread

This vegan cornbread, made with yellow cornmeal and whole kernel corn for texture, has just enough sweetness to eat by itself or stand up to a bowl of chili.

Yield:	Prep time:	Bake time:	Serving size:
1 (9×13-inch) loaf	20 minutes	30 to 40 minutes	1 (2½×2½-inch) piece

2 cups unbleached all-purpose flour

2 cups yellow cornmeal

2 TB. aluminum-free baking powder

1 tsp. baking soda

1 tsp. salt

Egg substitute for 3 large eggs

½ cup unbleached cane sugar

¾ cup canola oil

2 cups soy, rice, or almond milk

2 tsp. apple cider vinegar

1 (15-oz.) can whole kernel corn, drained

1. Preheat the oven to 350°F. Lightly coat a 9×13-inch baking pan with cooking oil spray.

2. Into a large bowl, whisk together unbleached all-purpose flour, cornmeal, aluminum-free baking powder, baking soda, and salt.

3. In a separate large bowl, whisk together egg substitute, unbleached cane sugar, canola oil, soy milk, and apple cider vinegar for 1 minute or until light and fluffy.

4. Add wet ingredients to dry ingredients, and mix to combine with a large rubber spatula. Fold in corn, and mix until batter is well blended, scraping the bowl as needed.

5. Pour batter into the prepared pan. Bake for 30 to 40 minutes or until a tooth-pick inserted into the center comes out clean.

6. Cool loaf for 15 to 20 minutes in the pan on a wire rack before serving warm. Wrap leftovers in plastic wrap, or freeze in zipper-lock bags for up to 3 months.

Variation: For **Savory Cornbread,** add 2 tablespoons minced fresh cilantro, ¼ cup diced chives, and 1 cup shredded cheddar cheese to the batter.

BATTER UP!

You can use either fine-ground yellow cornmeal for this recipe, or try using blue cornmeal for something really unique. Look for blue cornmeal in natural food stores.

Yeast Breads

In This Chapter

- Basic—but unbeatable!—breads
- Using yeast in yeast breads
- The least you *knead* to know about kneading

In this chapter, I give you a good selection of sweet breads, savory breads, and every-day sandwich breads. Basic breads such as white bread, whole-wheat bread, and rye bread will always be popular, and rightly so. Most of us grew up eating those breads at Mom's table. These doughs make great dinner rolls, too, so be sure to read Chapter 8 to see how they're made!

Feel free to make substitutions in these breads. Most of the recipes are flexible enough for changes, provided you don't change the structure of the bread. If you don't like raisins, leave them out of the Cinnamon Raisin Bread. Experiment with different herbs and spices in other doughs. Sweeteners can be changed as well, with the exception of molasses in savory herb breads like Sun-Dried Tomato and Olive Bread. Exchange agave, brown rice syrup, maple syrup, or honey if you're so inclined, keeping in mind that when you use substitutes, the flavor of the bread may come out different from what you expected.

Some ingredients may be new to you, but don't worry, you can find most of them at health food stores and co-ops in the bulk section, or in the organic aisle of large supermarkets. If you can't find liquid or granular soy lecithin or vital wheat gluten, you can just leave them out of the recipe. However, these ingredients give the bread its texture, lift, and structure, so your whole-grain breads might be a little heavier and more crumbly without them. Likewise, if you use too much whole-wheat flour, the bread won't be as light.

The Wonderful World of Yeast

Although many types of baker's yeast are used to make bread, the three most popular forms are compressed cake yeast, active dry yeast, and instant yeast. They all perform well, depending on the type of bread you're making, conditions in the kitchen, and availability.

Fresh yeast comes in a compressed cake and is very perishable. It needs to be refrigerated, tends to have a short shelf life, and needs to be activated in warm water before it can be used. Most home bakers have abandoned fresh yeast for these reasons.

Active dry yeast in the familiar yellow packets is sometimes found in the refrigerated section of the supermarket and should be refrigerated after it's been opened. Active dry yeast needs to be activated in warm (105°F to 115°F) water before mixing with the remaining ingredients. When using this yeast, you have to let the bread dough rise twice—once in the bowl, and again in the bread pans.

Instant yeast is—you guessed it—instant! Instant yeast is used most often in commercial bread recipes, and for ease of bread-making and consistency, most of the recipes that follow use it. Instant yeast doesn't have to be activated in warm water first, so it can go right into the bowl with the dry ingredients. The dough only has to rise once when you use instant yeast.

Instant yeast comes in 2¼ teaspoon packets, or 1-pound vacuum-packed bricks. It has a longer shelf life than fresh or active dry yeast, but after it's opened, package and seal it in an airtight container and store it in the refrigerator or freezer.

Substituting one form of yeast for another is easy, but there are ratios to take into account before baking. Substitute 25 percent less instant yeast for active dry yeast or, if substituting for fresh cake yeast, use 1 packet or 2¼ teaspoons instant yeast.

BATTER UP!

Most bread dough needs a warm place to rise before baking. Some people use their ovens. This works especially well with gas stoves because the pilot light provides just the right temperature for rising. For electric ovens, preheat to 150°F to 200°F for about 10 minutes. Turn off the heat, and place the unbaked bread inside until almost doubled in size. Just be sure to remove the bread prior to preheating the oven in preparation for baking; otherwise, it will begin to bake the bread before the oven and the bread is ready.

Hand-Kneading Versus Machine-Kneading

Making bread is a labor of love, and this labor is never so evident as in the act of kneading dough. Bread-baking is a creative passion for some … and a mundane task for others. Regardless, the dough needs to be kneaded. You can do that in a variety of ways: by hand, in an electric stand mixer, or in a bread machine.

The recipes in this chapter can be kneaded by hand or with a machine mixer. It takes roughly 12 to 15 minutes of hand-kneading to develop the bread dough properly. Unless you have strong arms and a good back, you might want to use a heavy-duty stand mixer fitted with a dough hook to knead the bread dough. Bread machines come with their own unique set of how-to instructions, so use these recipes as a guide for the ingredients, but follow the manufacturer's instructions for kneading and baking.

To knead dough by hand after mixing the dough, turn it out onto a well-floured surface. Press it down with both hands until the dough is flat. Fold it over onto itself. Working with the heels of your hands and firm pressure, push the dough forward and away from you. Fold the top of the dough over, turn ¼ turn, and push the dough again with the heels of your hands, adding small amounts of flour as needed if the dough is sticky. Fold it over again, push forward and fold, and turn the dough ¼ turn. Continue pushing, folding, and turning the dough for approximately 10 to 15 minutes or until the dough forms a membrane when stretched (sort of like a balloon that doesn't tear).

BAKER'S BONUS

Different varieties of bread may take longer to knead than others. To tell if the dough has been kneaded enough, press two fingers lightly into the dough. If it springs back up, the dough is done.

You can freeze leftover baked breads and rolls. Cool completely on wire racks, seal in plastic bags, and freeze for up to 6 months.

Homemade Sourdough Starter

Homemade sourdough is a tangy and bubbly living organism used to make all sorts of delicious baked goods. Basic sourdough bread is easy to make, provided you have a healthy, live starter. There are a few ways to make a sourdough starter. You can begin with a wild yeast starter, start with potato water and flour, or use this quick-and-easy version made with a little bit of yeast to jump-start the starter.

Yield:	Prep time:
2¼ cups	10 minutes

1 tsp. unbleached cane sugar

1 cup unbleached white flour, rye flour, or whole-wheat flour

1 cup warm (not hot) nonchlori-nated or spring water

1 tsp. instant yeast

1. In a clean, 8-cup glass jar, pottery crock, or plastic bucket, combine unbleached cane sugar, flour, water, and yeast. Cover with a kitchen towel, a loose piece of plastic wrap, or a loose-fitting lid; do not close tight. Set in a warm (70°F to 80°F) place, and let rest, undisturbed except when you stir it once or twice a day, for 3 or 4 days.

2. During that time, sourdough will smell tangy and yeasty and will be bubbly or foamy. It will rise and fall as it gives off gases. This is normal. Stir it down, cover, and refrigerate until ready to use.

3. Now that you've created a life, you need to feed and nurture it. At this point it's still a baby and needs to be cared for. As it gets older, it will soon be called "Mother" and has to be replenished each time you use "her." If you remove and use 1 cup starter, put 1 cup back. Replace with ½ cup flour and ½ cup water, mix in well, let her sit out for a few hours, cover, and put her back in the refrigerator. Once a month or so, add some room temperature potato water (cooking liquid left over after boiling potatoes) or ½ teaspoon yeast to help her along. You must remember to feed her often, or she will get moldy and die. Good sourdough smells pleasantly yeasty and tangy. Bad sourdough will have a moldy, musty smell, sometimes accompanying an off-color pinkish or yellow tinge. This means the sourdough has most likely gone bad and needs to be thrown away.

BATTER UP!

As your starter ages, you'll notice a brownish liquid that separates and floats to the top of the sourdough. This is called *hooch* and is perfectly normal, provided it smells pleasantly sour. If it smells foul—and you will know if it does—or it turns a different color or grows mold, throw it away and start again. Otherwise, stir the hooch back into the sourdough and feed as directed.

Sourdough Bread

This bread is an excellent way to experiment with Homemade Sourdough Starter. The older the starter, the tangier and yeastier tasting bread you'll have when it's done.

Yield:	Prep time:	Bake time:	Serving size:
2 large round loaves	30 to 60 minutes	25 to 35 minutes	1-inch slice

1 cup cold Homemade Sourdough Starter

1 cup hot water

2 TB. canola or vegetable oil

1 TB. agave, brown rice, or maple syrup

2 TB. liquid or granule soy lecithin

2 tsp. salt

3 TB. *vital wheat gluten*

1 cup whole-wheat flour

2⅔ cups bread flour

2 TB. instant yeast

1. Line a baking sheet with parchment paper, or spray with vegetable shortening spray.

2. In a large bowl, and using an electric mixer fitted with a dough hook attachment on low speed, combine Homemade Sourdough Starter, hot water, canola oil, agave syrup, and soy lecithin, or blend with a whisk. Add salt, vital wheat gluten, whole-wheat flour, bread flour, and instant yeast, and mix until dough forms a ball.

3. Knead by hand, or in mixer on low speed, for about 5 minutes, adding extra bread flour as needed if dough is too sticky. Stop the mixer, and push down dough if it starts to ride up the hook. Continue kneading 2 to 5 more minutes or until dough comes away from the sides of the bowl and forms a membrane when stretched (like a balloon that doesn't tear).

4. Turn out dough onto well-floured surface using bread flour, knead it by hand a few more times, and form it into a ball. Cover with a kitchen towel, and let it rest on the counter for 10 to 15 minutes.

5. Divide dough into 2 equal pieces, and roll each into a ball. Place seam side down on the prepared pan. Loosely cover dough with a kitchen towel and let rise in a warm place for 1 to 1½ hours or until double in size. Do not disturb bread or expose it to any drafts.

6. Halfway through the rise time, preheat the oven to 400°F.

7. Bake for 25 to 35 minutes or until bread sounds hollow when tapped lightly. Cool on wire racks.

VEGAN VOCAB

Vital wheat gluten, also known as instant gluten flour, is a powdered form of dehydrated pure wheat gluten (protein) used in the production of homemade bread. Heavier whole-grain bread doughs benefit from vital wheat gluten, because it strengthens the structure of the dough and gives it a better rise. Find it at a health food store or from an online baking ingredients company.

Rye Bread

This hearty and fragrant bread is made with rye flour, molasses, and caraway seeds and has a dense texture, perfect for making sandwiches.

Yield:	Prep time:	Bake time:	Serving size:
2 large round loaves	30 to 60 minutes	25 to 35 minutes	1-inch slice

2 cups warm water	4 TB. vital wheat gluten
2 TB. canola or vegetable oil	2 TB. caraway seeds
2 TB. molasses	3¼ cups bread flour
2 TB. liquid or granule *soy lecithin*	1¾ cups rye flour
2 tsp. salt	2 TB. instant yeast

1. Line a baking sheet with parchment paper, or spray with vegetable shortening spray.

2. In a large bowl, and using an electric mixer fitted with the dough hook attachment on low speed, combine warm water, canola oil, molasses, and soy lecithin, or blend with a whisk. Add salt, vital wheat gluten, caraway seeds, bread flour, rye flour, and instant yeast, and mix until dough forms a ball.

3. Knead by hand, or in mixer on low speed, for about 5 minutes, adding extra flour as needed if dough is too sticky. Stop the mixer, and push down dough if it starts to ride up the hook. Continue kneading 2 to 5 more minutes or until dough comes away from the sides of the bowl and forms a membrane when stretched (like a balloon that doesn't tear).

4. Turn out dough onto well-floured surface using bread flour, knead it by hand a few more times, and form it into a ball. Cover with a kitchen towel, and let it rest on the counter for 10 to 15 minutes.

5. Divide dough into 2 equal pieces, and roll each into a ball. Place seam side down on the prepared pan. Loosely cover dough with a kitchen towel and let rise in a warm place for 1 to 1½ hours or until double in size. Do not disturb bread or expose it to any drafts.

6. Halfway through the rise time, preheat the oven to 350°F.

7. Bake for 25 to 35 minutes or until bread sounds hollow when tapped lightly. Cool on wire racks.

Basic White Bread

This vegan sandwich bread is nice and soft inside, with a golden brown crust outside. It smells pleasantly yeasty and comforting and makes great dinner rolls.

Yield:	Prep time:	Bake time:	Serving size:
2 (9×5-inch) loaves	30 to 60 minutes	30 to 35 minutes	1-inch slice

¾ cup warm soy milk

¾ cup warm water

2 TB. canola or vegetable oil

2 TB. liquid or granule soy lecithin

4 TB. nonhydrogenated vegan margarine, melted

3 TB. unbleached cane sugar

2 TB. vital wheat gluten

1½ tsp. salt

4 cups *bread flour*

2 TB. instant yeast

1. Lightly coat 2 (9×5-inch) loaf pans with cooking oil spray.

2. In a large bowl, and using an electric mixer fitted with a dough hook attachment on low speed, combine soy milk, warm water, canola oil, soy lecithin, and vegan margarine, or blend with a whisk. Add unbleached cane sugar, vital wheat gluten, salt, bread flour, and instant yeast, and mix until dough forms a ball.

3. Knead by hand, or in mixer on low speed, for about 5 minutes, adding extra flour as needed if dough is too sticky. Stop the mixer, and push down dough if it starts to ride up the hook. Continue kneading 2 to 5 more minutes or until dough comes away from the sides of the bowl and forms a membrane when stretched (like a balloon that doesn't tear).

4. Turn out dough onto well-floured surface using bread flour, knead it by hand a few more times, and form it into a ball. Cover with a kitchen towel, and let it rest on the counter for 10 to 15 minutes.

5. Divide dough into 2 equal pieces, and roll each into a log, tucking ends underneath. Pinch seams with your fingers, and place bread seam side down on the prepared pans. Loosely cover bread with a kitchen towel and let rise in a warm place for 1 to 1½ hours or until double in size. Do not disturb bread or expose it to any drafts.

6. Halfway through the rise time, preheat the oven to 350°F.

7. Bake for 30 to 35 minutes or until bread sounds hollow when tapped lightly. Cool on wire racks.

VEGAN VOCAB

Bread flour is a high-gluten flour and is perfect for making breads where chewiness and loftiness are desired. It has a higher protein content than all-purpose flour, making it especially useful in heavier, whole-grain breads where that extra lift in the dough is needed. It's the gluten protein that, when mixed with water and agitated, creates elasticity and allows more stretch so the carbon dioxide from yeast fermentation is better contained. Although bread flour is excellent for some products, it's not a good choice for tender cakes and pastries.

Multi-Grain Bread

This multi-grain bread packed with fiber gets its texture and chewiness from corn-meal, oats, millet, flaxseed, couscous, sunflower seeds, rye flour, and buckwheat.

Yield:	Prep time:	Bake time:	Serving size:
2 (9×5-inch) loaves	30 to 60 minutes	30 to 35 minutes	1-inch slice

¼ cup cornmeal

¼ cup rolled oats

¼ cup millet

¼ cup sunflower seeds

¼ cup ground flaxseeds

¼ cup couscous

¼ cup rye flour

¼ cup buckwheat flour

2 cups warm water

3 TB. canola or vegetable oil

½ cup agave, brown rice, or maple syrup

2 TB. liquid or granule soy lecithin

1 cup grain and seed mix (see the following Batter Up!)

2 tsp. salt

3 TB. vital wheat gluten

1 cup whole-wheat flour

3 cups bread flour

2 TB. instant yeast

1. Lightly coat 2 (9×5-inch) loaf pans with cooking oil spray.

2. In a medium bowl, combine cornmeal, rolled oats, millet, sunflower seeds, flaxseeds, couscous, rye flour, and buckwheat flour.

3. In a large bowl, and using an electric mixer fitted with a dough hook attachment on low speed, combine warm water, canola oil, agave syrup, and soy lecithin, or blend with a whisk. Add grain and seed mix, salt, vital wheat gluten, whole-wheat flour, bread flour, and instant yeast, and mix until dough forms a ball.

4. Knead by hand, or in mixer on low speed, for about 5 minutes, adding extra flour as needed if dough is too sticky. Stop the mixer, and push down dough if it starts to ride up the hook. Continue kneading 2 to 5 more minutes or until dough comes away from the sides of the bowl and forms a membrane when stretched (like a balloon that doesn't tear).

5. Turn out dough onto well-floured surface using bread flour, knead it by hand a few more times, and form it into a ball. Cover with a kitchen towel, and let it rest on the counter for 10 to 15 minutes.

6. Divide dough into 2 equal pieces, and roll each into a log, tucking ends underneath. Pinch seams with your fingers, and place bread seam side down in the prepared pans.

7. Loosely cover the pans with a kitchen towel and let rise in a warm place for 1 to 1½ hours or until double in size. Do not disturb bread or expose it to any drafts.

8. Halfway through the rise time, preheat the oven to 350°F.

9. Bake for 30 to 35 minutes or until bread sounds hollow when tapped lightly. Cool on wire racks.

BATTER UP!

The grain and seed mix called for in this recipe can be whatever you can find in your pantry. Don't have millet or couscous? Substitute something else. Be sure to measure the grain mix before adding it to the bread dough. Store any remainder in a sealed container or zipper-lock plastic bag for another baking day.

Anadama Bread

This old-fashioned bread relies on molasses and cornmeal for its unique taste and texture. As the old folk tale goes, a fisherman was angry with his wife Anna for making the same gruel every day. When she added yeast and flour to the mix, he cursed her saying, "Anna, damn her."

Yield:	Prep time:	Bake time:	Serving size:
2 (9×5-inch) loaves	30 to 60 minutes	30 to 35 minutes	1 slice

2 cups warm water	3 TB. vital wheat gluten
3 TB. canola or vegetable oil	2 cups whole-wheat flour
¼ cup *blackstrap molasses*	2½ cups bread flour
2 TB. liquid or granule soy lecithin	⅔ cup cornmeal
2 tsp. salt	1½ TB. instant yeast

1. Grease or spray 2 (9×5-inch) loaf pans with cooking oil spray.

2. In a large bowl, and using an electric mixer fitted with a dough hook attachment on low speed, combine warm water, canola oil, blackstrap molasses, and soy lecithin, or blend with a whisk. Add salt, vital wheat gluten, whole-wheat flour, bread flour, cornmeal, and instant yeast, and mix until dough forms a ball.

3. Knead by hand, or in mixer on low speed, for about 5 minutes, adding extra flour as needed if dough is too sticky. Stop the mixer, and push down dough if it starts to ride up the hook. Continue kneading 2 to 5 more minutes or until dough comes away from the sides of the bowl and forms a membrane when stretched (like a balloon that doesn't tear).

4. Turn out dough onto well-floured surface using bread flour, knead it by hand a few more times, and form it into a ball. Cover with a kitchen towel, and let it rest on the counter for 10 to 15 minutes.

5. Divide dough into 2 equal pieces, and roll each into a log, tucking ends underneath. Pinch seams with your fingers, and place bread seam side down in the prepared pans.

6. Loosely cover the pans with a kitchen towel and let rise in a warm place for 1 to 1½ hours or until double in size. Do not disturb bread or expose it to any drafts.

7. Halfway through the rise time, preheat the oven to 350°F.

8. Bake for 30 to 35 minutes or until bread sounds hollow when tapped lightly. Cool on wire racks.

VEGAN VOCAB

Blackstrap molasses is the strongest-tasting molasses around. It's the thick, concentrated by-product left over after refining sugar cane into sugar, made from the third boiling of sugar syrup. Use it wherever you want a strong molasses flavor.

Cinnamon Raisin Bread

Your house will smell wonderful while this Cinnamon Raisin Bread bakes. Maple syrup, cinnamon, and plump raisins combined with whole-wheat flour makes delicious bread that makes great French toast!

Yield:	Prep time:	Bake time:	Serving size:
2 (9×5-inch) loaves	30 to 60 minutes	30 to 35 minutes	1 slice

1¼ cups seedless raisins	1 tsp. salt
½ cup water	1½ TB. ground cinnamon
1¾ cups warm water	2 TB. vital wheat gluten
2 TB. canola or vegetable oil	1 cup whole-wheat flour
¼ cup maple syrup	5 cups bread flour
2 TB. liquid or granule soy lecithin	1½ TB. instant yeast

1. Lightly coat 2 (9×5-inch) loaf pans with cooking oil spray.

2. In a small bowl, combine raisins and ½ cup water. Let soak for 15 minutes. Do not drain.

3. In a large bowl, and using an electric mixer fitted with a dough hook attachment on low speed, combine warm water, canola oil, maple syrup, and soy lecithin, or blend with a whisk. Add salt, ground cinnamon, vital wheat gluten, whole-wheat flour, bread flour, instant yeast, and raisins along with soaking water, and mix until dough forms a ball.

4. Knead by hand, or in mixer on low speed, for about 5 minutes, adding extra flour as needed if dough is too sticky. Stop the mixer, and push down dough if it starts to ride up the hook. Continue kneading 2 to 5 more minutes or until dough comes away from the sides of the bowl and forms a membrane when stretched (like a balloon that doesn't tear).

5. Turn out dough onto well-floured surface using bread flour, knead it by hand a few more times, and form it into a ball. Cover with a kitchen towel, and let it rest on the counter for 10 to 15 minutes.

6. Divide dough into 2 equal pieces, and roll each into a log, tucking ends underneath. Pinch seams with your fingers, and place bread seam side down in the prepared pans.

7. Loosely cover the pans with a kitchen towel and let rise in a warm place for 1 or 2 hours or until double in size. Do not disturb bread or expose it to any drafts.

8. Halfway through the rise time, preheat the oven to 350°F.

9. Bake for 30 to 35 minutes or until bread sounds hollow when tapped lightly. Cool on wire racks.

BATTER UP!

Soaking raisins in water before adding them to the bread dough makes them nice and plump. Don't drain off the soaking water though! It adds extra sweetness to the finished bread.

Whole-Wheat Bread

This lovely bread is made with wheat germ, agave syrup, and wheat flour for a hearty loaf that smells and tastes slightly nutty.

Yield:	Prep time:	Bake time:	Serving size:
2 (9×5-inch) loaves	30 to 60 minutes	30 to 35 minutes	1 slice

2 cups warm water

2½ TB. canola or vegetable oil

½ cup agave, brown rice, or maple syrup

2 TB. liquid or granule soy lecithin

1 tsp. salt

2 TB. wheat germ

3 TB. vital wheat gluten

6 cups whole-wheat bread flour

1½ TB. instant yeast

1. Lightly coat 2 (9×5-inch) loaf pans with cooking oil spray.

2. In a large bowl, and using an electric mixer fitted with a dough hook attachment on low speed, combine warm water, canola oil, agave syrup, and soy lecithin, or blend with a whisk. Add salt, wheat germ, vital wheat gluten, whole-wheat bread flour, and instant yeast, and mix until dough forms a ball.

3. Knead by hand, or in mixer on low speed, for about 5 minutes, adding extra flour as needed if dough is too sticky. Stop the mixer, and push down dough if it starts to ride up the hook. Continue kneading 2 to 5 more minutes or until dough comes away from the sides of the bowl and forms a membrane when stretched (like a balloon that doesn't tear).

4. Turn out dough onto well-floured surface, knead it by hand a few more times, and form it into a ball. Cover with a kitchen towel, and let it rest on the counter for 10 to 15 minutes.

5. Divide dough into 2 equal pieces, and roll each into a log, tucking ends underneath. Pinch seams with your fingers, and place bread seam side down in the prepared pans.

6. Loosely cover the pans with a kitchen towel and let rise in a warm place for 1 or 2 hours or until double in size. Do not disturb bread or expose it to any drafts.

7. Halfway through the rise time, preheat the oven to 350°F.

8. Bake for 30 to 35 minutes or until bread sounds hollow when tapped lightly. Cool on wire racks.

BATTER UP!

When mixing and kneading bread, it's important to be aware of weather conditions affecting your area at the time. Every day is different. Temperature and humidity play a big part in how much flour and water your bread will need. When adding water and/or flour during kneading, start with a few tablespoons at a time and see what happens before adding more.

Very Veggie Bread

Get all your veggies in one loaf of bread! This bread contains pops of green bell pepper, carrot, celery, and onion in a tomato-flavored bread. Oregano, basil, marjoram, and garlic add to this beautiful bread's awesome flavor.

Yield:	Prep time:	Bake time:	Serving size:
2 (9×5-inch) loaves	30 to 60 minutes	30 to 35 minutes	1-inch slice

½ green bell pepper, roughly chopped

1 large carrot, peeled, roughly chopped

2 stalks celery, roughly chopped

1 cup hot water

2½ TB. canola or vegetable oil

1½ TB. agave or brown rice syrup

2 TB. liquid or granule soy lecithin

½ cup tomato purée

2 tsp. salt

3 TB. vital wheat gluten

½ tsp. dried minced oregano leaves, or 1 tsp. fresh

½ tsp. dried minced basil leaves, or 1 tsp. fresh

¼ tsp. dried ground marjoram leaves, or 1 tsp. fresh

¾ tsp. garlic powder

2 TB. onion flakes

1½ cups whole-wheat flour

3½ cups bread flour

2 TB. instant yeast

1. Lightly coat 2 (9×5-inch) loaf pans with cooking oil spray.

2. In a food processor fitted with a cutting blade, coarsely grind green bell pepper, carrot, and celery, and measure to equal 1 cup.

3. In a large bowl, and using an electric mixer fitted with the dough hook attachment on low speed, combine hot water, canola oil, agave syrup, soy lecithin, and tomato purée, or blend with a whisk. Add salt, vital wheat gluten, oregano, basil, marjoram, garlic powder, onion flakes, whole-wheat flour, bread flour, instant yeast, and veggies, and mix until dough forms a ball.

4. Knead by hand, or in mixer on low speed, for about 5 minutes, adding extra flour as needed if dough is too sticky. Stop the mixer, and push down dough if it starts to ride up the hook. Continue kneading 2 to 5 more minutes or until dough comes away from the sides of the bowl and forms a membrane when stretched (like a balloon that doesn't tear).

5. Turn out dough onto well-floured surface using bread flour, knead it by hand a few more times, and form it into a ball. Cover with a kitchen towel, and let it rest on the counter for 10 to 15 minutes.

6. Divide dough into 2 equal pieces, and roll each into a log, tucking ends underneath. Pinch seams with your fingers, and place bread seam side down in the prepared pans.

7. Loosely cover the pans with a kitchen towel and let rise in a warm place for 1 or 2 hours or until double in size. Do not disturb bread or expose it to any drafts.

8. Halfway through the rise time, preheat the oven to 350°F.

9. Bake for 30 to 35 minutes or until bread sounds hollow when tapped lightly. Cool on wire racks.

BATTER UP!

Although dried herbs work just fine in this recipe, fresh herbs really add a special flavor. If you opt for fresh herbs, double the dried amounts called for in the recipe.

Spinach Garlic Bread

Savory and garlicky and oh-so-delicious, this stunning bread is studded with sautéed spinach and garlic. It goes great with an Italian dinner and will definitely impress your guests.

Yield:	Prep time:	Bake time:	Serving size:
2 (9×5-inch) loaves	30 to 60 minutes	30 to 35 minutes	1-inch slice

4 TB. canola or vegetable oil

3 TB. minced garlic

1 (10-oz.) pkg. frozen chopped spinach, thawed and drained well

2 cups warm water

1 TB. agave or brown rice syrup

2 TB. liquid or granule soy lecithin

1 TB. salt

3 TB. vital wheat gluten

1 TB. garlic powder

2 cups whole-wheat flour

3 cups bread flour

2 TB. instant yeast

1. Lightly coat 2 (9×5-inch) loaf pans with cooking oil spray.

2. Squeeze out as much liquid from spinach as much as possible.

3. In a medium frying pan over medium heat, heat 2 tablespoons canola oil. Add minced garlic and spinach, and sauté for 5 to 7 minutes or until garlic begins to brown and spinach starts to cook. Remove from heat, and set aside to cool for 15 to 20 minutes.

4. In a large bowl, and using an electric mixer fitted with a dough hook attachment on low speed, combine warm water, remaining 2 tablespoons canola oil, agave syrup, and soy lecithin, or blend with a whisk. Add salt, vital wheat gluten, garlic powder, whole-wheat flour, bread flour, instant yeast, and spinach-garlic mixture, and mix until dough forms a ball.

5. Knead by hand, or in mixer on low speed, for about 5 minutes, adding extra flour as needed if dough is too sticky. Stop the mixer, and push down dough if it starts to ride up the hook. Continue kneading 2 to 5 more minutes or until dough comes away from the sides of the bowl and forms a membrane when stretched (like a balloon that doesn't tear).

6. Turn out dough onto well-floured surface using bread flour, knead it by hand a few more times, and form it into a ball. Cover with a kitchen towel, and let it rest on the counter for 10 to 15 minutes.

7. Divide dough into 2 equal pieces, and roll each into a log, tucking ends underneath. Pinch seams with your fingers, and place bread seam side down in the prepared pans.

8. Loosely cover the pans with a kitchen towel and let rise in a warm place for 1 to 1½ hours or until double in size. Do not disturb bread or expose it to any drafts.

9. Halfway through the rise time, preheat the oven to 350°F.

10. Bake for 30 to 35 minutes or until bread sounds hollow when tapped lightly. Cool on wire racks.

BATTER UP!

If you have fresh spinach, you can use it in this bread. Finely chop and sauté clean, dry spinach as directed in the recipe. It takes approximately 1 pound fresh spinach to equal 1 (10-ounce) package frozen drained spinach.

Sun-Dried Tomato and Olive Bread

The combination of kalamata olives, sun-dried tomatoes, and rosemary give this bread a very unique flavor. The texture is so dense, it makes great bread for dipping in flavored olive oil.

Yield:	Prep time:	Bake time:	Serving size:
2 large round loaves	30 to 60 minutes	25 to 35 minutes	1-inch slice

2 cups warm water

2 TB. canola or vegetable oil

2 TB. agave or brown rice syrup

2 TB. liquid or granule soy lecithin

1 TB. salt

2 TB. vital wheat gluten

1 tsp. ground dried rosemary leaves

1 tsp. minced dried parsley flakes

1½ cups whole-wheat flour

3½ cups bread flour

2 TB. instant yeast

¾ cup chopped sun-dried tomatoes in oil, drained

¾ cup chopped pitted kalamata olives, drained

1. Line a baking sheet with parchment paper, or spray with vegetable shortening spray.

2. In a large bowl, and using an electric mixer fitted with a dough hook attachment on low speed, combine warm water, canola oil, agave syrup, and soy lecithin, or blend with a whisk. Add salt, vital wheat gluten, rosemary, parsley, whole-wheat flour, bread flour, and instant yeast, and mix until dough forms a ball.

3. Knead by hand, or in mixer on low speed, for about 5 minutes, adding extra flour as needed if dough is too sticky. Stop the mixer, and push down dough if it starts to ride up the hook. Add sun-dried tomatoes and kalamata olives. Continue kneading 2 to 5 more minutes or until dough comes away from the sides of the bowl and forms a membrane when stretched (like a balloon that doesn't tear).

4. Turn out dough onto well-floured surface, knead it by hand a few more times, and form it into a ball. Cover with a kitchen towel, and let it rest on the counter for 10 to 15 minutes.

5. Divide dough into 2 equal pieces, and roll each into a tight ball, tucking ends underneath. Place seam side down on the prepared pan.

6. Loosely cover bread with a kitchen towel and let rise in a warm place for 1 to 1½ hours or until double in size. Do not disturb bread or expose it to any drafts.

7. Halfway through the rise time, preheat the oven to 400°F.

8. Bake for 25 to 35 minutes or until bread sounds hollow when tapped lightly. Cool on wire racks.

BATTER UP!

You can make this bread in either free-form loaves on a baking sheet or formed into loaves and placed in regular-size bread pans. If making into loaves, bake at 350°F for 30 to 35 minutes.

Rolls and Sweet Breads

8

In This Chapter

- Savory and sweet rolls
- Beautiful biscuits and buns
- Making rolls from bread recipes

Now we're on a roll! Rolls make great mini sandwiches, mini sliders, and dinner rolls, or you can eat them as is, just because you can! When most people think of rolls and biscuits, they think of plain white dinner rolls. The rolls in this chapter will change your mind about that and get you drooling for sweet and savory buns. Try them all, and you'll see vegan baking doesn't have to be boring anymore!

Doing Double Duty from Breads to Rolls

With the exception of Irish Soda Bread, all the breads in Chapter 7 can do double duty and make mini breads, sandwich rolls, or dinner rolls. The dough is made the same way, and you can throw in a few extra herbs and spices for variety.

A regular-size loaf of bread weighs approximately 24 ounces. Mini breads weigh about 8 ounces, sandwich rolls weigh roughly 3 ounces, and dinner rolls weigh between 1¾ and 2 ounces. One loaf of bread yields approximately 3 mini breads, 8 sandwich rolls, or 12 to 16 dinner rolls, give or take. Mini breads and rolls bake at the same temperature as the large breads, but the baking time is reduced to 20 to 25 minutes for minis and 18 to 22 minutes for rolls, or until they're golden brown and baked through.

Snowflake Rolls

Also known as Fairy Rolls, these deliciously yeasty-smelling rolls have "snowy" flour sprinkled on top.

Yield:	Prep time:	Bake time:	Serving size:
24 rolls	30 to 40 minutes	22 to 25 minutes	1 roll

¾ cup warm soy milk	1 tsp. aluminum-free baking powder
¾ cup warm water	
1 TB. canola or vegetable oil	1 tsp. salt
6 TB. nonhydrogenated vegan margarine, melted	4 cups bread flour
	1 TB. instant yeast
2 TB. unbleached cane sugar	½ cup unbleached all-purpose flour

1. Line a baking sheet with parchment paper, or spray with vegetable shortening spray.

2. In a large bowl, and using an electric mixer fitted with a dough hook attachment on low speed, combine warm soy milk, warm water, canola oil, and vegan margarine, or blend with a whisk. Add unbleached cane sugar, aluminum-free baking powder, salt, bread flour, and instant yeast, and mix until dough forms a ball.

3. Knead by hand, or in mixer on low speed, for about 5 minutes, adding extra flour as needed if dough is too sticky. Stop the mixer, and push down dough if it starts to ride up the hook. Continue kneading 2 to 5 more minutes or until dough comes away from the sides of the bowl and forms a membrane when stretched (like a balloon that doesn't tear).

4. Turn out dough onto well-floured surface using unbleached all-purpose flour, knead it by hand a few more times, and form it into a ball. Cover with a kitchen towel, and let it rest on the counter for 10 minutes.

5. Divide dough into 4 equal pieces and then divide each into 6 more pieces. Roll 2 at a time, one in each hand, in a circular motion on a lightly oiled surface until dough balls are tight and compact. Dip each ball into unbleached all-purpose flour, shake off excess, and place almost next to each other on the prepared pan.

6. Loosely cover with a kitchen towel, and let rise in a warm place for about 1 hour or until double in size. Do not disturb bread or expose to any drafts.

7. Halfway through the rise time, preheat the oven to 350°F.

8. Bake for 22 to 25 minutes or until rolls are lightly browned. Cool on wire racks.

 BATTER UP!

Don't be surprised to see baking powder *and* yeast in this recipe. One of the reasons the Snowflake Rolls are so light and fluffy is because they're made with two leavening agents.

Sweet Potato Rolls

Sweet potatoes, thyme, and garlic powder combine in these flavorful and delicious rolls perfect for holiday dinners. A small amount of potato flakes makes them soft and tender.

Yield:	Prep time:	Bake time:	Serving size:
24 rolls	30 to 40 minutes	22 to 25 minutes	1 roll

1½ cups very warm water

2 TB. canola or vegetable oil

2 TB. agave, brown rice, or maple syrup

2 TB. liquid or granule soy lecithin

2 tsp. salt

3 TB. vital wheat gluten

2 tsp. ground dried thyme leaves

½ tsp. garlic powder

1¾ cups whole-wheat flour

2¾ cups bread flour

2½ TB. instant yeast

⅔ cups sweet potatoes, canned or freshly cooked and mashed, firmly packed

3 TB. instant mashed potato flakes

1. Line a baking sheet with parchment paper, or spray with vegetable shortening spray.

2. In a large bowl, and using an electric mixer fitted with a dough hook attachment on low speed, combine very warm water, canola oil, agave syrup, and soy lecithin, or blend with a whisk. Add salt, vital wheat gluten, ground thyme leaves, garlic powder, whole-wheat flour, bread flour, instant yeast, sweet potatoes, and instant potato flakes, and mix until dough forms a ball.

3. Knead by hand, or in mixer on low speed, for about 5 minutes, adding extra flour as needed if dough is too sticky. Stop the mixer, and push down dough if it starts to ride up the hook. Continue kneading 2 to 5 more minutes or until dough comes away from the sides of the bowl and forms a membrane when stretched (like a balloon that doesn't tear).

4. Turn out dough onto well-floured surface using bread flour, knead it by hand a few more times, and form it into a ball. Cover with a kitchen towel, and let it rest on the counter for 10 minutes.

5. Divide dough into 4 equal pieces and then divide each into 6 more pieces. Roll 2 at a time, one in each hand, in a circular motion on a lightly oiled surface until dough balls are tight and compact. Place almost next to each other on the prepared pan.

6. Loosely cover with a kitchen towel, and let rise in a warm place for about 1 hour or until double in size. Do not disturb bread or expose to any drafts.

7. Halfway through the rise time, preheat the oven to 350°F.

8. Bake for 22 to 25 minutes or until rolls are lightly browned. Cool on wire racks.

BAKER'S BONUS

You can use either canned or fresh sweet potatoes or yams in this recipe. Drain canned sweet potatoes before using and mash slightly with a fork. If using fresh potatoes, bake 1 large clean sweet potato in a 375°F conventional oven for 60 minutes or until a fork pierces the potato easily. Peel and mash the potato with a fork until smooth. Or microwave the sweet potato for 10 to 15 minutes or until done.

Cheesy Rolls

Thanks to rice cheddar cheese and *nutritional yeast*, you won't believe there's no dairy cheese in these rolls! Add a little garlic powder and parsley, and these rolls will soon become a favorite.

Yield:	Prep time:	Bake time:	Serving size:
24 rolls	20 to 30 minutes	22 to 25 minutes	1 roll

2 cups warm water

2½ TB. canola or vegetable oil

2 tsp. agave or brown rice syrup

2 TB. liquid or granule soy lecithin

1½ tsp. salt

3 TB. vital wheat gluten

5 TB. nutritional yeast flakes

1 TB. dried parsley flakes

2 tsp. garlic powder

½ tsp. fresh or dried minced dill

1 cup whole-wheat flour

4 cups bread flour

2 TB. instant yeast

1½ cups rice cheddar cheese, shredded

1. Line a baking sheet with parchment paper, or spray with vegetable shortening spray.

2. In a large bowl, and using an electric mixer fitted with a dough hook attachment on low speed, combine warm water, canola oil, agave syrup, and soy lecithin, or blend with a whisk. Add salt, vital wheat gluten, nutritional yeast flakes, parsley flakes, garlic powder, dill, whole-wheat flour, bread flour, instant yeast, and rice cheddar cheese, and mix until dough forms a ball.

3. Knead by hand, or in mixer on low speed, for about 5 minutes, adding extra bread flour as needed if dough is too sticky. Stop the mixer, and push down dough if it starts to ride up the hook. Continue kneading 2 to 5 more minutes or until dough comes away from the sides of the bowl and forms a membrane when stretched (like a balloon that doesn't tear).

4. Turn out dough onto well-floured surface using bread flour, knead it by hand a few more times, and form it into a ball. Cover with a kitchen towel, and let it rest on the counter for 10 minutes.

5. Divide dough into 4 equal pieces and then divide each into 6 more pieces. Roll 2 at a time, one in each hand, in a circular motion on a lightly oiled surface until dough balls are tight and compact. Place almost next to each other on the prepared pan.

6. Loosely cover with a kitchen towel, and let rise in a warm place for 1 to 1½ hours or until double in size. Do not disturb bread or expose to any drafts.

7. Halfway through the rise time, preheat the oven to 350°F.

8. Bake for 22 to 25 minutes or until rolls are lightly browned. Cool on wire racks.

VEGAN VOCAB

Nutritional yeast is inactive yeast with a nutty, cheeselike flavor. It comes in large and small flakes, or the powdered variety. These Cheesy Rolls are best made with nutritional yeast flakes—either size is fine. You can find nutritional yeast in health food stores or through online baking sites.

Herb Rolls

These rolls are so full of flavor, thanks to the parsley, sage, rosemary, and thyme, they'll make your house smell unbelievably yummy while they're baking.

Yield:	Prep time:	Bake time:	Serving size:
24 rolls	20 to 30 minutes	22 to 25 minutes	1 roll

2 cups warm water

2½ TB. canola or vegetable oil

1 TB. agave or brown rice syrup

2 TB. liquid or granule soy lecithin

2 TB. wheat germ

1 tsp. salt

3 TB. vital wheat gluten

1 TB. parsley flakes

1 tsp. ground sage

1 tsp. ground rosemary

1 tsp. minced thyme leaves

1 tsp. minced dried garlic

1 cup whole-wheat flour

4 cups bread flour

2 TB. instant yeast

1. Line a baking sheet with parchment paper, or spray with vegetable shortening spray.

2. In a large bowl, and using an electric mixer fitted with a dough hook attachment on low speed, combine warm water, canola oil, agave syrup, and soy lecithin, or blend with a whisk. Add wheat germ, salt, vital wheat gluten, parsley flakes, ground sage, ground rosemary, minced thyme, minced garlic, whole-wheat flour, bread flour, and instant yeast, and mix until dough forms a ball.

3. Knead by hand, or in mixer on low speed, for about 5 minutes, adding extra bread flour as needed if dough is too sticky. Stop the mixer, and push down dough if it starts to ride up the hook. Continue kneading 2 to 5 more minutes or until dough comes away from the sides of the bowl and forms a membrane when stretched (like a balloon that doesn't tear).

4. Turn out dough onto well-floured surface using bread flour, knead it by hand a few more times, and form it into a ball. Cover with a kitchen towel, and let it rest on the counter for 10 minutes.

5. Divide dough into 4 equal pieces and then divide each into 6 more pieces. Roll 2 at a time, one in each hand, in a circular motion on a lightly oiled surface until dough balls are tight and compact. Place almost next to each other on the prepared pan.

6. Loosely cover with a kitchen towel, and let rise in a warm place for 1 to 1½ hours or until double in size. Do not disturb bread or expose to any drafts.

7. Halfway through the rise time, preheat the oven to 350°F.

8. Bake for 22 to 25 minutes or until rolls are lightly browned. Cool on wire racks.

BATTER UP!

Looking for a different taste combination? Use this recipe to experiment with a variety of herbs, and even spices, for a totally unique roll. Try dill, parsley, and chives together, or a combination of basil, oregano, garlic powder, and onion powder. Tarragon, chives, basil, and garlic also works, as does cilantro, chili powder or cumin, and chives. Experiment!

Cinnamon Rolls

These big soft and sweet rolls are made with whole-wheat flour; rolled and filled with vegan butter, cinnamon, and brown sugar; baked until golden brown; and iced with confectioners' sugar icing. No need to go to a bakery!

Yield:	Prep time:	Bake time:	Serving size:
20 rolls	20 to 30 minutes	25 to 28 minutes	1 roll

2 cups warm water

2½ TB. canola or vegetable oil

½ cup maple, agave, or brown rice syrup

2 TB. liquid or granule soy lecithin

1½ tsp. salt

3 TB. vital wheat gluten

2 TB. wheat germ

8 TB. ground cinnamon

2 cups whole-wheat flour

4 cups bread flour

2 TB. instant yeast

½ cup nonhydrogenated vegan margarine, softened

1 cup light brown sugar, firmly packed

Confectioners' Sugar Icing (recipe in Chapter 22)

1. Line 2 baking sheets with parchment paper, or spray with vegetable shortening spray.

2. In a large bowl, and using an electric mixer fitted with a dough hook attachment on low speed, combine warm water, canola oil, maple syrup, and soy lecithin, or blend with a whisk. Add salt, vital wheat gluten, wheat germ, 2 tablespoons ground cinnamon, whole-wheat flour, bread flour, and instant yeast, and mix until dough forms a ball.

3. Knead by hand, or in mixer on low speed, for about 5 minutes, adding extra bread flour as needed if dough is too sticky. Stop the mixer, and push down dough if it starts to ride up the hook. Continue kneading 2 to 5 more minutes or until dough comes away from the sides of the bowl and forms a membrane when stretched (like a balloon that doesn't tear).

4. Turn out dough onto well-floured surface using bread flour, knead it by hand a few more times, and form it into a ball. Cover with a kitchen towel, and let it rest on the counter for 10 minutes.

5. In a medium bowl, combine vegan margarine, remaining 6 tablespoons ground cinnamon, and light brown sugar, and mix with a wooden spoon or a rubber spatula until creamy.

6. Divide dough into 2 equal pieces. Using a rolling pin, roll out each piece into a large rectangle approximately 12 inches long by 18 inches wide, with the 18-inch-wide side facing you. Using a rubber spatula or an offset spatula, spread 1/2 of brown sugar mixture over dough, leaving 1 inch on all sides bare. Starting with widest side of dough nearest you, roll up tightly, jelly-roll style, until you get to the end. Pinch seams all along edge to seal. Smooth roll so it's even from one end to the other. Repeat with second piece of dough and remaining brown sugar spread.

7. With a sharp, serrated knife, cut off any straggly pieces at the very end on each side. Cut roll in half, and cut each half in 5 equal slices approximately 1 1/2 inches thick. Place 10 cinnamon buns almost next to each other on each of the prepared pans. Cover with a kitchen towel, and let rolls rise in a warm place for 1 to 1 1/2 hours or until double in size. Do not disturb rolls or expose to any drafts.

8. Halfway through the rise time, preheat the oven to 350°F.

9. Bake for 25 to 28 minutes or until rolls are golden brown and puffy. Cool on wire racks. When completely cool, ice with Confectioners' Sugar Icing.

BAKER'S BONUS

This is a big batch of Cinnamon Rolls! If you don't need or want all Cinnamon Rolls, make one or two pans of Maple Sticky Buns (recipe follows) with some of the Cinnamon Roll dough. That way you have the best of both sweet worlds!

Maple Sticky Buns

Big, soft cinnamon rolls are baked in a mixture of toasted pecans, vegan butter, and cinnamon maple syrup—totally yummy! Work quickly with this recipe, though! By the time Cinnamon Rolls are rolled, the pans should be filled with maple syrup mixture.

Yield:	Prep time:	Bake time:	Serving size:
3 (9-inch pans), or about 20 rolls	20 to 30 minutes	25 to 28 minutes	1 roll

1 batch Cinnamon Rolls (recipe earlier in this chapter)

1½ cups nonhydrogenated vegan margarine, melted

1½ cups pure maple syrup

¾ cup agave or brown rice syrup

2¼ cups toasted pecan walnut halves

Confectioners' Sugar Icing (recipe in Chapter 22)

1. Prepare Cinnamon Rolls according to the recipe, but do not slice, bake, or let them rise yet.

2. Preheat the oven to 350°F. Spray 3 (9-inch) cake pans with vegetable shortening spray.

3. In a large bowl, and using a large spatula or wooden spoon, combine melted vegan margarine, pure maple syrup, and agave syrup. Pour 1¼ cups maple syrup mixture into each of the prepared pans. Sprinkle ¾ cup toasted pecan halves on top of syrup.

4. Slice each Cinnamon Roll log into 10 rolls. Arrange 6 or 7 rolls in each of the pans on top of maple syrup mixture, making sure they all fit in 3 pans.

5. Bake for 25 to 28 minutes or until golden brown on top and syrup is bubbly.

6. Cool on wire racks for 10 minutes, and loosen around the edges with a sharp knife. Place a serving plate upside down over the pan of sticky buns, and with a firm hand on the plate, quickly flip it over, releasing buns. Spread any leftover sticky goo onto buns, and cool completely before spreading with Confectioners' Sugar Icing.

Variation: Instead of making all-pecan sticky buns, use walnuts, almonds, cashews, or raisins instead.

BAKER'S BONUS

Can't eat them all? These Maple Sticky Buns can be double-wrapped in plastic and frozen for up to 3 months.

Flatbreads and Crackers

In This Chapter

- Fantastic flatbreads
- Perfect pitas and pizza dough
- Sweet and savory crackers

Everyone loves snacks, so much so that commercial, store-bought crackers and flatbreads are a huge money-making business. As good as they taste, many of them are so full of preservatives and junk, it can be scary just reading the ingredient list. The solution? Make your own! Not only will you save money, but you'll know exactly what's going into your yummy snacks—and your body.

Flatbreads are simple, humble breads that can include unleavened varieties like crackers or yeast breads like focaccia. Savory flatbreads are often seasoned with herbs and spices, onions, garlic, kosher salt, etc.

The flatbread recipes in this chapter are perfect for experimentation. Substitute unusual seeds, flours, or finely chopped nuts for the traditional. Mix and match spices. Try adding your favorite dried or fresh-from-the-garden herbs.

Not all flatbreads are savory, however. Depending on what your sweet tooth craves, the homemade Sweet Graham Crackers, made with pure maple syrup, can be adapted to Chocolate Graham Crackers with the addition of cocoa, or add cinnamon sugar for Cinnamon Graham Crackers.

And best of all? They're all vegan!

Multi-Seed Flatbread

This crispy flatbread is packed full of toasted sesame and sunflower seeds, poppy seeds, and caraway seeds, plus a garlicky flavor for extra pizzazz. This is great for use with dips or flavored oils.

Yield:	Prep time:	Bake time:	Serving size:
1 (9×14-inch) flatbread	30 to 40 minutes	20 to 22 minutes	1 piece

1 cup warm water

2 TB. canola or vegetable oil

½ tsp. agave or brown rice syrup

¾ tsp. salt

1 TB. vital wheat gluten

1 tsp. garlic powder

1 TB. plus 2 tsp. toasted sesame seeds

1 TB. plus 1 tsp. toasted, hulled sunflower seeds

1 TB. plus 1 tsp. poppy seeds

1 TB. plus 1 tsp. caraway seeds

2½ cups bread flour

1 tsp. instant yeast

1 or 2 TB. water

1. Line a baking sheet with parchment paper, or spray with vegetable shortening spray.

2. In a large bowl, and using an electric mixer fitted with a dough hook attachment on low speed, combine warm water, canola oil, and agave syrup, or blend with a whisk. Add salt, vital wheat gluten, garlic powder, 1 tablespoon sesame seeds, 1 tablespoon sunflower seeds, 1 tablespoon poppy seeds, 1 tablespoon caraway seeds, bread flour, and instant yeast, and mix until dough forms a ball.

3. Knead by hand, or in mixer on low speed, for about 5 minutes, adding extra bread flour as needed if dough is too sticky. Stop the mixer, and push down dough if it starts to ride up the hook. Continue kneading 2 to 5 more minutes or until dough comes away from the sides of the bowl and forms a membrane when stretched (like a balloon that doesn't tear).

4. Turn out dough onto well-floured surface, knead it by hand a few more times, and form it into a ball. Cover with a kitchen towel, and let it rest on the counter for 10 minutes.

5. In a small bowl, combine remaining 2 teaspoons sesame seeds, 1 teaspoon sunflower seeds, 1 teaspoon poppy seeds, and 1 teaspoon caraway seeds.

6. Roll dough into a rectangle about 9×14×¼ inch thick. Brush very lightly with 1 or 2 tablespoons water, and sprinkle remaining seeds mixture evenly over the top, pressing down into dough carefully. Place on the prepared pan.

7. Loosely cover with a kitchen towel and let rise in a warm place for 15 to 20 minutes. Do not disturb dough or expose it to any drafts.

8. Preheat the oven to 350°F.

9. Bake for 20 to 22 minutes or until flatbread is lightly browned. Cool on a wire rack before cutting into pieces with scissors or knife. This is best eaten the same day, but you can also store it in a plastic bag to enjoy later.

BAKER'S BONUS

This flatbread is also good grilled. Instead of brushing the top with water, substitute with 1 or 2 tablespoons olive oil and then sprinkle with seeds. After it's been rising for about 20 minutes, slap it on a hot grill, and close the lid. Reduce the heat to medium, and grill flatbread for 3 to 5 minutes, checking the underside occasionally to see if it's burning. When it's done, flip it over gently so you don't disturb too many of the seeds, and grill for 1 to 3 more minutes.

Rosemary Focaccia

This easy bread is flavored with fresh rosemary and garlic-infused olive oil. It can be eaten as is or topped with vegan cheese, caramelized onions, fresh tomatoes, roasted red peppers, and anything else you like.

Yield:	Prep time:	Bake time:	Serving size:
1 (8×12-inch) focaccia	30 to 40 minutes	15 to 20 minutes	1 piece

1 cup warm water

1 TB. olive oil

1 tsp. agave syrup

2 tsp. soy lecithin

1 tsp. salt

1 TB. vital wheat gluten

½ tsp. freshly ground black pepper

1 tsp. fresh minced garlic

1½ tsp. plus 1 TB. freshly minced rosemary

1 tsp. garlic powder

2½ cups bread flour

2 tsp. instant yeast

2 TB. garlic oil

½ to 1 tsp. kosher salt

1. Spray or grease a baking sheet with vegetable shortening.

2. In a large bowl, and using an electric mixer fitted with a dough hook attachment on low speed, combine warm water, olive oil, agave syrup, and soy lecithin, or blend with a whisk. Add salt, vital wheat gluten, black pepper, garlic, 1½ teaspoons rosemary, garlic powder, bread flour, and instant yeast, and mix until dough forms a ball.

3. Knead by hand, or in mixer on low speed, for about 5 minutes, adding extra flour as needed if dough is too sticky. Stop the mixer, and push down dough if it starts to ride up the hook. Continue kneading 2 to 5 more minutes or until dough comes away from the sides of the bowl and forms a membrane when stretched (like a balloon that doesn't tear).

4. Turn out dough onto well-floured surface, knead it by hand a few more times, and form it into a ball. Cover with a kitchen towel, and let it rest on the counter for 10 minutes.

5. Using a rolling pin or your hands, roll or pat dough into a rectangle, about 8×12×¾ inch thick. Press your oiled fingers into dough to make dimples, and spread with garlic oil. Sprinkle remaining 1 tablespoon rosemary and kosher salt evenly over the top, pressing down into dough carefully. Place on the prepared pan.

6. Loosely cover *focaccia* with a kitchen towel and let rise in a warm place for about 30 minutes. Do not disturb dough or expose to any drafts.

7. Preheat the oven to 400°F.

8. Bake for 15 to 20 minutes or until focaccia is lightly browned. Cool on a wire rack, or eat warm. Cut into 6 to 8 slices. This is best eaten the same day, but you can also store it in a plastic bag to enjoy later.

Variation: This focaccia pairs well with any fresh or dried herbs. Also try experimenting with a variety of flavored oils, like sesame oil, basil oil, or chili pepper oil for a real hot bite!

VEGAN VOCAB

Similar to pizza, **focaccia** is a flat, oven-baked bread usually seasoned with olive oil and herbs, and sometimes topped with onions, vegetables, cheese, and salt. Before baking, it is often "docked" by pressing oiled fingers into the dough to create dimples after which more olive oil is brushed on so it can settle in the dimples. Focaccia can be eaten as is or used to make sandwiches.

Whole-Wheat Pitas

If you've never tried making pita breads, now is the time! This simple and humble whole-wheat bread has a slightly nutty flavor, and the hollow interior is just right for making a pita pocket sandwich.

Yield:	Prep time:	Bake time:	Serving size:
8 pitas	30 to 40 minutes	4 to 7 minutes	1 pita

1¼ cups warm water	1¾ cups whole-wheat flour
2 TB. canola or olive oil	1¼ cups bread flour
½ tsp. unbleached cane sugar	2 tsp. instant yeast
1½ tsp. salt	

1. Have 1 or 2 small ovenproof wire racks handy.

2. In a large bowl, and using an electric mixer fitted with a dough hook attachment on low speed, combine warm water, canola oil, unbleached cane sugar, and salt, or blend with a whisk. Add whole-wheat flour, bread flour, and instant yeast, and mix until dough forms a ball.

3. Knead by hand, or in mixer on low speed, for about 5 minutes, adding extra bread flour as needed if dough is too sticky. Stop the mixer, and push down dough if it starts to ride up the hook. Continue kneading 2 to 5 more minutes or until dough comes away from the sides of the bowl and forms a membrane when stretched (like a balloon that doesn't tear).

4. Turn out dough onto well-floured surface using bread flour, knead it by hand a few more times, and form it into a ball. Cover with a kitchen towel, and let it rest on the counter for 10 minutes.

5. Preheat oven to 450°F.

6. Divide dough into 8 equal pieces, and press each into a round disc. Using a rolling pin, roll each piece of dough into a round circle about 5 or 6 inches in diameter, and ½ inch thick.

7. Loosely cover with a kitchen towel, and let rise in a warm place for about 20 minutes. Do not disturb bread or expose to any drafts.

8. When the oven is hot and dough is risen, place a few pita breads on a wire rack, and place pita and rack in the oven. Bake for 4 to 7 minutes or until pitas have ballooned and shell is golden brown. Do not overbake, or pita could become hard and brittle.

9. Cool on a separate wire rack for about 30 minutes. Cover with a kitchen towel so pitas will soften and be easier to slice open. Store in a plastic zipper-lock bag.

BAKER'S BONUS

If you don't have wire racks, you can bake your pitas on a stone or a baking sheet. If you use either of these, flip the pitas over about halfway through the bake time so both sides bake evenly.

Pizza Dough

Stop buying pizza dough and make your own! This is a basic, easy-to-make pizza dough you can top with all your favorite toppings. (The whole-wheat version is a little heavier, so you add a bit of vital wheat gluten and soy lecithin to lighten it up.)

Yield:	Prep time:	Bake time:	Serving size:
2 (8- to 12-inch) pizzas	30 to 40 minutes	5 to 7 minutes	1 slice

1 cup warm water

1 TB. flavored or extra-virgin olive oil

1 tsp. unbleached cane sugar

1 tsp. salt

3 cups bread flour

2½ tsp. instant yeast

1. Line a baking sheet with parchment paper, spray with vegetable shortening spray, or have a (12- to 14-inch) pizza stone ready.

2. In a large bowl, and using an electric mixer fitted with a dough hook attachment on low speed, combine warm water, flavored oil, unbleached cane sugar, and salt, or blend with a whisk. Add bread flour and instant yeast, and mix until dough forms a ball.

3. Knead by hand, or in mixer on low speed, for about 5 minutes, adding extra bread flour as needed if dough is too sticky. Stop the mixer, and push down dough if it starts to ride up the hook. Continue kneading 2 to 5 more minutes or until dough comes away from the sides of the bowl and forms a membrane when stretched (like a balloon that doesn't tear).

4. Turn out dough onto well-floured surface, knead it by hand a few more times, and form it into a ball. Cover with a kitchen towel, and let it rest on the counter for 10 to 15 minutes.

5. Divide dough into 2 equal pieces, and roll each into whatever pizza shape you'd like. Place on the prepared pan.

6. Loosely cover with a kitchen towel and let rise in a warm place for 15 to 30 minutes. Do not disturb bread or expose to any drafts.

7. Preheat the oven to 400°F if you're baking on a sheet pan. Preheat to 450°F if using a pizza stone.

8. Bake for 10 to 20 minutes or until nicely browned.

9. Follow your favorite pizza recipe. Or divide dough into two pieces, and on a lightly floured surface sprinkled with a little cornmeal, roll and stretch dough with lightly oiled hands, or a rolling pin, shaping into two 8- to 10-inch circles. Let rest for 5 to 10 minutes. Top pizzas as desired, and bake for 10 to 20 minutes depending on size and method, or until crust is nicely browned and topping is done. Pizza is best eaten the same day, although it can be wrapped in plastic wrap or foil, and stored in the refrigerator.

Variation: For **Whole-Wheat Pizza Dough,** substitute whole-wheat flour for the bread flour, and add 2 tablespoons vital wheat gluten and 1½ teaspoons soy lecithin to the dough.

BAKER'S BONUS

You can make this pizza dough ahead of time and refrigerate it in a zipper-lock plastic bag for up to 24 hours. If freezing, flatten dough into round discs, place in zipper-lock plastic bags, and freeze for up to 3 months. Thaw in the bag overnight under refrigeration, or for 2 to 4 hours on the counter.

Sesame Crackers

Crackers are so easy to make at home. They're basically unleavened bread that's baked thin and flat. This version is loaded with toasted sesame seeds, with an extra kick from the sesame oil.

Yield:	Prep time:	Bake time:	Serving size:
30 to 36 crackers	30 to 40 minutes	15 to 18 minutes	4 crackers

1 cup unbleached all-purpose flour

½ cup semolina flour

¼ tsp. aluminum-free baking powder

¼ tsp. ground turmeric

¼ tsp. ground cumin

1 tsp. kosher salt

¼ cup nonhydrogenated vegan margarine, cold

1 tsp. agave or brown rice syrup

⅓ cup soy milk

1 or 2 TB. water

1½ tsp. sesame oil

⅓ cup toasted, hulled sesame seeds

2 TB. toasted, hulled black sesame seeds

1. Preheat the oven to 325°F. Line baking sheet with parchment paper, or spray with vegetable shortening spray.

2. Into a large bowl, sift unbleached all-purpose flour, semolina flour, aluminum-free baking powder, ground turmeric, ground cumin, and kosher salt, or blend with a wire whisk. Add vegan margarine, and using a pastry blender, cut in until mixture resembles meal.

3. In a small cup, and using a spoon or small whisk, combine agave syrup, soy milk, 1 tablespoon water, and sesame oil.

4. Make a well in middle of dough, and add liquid, followed by sesame seeds. Using your hands or a rubber spatula, mix gently, making sure all dry ingredients are incorporated. Add remaining 1 tablespoon water if needed, mixing until dough comes together.

5. Turn out dough onto a lightly floured surface, and using a rolling pin, roll out to ¹⁄₁₆ inch thick. Sprinkle black sesame seeds on top, and press into dough. With a pizza cutter, cookie cutter, or knife, cut into round or square crackers, and place on the prepared pan.

6. Bake for 15 to 18 minutes or until crackers are lightly browned. Cool completely on wire racks. Store in zipper-lock bags for 5 to 7 days.

> **BATTER UP!**
>
> To toast sesame seeds, add them to a medium skillet over medium heat. Cook, stirring constantly, until seeds start to turn brown. The seeds toast very quickly, and easily burn, so watch them carefully. Remove from pan immediately, as seeds will continue to cook in the pan.

Savory Herbed Crackers

These homemade crackers, made with rye and wheat flour and flavored with basil, oregano, marjoram, and a touch of garlic, are perfect with dips or topped with vegan cheese.

Yield:	Prep time:	Bake time:	Serving size:
30 to 36 crackers	30 to 40 minutes	12 to 15 minutes	4 crackers

¾ cup unbleached all-purpose flour

½ cup whole-wheat pastry flour

¼ cup rye flour

1 tsp. garlic powder

¼ tsp. aluminum-free baking powder

¼ cup nonhydrogenated vegan margarine, cold

2 tsp. dried chopped parsley

½ tsp. dried minced basil leaves

½ tsp. dried minced oregano leaves

½ tsp. dried minced marjoram leaves

½ tsp. salt

½ cup water

1. Preheat the oven to 350°F. Line a baking sheet with parchment paper, or spray with vegetable shortening spray.

2. Into a large bowl, sift unbleached all-purpose flour, whole-wheat pastry flour, rye flour, garlic powder, and aluminum-free baking powder, and blend with a wire whisk. Add vegan margarine, and using a pastry blender, cut in until mixture resembles meal. Add parsley, basil, oregano, marjoram, and salt.

3. Make a well in middle of dough, and add water. Using your hands or a rubber spatula, mix gently, making sure all dry ingredients are incorporated and dough comes together.

4. Turn out dough onto a lightly floured surface with all-purpose flour. Using a rolling pin, carefully roll dough to ⅛ inch thick. Cut into desired shapes, and place on the prepared baking sheets.

5. Bake for 12 to 15 minutes or until golden brown and crispy. Cool completely on wire racks before storing in zipper-lock bags for 5 to 7 days.

BATTER UP!

Be creative with the herbs in this recipe. Try adding sage, rosemary, thyme, dill, tarragon, and chives. Or try Italian seasoning. You could also sprinkle flavored salts on the top of crackers before baking. Crackers last for quite a while, so make a large batch, mixing and matching the flavors, and package them for later use.

Sweet Graham Crackers

These homemade graham crackers are made with *graham flour*, maple syrup, and brown sugar, and sprinkled with cinnamon sugar, so they're sweet, fresh, and tender.

Yield:	Prep time:	Bake time:	Serving size:
24 to 30 crackers	30 to 40 minutes	13 to 15 minutes	1 graham cracker

¼ cup pure maple syrup

1 tsp. pure vanilla extract

½ cup plus 2 TB. soy milk

1 cup whole-wheat pastry flour

1 cup unbleached all-purpose flour

1 cup graham flour

Pinch salt

¾ tsp. aluminum-free baking powder

½ tsp. baking soda

½ cup light brown sugar, firmly packed

½ cup cubed nonhydrogenated vegan margarine, cold

3 TB. unbleached cane sugar

1. Into a small bowl, whisk together maple syrup, vanilla extract, and ½ cup soy milk.

2. In a food processor fitted with a cutting blade, combine whole-wheat pastry flour, unbleached all-purpose flour, graham flour, salt, aluminum-free baking powder, baking soda, and light brown sugar. Pulse on and off 5 or 6 times until well blended.

3. Turn food processor to low, and add vegan margarine 2 tablespoons at a time until mixture resembles cornmeal. With food processor still running, add maple syrup mixture in a steady stream until dough comes together. Turn off food processor, and scrape down the bowl with a rubber spatula. Pulse a few more times until dough forms a ball. Remove dough from the bowl, wrap in plastic, and chill for 4 hours or overnight.

4. Preheat the oven to 350°F. Line 2 baking sheets with parchment paper, or spray with vegetable shortening spray.

5. Turn out dough onto a lightly floured surface. Divide dough into 2 equal pieces, and roll each piece into a rectangle ⅛ inch thick. Cut dough into 3×3-inch squares, and place on the prepared baking sheet.

6. Lightly brush crackers with remaining 2 tablespoons soy milk, sprinkle evenly with unbleached cane sugar, and prick a few times with the tines of a fork.

7. Bake for 13 to 15 minutes or until fragrant and golden brown. Cool completely on wire racks before storing in an airtight container.

Variations: For **Cinnamon Graham Crackers,** add 1 teaspoon ground cinnamon to the dry ingredients. Before baking, mix 3 tablespoons unbleached cane sugar with ½ teaspoon cinnamon, and sprinkle on top of crackers. For **Chocolate Graham Crackers,** decrease the graham flour to ¾ cup and add ¼ cup natural cocoa powder to the dry ingredients. Before baking, sprinkle crackers with 3 tablespoons unbleached cane sugar.

VEGAN VOCAB

Graham flour is a type of wheat flour used in—you guessed it!—graham crackers. It's available in health food stores and most large supermarkets. If you can't find it, substitute all-purpose flour and whole-wheat flour in equal parts.

Cookies, Brownies, and Bars

Have a sweet tooth that's waiting to be satisfied, but you just can't find anything at your local bakery that doesn't contain animal products? There's no need to do without when vegan bake-shop sweets are so quick and easy to make at home—and using ingredients readily available from your local supermarket or natural food store.

The tasty cookie, brownie, and other sweet treat recipes in Part 4 will make a vegan dessert lover out of you in no time! The vegan cookies range from the easy scoop-and-bake variety, to festive formed cookies. Then there are the rich, chocolaty brownies we all love. Fruit bars and lemon bars are all dairy and egg free and good for a sweet pick-me-up.

In Part 4, you'll also find a few recipes you can make without ever turning on the oven!

Cookie Jar Classics

In This Chapter

- Cookies to please every sweet tooth
- Drop and bake cookies
- Chocolate cookies, spicy cookies, and everything in between

Cookies are comfort food, plain and simple. Vegans love cookies, too, but most associate dairy-free, egg-free cookies with dry, tasteless globs of baked dough. That couldn't be further from the truth! This chapter shows you just how good a vegan cookie can be.

What's your favorite cookie? Is it a chocolate-chip cookie with a rich, "buttery" flavor with just the right amount of chocolate chips in every bite? Is it a soft molasses cookie with spices that reminds you of Grandma's cookie jar? Or is it a melt-in-your-mouth sugar cookie topped with colored sprinkles? Whatever your preference, you can feel good about making these cookies, because not only are they vegan, they taste good, too!

Tips for Baking Vegan Cookies

Because vegan cookies and brownies have no dairy products in them, they must rely on substitutes and flavors to make them taste buttery and delicious. Nonhydrogenated vegan margarine comes in a buttery flavor, making all you bake taste wonderful.

6. Bake for 10 to 12 minutes or until slightly firm around the edges. Cookies will continue to bake for a few minutes after they're removed from the oven. Allow them to sit for a few minutes before transferring to wire racks. Cool cookies completely before storing in an airtight container or in zipper-lock plastic bags.

Variations: For **Chocolate-Chip Walnut Cookies,** add ½ cup chopped walnuts to cookie dough when adding vegan chocolate chips. For **White Chocolate-Chip Cookies,** substitute an equal amount of vegan white chocolate chips for semisweet chocolate chips.

BATTER UP!

Vegan chocolate chips are available at natural food stores. Generally sold in 12-ounce packages, they come in different flavors like semisweet and white chocolate. They taste similar to real chocolate chips but are completely vegan and dairy free.

Peanut Butter Cookies

These cookie jar favorites are a little soft on the inside, a little crumbly on the outside, dipped in sugar, and marked with a fork in a classic criss-cross pattern. Make them with crunchy peanut butter and chopped peanuts for more crunch in every bite!

Yield:	Prep time:	Bake time:	Serving size:
24 to 30 cookies	20 to 25 minutes	12 to 15 minutes	1 cookie

1½ cups unbleached all-purpose flour	Egg substitute for 1 large egg
¾ tsp. baking soda	1½ cups smooth or chunky peanut butter
½ cup nonhydrogenated vegan margarine, at room temperature	2 tsp. pure vanilla extract
½ cup light brown sugar, firmly packed	½ cup chopped peanuts (optional)
½ cup Florida Crystals or unbleached cane sugar	½ cup unbleached cane sugar (optional)

1. Preheat the oven to 350°F. Lightly oil or spray 2 baking sheets with vegetable shortening, or line with parchment paper.

Cookie Jar Classics

In This Chapter

- Cookies to please every sweet tooth
- Drop and bake cookies
- Chocolate cookies, spicy cookies, and everything in between

Cookies are comfort food, plain and simple. Vegans love cookies, too, but most associate dairy-free, egg-free cookies with dry, tasteless globs of baked dough. That couldn't be further from the truth! This chapter shows you just how good a vegan cookie can be.

What's your favorite cookie? Is it a chocolate-chip cookie with a rich, "buttery" flavor with just the right amount of chocolate chips in every bite? Is it a soft molasses cookie with spices that reminds you of Grandma's cookie jar? Or is it a melt-in-your-mouth sugar cookie topped with colored sprinkles? Whatever your preference, you can feel good about making these cookies, because not only are they vegan, they taste good, too!

Tips for Baking Vegan Cookies

Because vegan cookies and brownies have no dairy products in them, they must rely on substitutes and flavors to make them taste buttery and delicious. Nonhydrogenated vegan margarine comes in a buttery flavor, making all you bake taste wonderful.

Substituting butter, eggs, and honey is easy in vegan baking. Most of the time it's a 1:1 ratio. However, there are exceptions to the rule, so be sure to check the recipe before cranking up your oven. Refer to Chapter 1 for suggestions on how to substitute the ingredients you love to make these vegan cookies.

Most cookies can be stored in the cookie jar for up to a week before losing their crunch or softness. Cool cookies completely before storing them in an airtight container. If you want to store them longer, freezing is the way to go.

BAKER'S BONUS

When working with extra-sticky cookies, layer them between sheets of waxed paper or paper towels before placing in airtight containers or zipper-lock bags.

Classic Chocolate-Chip Cookies

These classic "buttery" cookies are soft on the inside with just the right chocolate chip–cookie dough ratio. Eat them warm from the oven, when the vegan semisweet chocolate morsels are still super soft.

Yield:	Prep time:	Bake time:	Serving size:
24 to 30 cookies	20 to 25 minutes	10 to 12 minutes	1 cookie

2½ cups unbleached all-purpose flour

½ tsp. salt

1 tsp. baking soda

1 cup nonhydrogenated vegan margarine, at room temperature

¾ cup light brown sugar, firmly packed

¾ cup Florida Crystals or unbleached cane sugar

Egg substitute for 2 large eggs

1 tsp. pure vanilla extract

2 cups vegan semisweet chocolate chips

1. Preheat the oven to 350°F. Lightly oil or spray 2 baking sheets with vegetable shortening, or line with parchment paper.

2. In a large bowl, combine unbleached all-purpose flour, salt, and baking soda with a wooden spoon or whisk. Set aside.

3. In a separate large bowl, and using an electric mixer fitted with the beater attachment on medium speed, beat vegan margarine, light brown sugar, and Florida Crystals until creamy, scraping the bowl as needed with a rubber spatula. Add egg substitute and vanilla extract, and beat again until light and fluffy. Scrape down the bowl, and beat again until batter is nice and smooth.

4. Reduce speed to low, add ½ of dry ingredients to batter, and mix to combine. Add remaining dry ingredients, and mix until dough is smooth, scraping the bowl as needed. Add vegan chocolate chips, and mix only enough to combine. (If your kitchen is especially warm or humid, cover and chill dough for 30 minutes before scooping and baking.)

5. Using a ¼ cup ice cream scoop or a tablespoon, scoop out cookie dough and place on the prepared baking sheets, leaving enough room for cookies to spread, about 1 inch apart.

6. Bake for 10 to 12 minutes or until slightly firm around the edges. Cookies will continue to bake for a few minutes after they're removed from the oven. Allow them to sit for a few minutes before transferring to wire racks. Cool cookies completely before storing in an airtight container or in zipper-lock plastic bags.

Variations: For **Chocolate-Chip Walnut Cookies,** add ½ cup chopped walnuts to cookie dough when adding vegan chocolate chips. For **White Chocolate-Chip Cookies,** substitute an equal amount of vegan white chocolate chips for semisweet chocolate chips.

BATTER UP!

Vegan chocolate chips are available at natural food stores. Generally sold in 12-ounce packages, they come in different flavors like semisweet and white chocolate. They taste similar to real chocolate chips but are completely vegan and dairy free.

Peanut Butter Cookies

These cookie jar favorites are a little soft on the inside, a little crumbly on the outside, dipped in sugar, and marked with a fork in a classic criss-cross pattern. Make them with crunchy peanut butter and chopped peanuts for more crunch in every bite!

Yield:	Prep time:	Bake time:	Serving size:
24 to 30 cookies	20 to 25 minutes	12 to 15 minutes	1 cookie

1½ cups unbleached all-purpose flour

¾ tsp. baking soda

½ cup nonhydrogenated vegan margarine, at room temperature

½ cup light brown sugar, firmly packed

½ cup Florida Crystals or unbleached cane sugar

Egg substitute for 1 large egg

1½ cups smooth or chunky peanut butter

2 tsp. pure vanilla extract

½ cup chopped peanuts (optional)

½ cup unbleached cane sugar (optional)

1. Preheat the oven to 350°F. Lightly oil or spray 2 baking sheets with vegetable shortening, or line with parchment paper.

2. In a large bowl, combine unbleached all-purpose flour and baking soda with a wooden spoon or whisk. Set aside.

3. In a separate large bowl, and using an electric mixer fitted with the beater attachment on medium speed, beat vegan margarine, light brown sugar, and Florida Crystals until creamy, scraping the bowl as needed with a rubber spatula. Add egg substitute, peanut butter, and vanilla extract, and beat again until light and fluffy. Scrape down the bowl, and beat again until batter is nice and smooth.

4. Reduce speed to low, add ½ of dry ingredients to batter, and mix to combine. Add remaining dry ingredients, and mix until dough is smooth, scraping the bowl as needed. Add chopped peanuts (if using), and mix only enough to combine. (If your kitchen is especially warm or humid, cover and chill dough for 30 minutes before scooping and baking.)

5. Using a ¼ cup ice cream scoop or a tablespoon, scoop out cookie dough and roll into balls. Roll balls in ½ cup unbleached cane sugar (if using), and place on the prepared baking sheets, leaving enough room for cookies to spread a little, about 1 inch apart. With a fork, press down lightly on cookie, turn fork ¼ turn, and press again, making a criss-cross pattern.

6. Bake cookies for 12 to 15 minutes or until slightly firm around edges and very lightly browned. Remove cookies from the oven, and allow them to sit for a few minutes before transferring to wire racks. Cool cookies completely before storing in an airtight container or in zipper-lock plastic bags.

Variation: For **Peanut Butter Chocolate-Chip Cookies,** add 1 cup vegan semisweet chocolate chips to the dough just before baking.

DOUGH-NOT

Peanut butter cookies are best served slightly soft, so be sure not to overbake them. They'll continue to bake for a few minutes after they're removed from the oven.

Snickerdoodles

Rolled in cinnamon sugar before they're baked, these old-fashioned, melt-in-your-mouth cookies are soft on the inside and slightly crisp on the outside.

Yield:	Prep time:	Bake time:	Serving size:
24 to 30 cookies	50 to 85 minutes	13 to 16 minutes	1 cookie

2¼ cups unbleached all-purpose flour	1 cup nonhydrogenated vegan margarine, at room temperature
2 tsp. *cream of tartar*	2 cups unbleached cane sugar
1 tsp. baking soda	Egg substitute for 2 large eggs
½ tsp. salt	2 tsp. ground cinnamon, or to taste

1. In a large bowl, combine unbleached all-purpose flour, cream of tartar, baking soda, and salt with a wooden spoon or whisk. Set aside.

2. In a separate large bowl, and using an electric mixer fitted with the beater attachment on medium speed, beat vegan margarine and 1½ cups unbleached cane sugar until creamy, scraping the bowl as needed with a rubber spatula. Add egg substitute, and beat again until light and fluffy. Scrape down the bowl, and beat again until batter is nice and smooth.

3. Reduce speed to low, add ½ of dry ingredients to batter, and mix to combine. Add remaining dry ingredients, and mix until dough is smooth, scraping the bowl as needed.

4. Cover cookie dough with plastic wrap, and refrigerate for 30 to 60 minutes.

5. Preheat the oven to 350°F. Lightly oil or spray 2 baking sheets with vegetable shortening, or line with parchment paper.

6. In a small bowl, mix remaining ½ cup unbleached cane sugar and cinnamon.

7. Using a ¼ cup ice cream scoop or a tablespoon, scoop out chilled cookie dough and roll into balls. Roll dough in cinnamon-sugar mixture, and place on the prepared baking sheets, leaving enough room for cookies to spread a little, about 1 inch apart.

8. Bake for 13 to 16 minutes or until outside of cookies feel slightly firm to the touch. Remove cookies from the oven, and allow them to sit for a few minutes before transferring to wire racks. Cool cookies completely before storing in an airtight container or in zipper-lock plastic bags.

> **VEGAN VOCAB**
>
> **Cream of tartar** is a by-product of winemaking, the potassium acid salt of tartaric acid, a carboxylic acid. It's a white, odorless, acidic powder used for many culinary and other household purposes; in this case, it is needed to create carbon dioxide with the baking soda to leaven.

Soft Molasses Cookies

These soft, chewy cookies are flavored with cinnamon, cloves, ginger, and molasses all rolled in sugar and baked.

Yield:	Prep time:	Bake time:	Serving size:
24 to 30 cookies	50 to 55 minutes	11 to 13 minutes	1 cookie

2 cups unbleached all-purpose flour

2 tsp. baking soda

1 tsp. ground cinnamon

¾ tsp. ground cloves

¾ tsp. ground ginger

¼ tsp. salt

10 TB. nonhydrogenated vegan margarine, at room temperature

1 cup light brown sugar, firmly packed

¼ cup molasses

Egg substitute for 1 large egg

½ cup raisins (optional)

⅓ cup chopped walnuts (optional)

½ cup Florida Crystals or unbleached cane sugar

1. Preheat the oven to 350°F. Lightly oil or spray 2 baking sheets with vegetable shortening, or line with parchment paper.

2. In a large bowl, combine unbleached all-purpose flour, baking soda, ground cinnamon, ground cloves, ground ginger, and salt with a wooden spoon or whisk. Set aside.

3. In a separate large bowl, and using an electric mixer fitted with the beater attachment on medium speed, beat vegan margarine, light brown sugar, and molasses until creamy, scraping the bowl as needed with a rubber spatula. Add egg substitute, and beat again until light and fluffy. Scrape down the bowl, and beat again until batter is nice and smooth.

4. Reduce speed to low, add ½ of dry ingredients to batter, and mix to combine. Add remaining dry ingredients, and mix until dough is smooth, scraping the bowl as needed. Add raisins (if using) and walnuts (if using), and mix only enough to combine. (If your kitchen is especially warm or humid, cover and chill the dough for 30 minutes before scooping and baking.)

5. Using a ¼ cup ice cream scoop or a tablespoon, scoop out cookie dough and roll into balls. Roll cookie in Florida Crystals, and place on the prepared baking sheets, leaving enough room for cookies to spread a little, about 1 inch apart.

6. Bake for 11 to 13 minutes or until edges feel slightly firm. Remove cookies from the oven, and allow them to sit for a few minutes before transferring to wire racks. Cool cookies completely before storing in an airtight container or in zipper-lock plastic bags.

BAKER'S BONUS

You can use one of two types of molasses in this recipe. If you like a strong molasses flavor, try using blackstrap molasses—a dark, concentrated liquid sweetener that's a by-product of processing sugar cane or sugar beets into sugar. Use a lighter molasses like Grandma's Molasses for a mellower flavor.

Soft Sugar Cookies

These simple "buttery" cookies—made with confectioners' sugar, which lends a smooth, tender crumb inside—are perfect for the holidays or any day, and kids of any age will enjoy rolling the cookies in colored sugar and sprinkles.

Yield:	Prep time:	Bake time:	Serving size:
24 to 30 cookies	50 to 55 minutes	8 to 10 minutes	1 cookie

2⅛ cups unbleached all-purpose flour

½ tsp. baking soda

½ tsp. cream of tartar

¼ tsp. salt

½ cup nonhydrogenated vegan margarine, at room temperature

½ cup unbleached cane sugar

6 TB. vegan confectioners' sugar

Egg substitute for 1 large egg (Ener-G Egg Replacer is best in this recipe)

1 tsp. pure vanilla extract

½ cup canola or vegetable oil

½ cup colored sugar or sprinkles

1. Preheat the oven to 350°F. Lightly oil or spray 2 baking sheets with vegetable shortening, or line with parchment paper.

2. In a large bowl, combine unbleached all-purpose flour, baking soda, cream of tartar, and salt with a wooden spoon or whisk. Set aside.

3. In a separate large bowl, and using an electric mixer fitted with the beater attachment on medium speed, beat vegan margarine, unbleached cane sugar, and confectioners' sugar until light and fluffy, scraping the bowl as needed with a rubber spatula. Add egg substitute and vanilla extract, and beat again.

4. Reduce speed to low, add canola oil, and beat until smooth and no lumps remain. Add ½ of dry ingredients to batter, and mix to combine. Add remaining dry ingredients, and mix until dough is nice and smooth, scraping the bowl as needed. (If your kitchen is especially warm or humid, cover and chill the dough for 30 minutes before scooping and baking.)

5. Using a ¼ cup ice cream scoop or a tablespoon, scoop out cookie dough and roll into balls. Roll balls in colored sugar or sprinkles until they're completely covered, and place on the prepared baking sheets, leaving enough room for cookies to spread a little, about 1 inch apart.

6. Bake for 8 to 10 minutes or until outside of cookies feel slightly firm to the touch. Remove cookies from the oven, and allow them to sit for a few minutes before transferring to wire racks. Cool cookies completely before storing in an airtight container or in zipper-lock plastic bags.

> **BAKER'S BONUS**
>
> Save money by making your own colored sugar! Add a few drops of natural food coloring to unbleached cane sugar. Then, simply mix with a spoon until the color coats all the sugar. Store extra colored sugar in a glass jar or airtight container.

Oatmeal Raisin Cookies

These old-fashioned, sweet, and chewy cookies are made with sugar and spice and everything nice, just like the cookies in Grandma's cookie jar.

Yield:	Prep time:	Bake time:	Serving size:
24 to 30 cookies	50 to 55 minutes	10 to 12 minutes	1 cookie

2 cups unbleached all-purpose flour	1 cup Florida Crystals or unbleached cane sugar
1¼ cups rolled oats	1 cup light brown sugar, firmly packed
1 tsp. baking soda	Egg substitute for 2 large eggs
1 tsp. ground *cinnamon*	1 tsp. pure vanilla extract
¼ tsp. ground nutmeg	1½ cups raisins
¼ tsp. salt	
1 cup nonhydrogenated vegan margarine, softened	

1. Preheat the oven to 350°F. Lightly oil or spray 2 baking sheets with vegetable shortening, or line with parchment paper.

2. In a large bowl, combine unbleached all-purpose flour, rolled oats, baking soda, ground cinnamon, ground nutmeg, and salt with a wooden spoon or whisk. Set aside.

3. In a separate large bowl, and using an electric mixer fitted with the beater attachment on medium speed, beat vegan margarine, Florida Crystals, and light brown sugar until light and fluffy, scraping the bowl as needed with a rubber spatula. Add egg substitute and vanilla extract, and beat again.

4. Reduce speed to low, add ½ of dry ingredients to batter, and mix to combine. Add remaining dry ingredients and raisins, and mix only enough to combine, scraping the bowl as needed. (If your kitchen is especially warm or humid, cover and chill dough for 30 minutes before scooping and baking.)

5. Using a ¼ cup measure or a tablespoon, scoop out cookie dough and place on the prepared baking sheets, leaving enough room for cookies to spread a little, about 1 inch apart.

6. Bake for 10 to 12 minutes or until slightly firm around the edges. Do not over-bake. Cookies will continue to bake for a few minutes after they're removed from the oven. Remove cookies from the oven, and allow them to sit for a few minutes before transferring to wire racks. Cool cookies completely before storing in an airtight container or in zipper-lock plastic bags.

Variations: For **Oatmeal Craisin Cookies,** substitute dried sweetened cranberries for the raisins. For **Oatmeal Chocolate-Chip Walnut Cookies,** substitute vegan chocolate chips for the raisins, and add ½ cup chopped walnuts.

VEGAN VOCAB

Cinnamon is a rich, aromatic spice commonly used in baking or desserts. It can also be used for delicious and interesting entrées.

White Chocolate Macadamia Cookies

These cookies have a rich "buttery" flavor that's made even better with sweet vegan white chocolate chips. The nutty macadamias bring an exotic texture and taste.

Yield:	Prep time:	Bake time:	Serving size:
24 to 30 cookies	20 to 25 minutes	10 to 12 minutes	1 cookie

2¼ cups unbleached all-purpose flour

1 tsp. baking soda

1 tsp. salt

1 cup nonhydrogenated vegan margarine, at room temperature

¾ cup light brown sugar, firmly packed

½ cup unbleached cane sugar

Egg substitute for 2 large eggs

1½ tsp. pure vanilla extract

1 cup vegan white chocolate chips or chunks

⅔ cup chopped macadamia nuts

1. Preheat the oven to 350°F. Lightly oil or spray 2 baking sheets with vegetable shortening, or line with parchment paper.

2. In a large bowl, combine unbleached all-purpose flour, baking soda, and salt with a wooden spoon or whisk. Set aside.

3. In a separate large bowl, and using an electric mixer fitted with the beater attachment on medium speed, beat vegan margarine, light brown sugar, and unbleached cane sugar until creamy, scraping the bowl as needed with a rubber spatula. Add egg substitute and vanilla extract, and beat again until light and fluffy. Scrape down the bowl, and beat again until batter is nice and smooth.

4. Reduce speed to low, add ½ of dry ingredients to batter, and mix to combine. Add remaining dry ingredients, and mix until dough is smooth, scraping the bowl as needed. Add vegan white chocolate chips and macadamia nuts, and mix only enough to combine. (If your kitchen is especially warm or humid, cover and chill dough for 30 minutes before scooping and baking.)

5. Using a ¼ cup ice cream scoop or a tablespoon, scoop out cookie dough and place on the prepared baking sheets, leaving enough room for cookies to spread, about 1 inch apart.

6. Bake cookies for 10 to 12 minutes or until slightly firm around the edges. Cookies will continue to bake for a few minutes after they're removed from the oven. Remove cookies from the oven, and allow them to sit for a few minutes before transferring to wire racks. Cool cookies completely before storing in an airtight container or in zipper-lock plastic bags.

BATTER UP!

Unlike regular white chocolate, which contains milk solids, vegan white chocolate chips contain non–bone char refined sugar, partially hydrogenated palm kernel oil, sorbitan monostearate (vegetarian source), soy lecithin, and vanillin. Most commercial white chocolate chips include whole milk powder and may contain trace amounts of eggs, making them unsuitable for vegan diets.

Chocolate No-Bake Cookies

You don't need to turn on your oven for these dark and chocolaty cookies made with peanut butter, walnuts, coconut, and a hint of cinnamon. Simply mix everything in a saucepan, and let the cookies firm a little before eating.

Yield:	Prep time:	Cool time:	Serving size:
20 to 24 cookies	20 to 25 minutes	20 to 30 minutes	1 cookie

2 cups unbleached cane sugar

4 TB. Dutch cocoa powder

½ cup nonhydrogenated vegan margarine

½ cup plain or chocolate soy milk

Pinch salt

½ cup smooth or chunky peanut butter

½ tsp. ground cinnamon

1 tsp. pure vanilla extract

3 cups rolled oats

½ cup chopped walnuts

¾ cup shredded sweetened coconut

1. Lightly oil or spray 2 baking sheets with vegetable shortening, or line with parchment paper.

2. In a large saucepan over medium heat, combine unbleached cane sugar, Dutch cocoa powder, vegan margarine, soy milk, and salt. Bring to a boil, boil for 30 seconds, and remove the pan from the stove. Using a large wooden spoon or spatula, add peanut butter, ground cinnamon, and vanilla extract, and mix well.

3. Add rolled oats, chopped walnuts, and shredded coconut, and stir well, using a rubber spatula to scrape the edges.

4. Allow cookie mixture to cool slightly, about 10 minutes.

5. Using a ¼ cup measure or a tablespoon, scoop out warm cookie dough and place on the prepared baking sheets. Press down to flatten cookies just a little with oiled hands. No-bake cookies don't spread much, but they still need a little room between each other, about 1 inch apart.

6. Let cookies cool and firm up completely on the baking sheet before wrapping in plastic wrap, storing in an airtight container, or in zipper-lock plastic bags.

BAKER'S BONUS

No need to dirty extra bowls or pans with this cookie recipe. Save cleanup time by making the entire recipe in one saucepan.

Specialty Cookies

In This Chapter

- Fancy and nutty cookies
- Molded and rolled cookies
- Unbelievable biscotti

Want to impress your guests with something a little elegant, but only have time to make cookies? Or have you been asked to bring a cookie platter to the company party and are looking for something special? If you want pretty, festive sweets on your cookie plate, but without all the dairy and eggs, this chapter is for you.

Choose a nice selection of cookies with lots of color that will make your cookie platter stand out among the rest of the desserts on the table. Thumbprint Cookies rolled in chopped nuts and filled with red and green jam will sparkle for the holidays. Pink Cherry Valentine Cookies decked out with chopped red cherries are perfect for the holiday of love, Mother's Day, or even Christmas. And who doesn't love snowy-white Pecan Butterballs made with ground pecans and coated in vegan confectioners' sugar?

Speaking of nuts, a few of these vegan cookie recipes have toasted chopped nuts in them. If you don't like pecans, try substituting almonds or walnuts. Grinding nuts can be as easy as putting them in the food processor and giving it a whirl to achieve the size of nut you need. Refer to the recipes for instructions on how to toast nuts.

Cherry Valentine Cookies

These cookies are pretty and pink with an almond flavor and sweet maraschino cherries. Add a vegan chocolate kiss or candy disc on top for a little something extra!

Yield:	Prep time:	Bake time:	Serving size:
25 to 30 cookies	50 to 60 minutes	10 to 12 minutes	1 cookie

1 cup nonhydrogenated vegan margarine, softened

1 cup vegan confectioners' sugar

1 TB. maraschino cherry juice

½ tsp. pure almond extract

2 drops natural red food coloring

¼ tsp. salt

2½ cups unbleached all-purpose flour

½ cup drained and chopped maraschino cherries

25 to 30 vegan chocolate kisses or candy discs

1. Preheat the oven to 350°F. Lightly oil or spray 2 baking sheets with vegetable shortening, or line with parchment paper.

2. In a large bowl, and using an electric mixer fitted with the beater attachment on medium speed, beat vegan margarine and confectioners' sugar until light and fluffy, scraping the bowl as needed with a rubber spatula. Add maraschino cherry juice, almond extract, red food coloring, and salt, and beat again.

3. Reduce speed to low, add ½ of unbleached all-purpose flour, and mix to combine. Add remaining flour, scraping the bowl as needed. Add maraschino cherries, and mix only enough to combine. (If your kitchen is especially warm or humid, cover and chill dough for 30 minutes before scooping and baking.)

4. Using a small ice cream scoop or tablespoon, scoop out cookie dough and place on the prepared baking sheets, leaving enough room for cookies to spread a little, about 1 inch apart. Do not flatten cookies.

5. Bake for 10 to 12 minutes or until slightly firm and slightly browned around the edges. Remove cookies from the oven, and immediately place an unwrapped chocolate kiss or chocolate disc on the top of each cookie, pressing down slightly. Transfer cookies to wire racks, and cool completely before storing in an airtight container or in zipper-lock plastic bags.

BATTER UP!

Look for vegan and gluten-free all-natural red food coloring. Natural food colors contain vegetable-, fruit-, and plant-based dyes without all the harmful additives. If you can find natural gel cake coloring, even better. A little goes a long way.

Thumbprint Cookies

These Christmas cookie favorites are filled with raspberry jam and rolled in toasted nuts. Brown sugar and a touch of almond extract take them over the top!

Yield:	Prep time:	Bake time:	Serving size:
25 to 30 cookies	30 to 55 minutes	10 to 14 minutes	1 cookie

2 cups toasted nuts (walnuts, almonds, pecans, etc.)

2¾ cups unbleached all-purpose flour

1 tsp. aluminum-free baking powder

1 cup nonhydrogenated vegan margarine, softened

½ cup light brown sugar, firmly packed

Egg substitute for 2 large eggs

½ tsp. pure almond extract

2 TB. agave syrup

2 TB. water

¾ to 1 cup raspberry jam (or your choice jam or marmalade)

1. Preheat the oven to 350°F. Lightly oil or spray 2 baking sheets with vegetable shortening, or line with parchment paper.

2. Grind toasted nuts in a food processor or chop on a cutting board with a sharp knife until fine. Set aside.

3. In a large bowl, combine unbleached all-purpose flour and aluminum-free baking powder with a wooden spoon or whisk.

4. In a separate large bowl, and using an electric mixer fitted with the beater attachment on medium speed, beat vegan margarine and light brown sugar until light and fluffy, scraping the bowl as needed with a rubber spatula. Add egg substitute and almond extract, and beat again.

5. Reduce speed to low, add ½ of dry ingredients, and mix to combine. Add remaining dry ingredients, and mix only enough to combine, scraping the bowl as needed. (If your kitchen is especially warm or humid, cover and chill the dough for 30 minutes before scooping and baking.)

6. In a small bowl, whisk together agave syrup and water until blended.

7. Using a tablespoon, scoop out cookie dough and form into 1¼-inch-round balls. Dip each cookie in agave syrup mixture, and roll in toasted chopped nuts, coating completely.

8. Place cookies on the prepared baking sheets, leaving a little room for cookies to spread, about 1 inch apart. Press the back of a teaspoon or your thumb into cookie, creating a shallow well. Fill indentation with a little jam.

9. Bake for 10 to 14 minutes or until slightly firm around the edges. Do not overbake. Cookies will continue to bake for a few minutes after they're removed from the oven. Remove cookies from the oven, and allow them to sit for a few minutes before transferring to wire racks. Cool cookies completely before layering between waxed paper or parchment and storing in an airtight container.

Variation: For **Chocolate Thumbprints,** omit the jam and bake the cookies first. Immediately upon removing the pan from the oven, place 1 vegan semisweet chocolate disc or chocolate kiss in the center and press down lightly.

BAKER'S BONUS

Get festive! Vary the flavor and color of the jam according to the season. Peach, blueberry, and strawberry jams are not only refreshing for the summer, but beautiful as well. Make Christmas colors of green and red by using green mint jelly in half the cookies and red raspberry jam in the remaining half. Orange marmalade is a good choice, as is grape jelly. For a special cookie platter, line the plate with a pretty doily or napkin and fill the cookies with 4 or 5 different jams and jellies.

Shortbread Cookies

"Buttery" shortbread cookies are a classic holiday favorite. But you can enjoy these tender, melt-in-your-mouth cookies all year round by varying the flavors and shapes.

Yield:	Prep time:	Bake time:	Serving size:
48 to 60 cookies	20 to 25 minutes	30 to 40 minutes	1 cookie

4 cups unbleached all-purpose flour	2 cups nonhydrogenated vegan margarine, softened
½ tsp. aluminum-free baking powder	1 cup vegan confectioners' sugar
½ tsp. salt	2 tsp. pure vanilla extract

1. Preheat the oven to 350°F. Lightly oil or spray a 9×13 baking pan with vegetable shortening, or line with parchment paper.

2. In a large bowl, combine unbleached all-purpose flour, aluminum-free baking powder, and salt with a wooden spoon or whisk.

3. In a separate large bowl, and using an electric mixer fitted with the beater attachment on medium speed, beat vegan margarine and confectioners' sugar until light and fluffy, scraping the bowl as needed with a rubber spatula. Add vanilla extract, and beat again.

4. Reduce speed to low, add ½ of dry ingredients, and mix to combine. Add remaining flour, scraping the bowl as needed.

5. Press cookie dough into prepared baking pan. With a small, sharp knife, *score* dough into 1×3-inch "fingers." Do not cut all the way through; just the top third of the dough. Using a fork, *prick* the top all over.

6. Bake for 30 to 40 minutes or until shortbread is very light brown and fragrant. Remove from the oven, and cool for 10 minutes in the pan on a wire rack. Carefully remove shortbread from the pan, place on a cutting board, and cut through score marks. Cool completely on wire rack before storing in an airtight container or in zipper-lock bags.

Variations: For **Flavored Shortbread Cookies,** substitute pure almond, rum, or maple extract for the vanilla extract. For **Chocolate Dipped Shortbread Cookies,** dip the end of a completely cooled baked shortbread cookie into melted vegan chocolate ganache.

VEGAN VOCAB

To **score** means to make shallow cuts in the surface of a food. To **prick** means to make small holes in the surface of a food so it won't rise or blister. This is usually done with the tines of a fork.

Pecan Butterballs

These snow-white cookies are made with ground pecans and rolled in confectioners' sugar. They're so melt-in-your-mouth tender, it's hard to stop at just one! They look great on a holiday cookie platter, too.

Yield:	Prep time:	Bake time:	Serving size:
30 cookies	20 to 30 minutes	13 to 15 minutes	1 cookie

1 cup toasted pecans	2 tsp. pure vanilla extract
1 cup nonhydrogenated vegan margarine, softened	¼ tsp. salt
1½ cups vegan confectioners' sugar	2 cups unbleached all-purpose flour

1. Preheat the oven to 350°F. Lightly oil or spray 2 baking sheets with vegetable shortening, or line with parchment paper.

2. Grind toasted pecans in a food processor or chop on a cutting board with a sharp knife until very fine.

3. In a large bowl, and using an electric mixer fitted with the beater attachment on high speed, beat vegan margarine for 1 or 2 minutes or until fluffy. Add ½ cup confectioners' sugar, and beat again, scraping the sides of the bowl as necessary with a rubber spatula. Add vanilla extract and salt, and beat again.

4. Reduce speed to low, add ½ of all-purpose flour, and mix to combine. Add remaining flour and ground pecans, and mix until dough is smooth, scraping the bowl as needed.

5. Using a small ice cream scoop, or tablespoon, scoop out cookie dough in 1-inch balls, and place on the prepared baking sheets, leaving a little room for cookies to spread, about 1 inch apart.

6. Bake for 13 to 15 minutes or until cookies are almost firm and edges are lightly browned. Remove from the oven, and let cool on the baking sheet just enough to handle.

7. Place remaining 1 cup confectioners' sugar in a medium bowl. Roll warm cookies in confectioners' sugar until completely coated. Shake off excess sugar, and place cookies back on the baking sheet. Cool cookies completely before storing in an airtight container. Pecan Butterballs may need a second coating of confectioners' sugar before they're served.

BAKER'S BONUS

To toast pecans, place them in a single layer on an ungreased, lipped baking sheet, and bake in a preheated 350°F oven for 8 to 12 minutes, stirring every 3 or 4 minutes, or until they smell fragrant and start to turn golden brown. Let cool completely before grinding in a food processor or chopping on a cutting board with a sharp knife until fine. Try toasting almonds, walnuts, hazelnuts, macadamias, and other nuts as well for variety.

Coconut Lime Biscotti

These refreshing twice-baked cookies—made with fresh lime *zest*, sweet coconut, and a touch of coconut extract, and drizzled with vegan white chocolate—will make you feel like you're in the islands.

Yield:	Prep time:	Bake time:	Serving size:
30 to 36 cookies	60 to 70 minutes	35 to 45 minutes	1 cookie

1½ cups unbleached all-purpose flour

1½ tsp. aluminum-free baking powder

½ cup yellow cornmeal

¼ tsp. salt

½ cup nonhydrogenated vegan margarine, softened

1 cup unbleached cane sugar

Egg substitute for 2 large eggs

Grated zest of 1 lime

1½ tsp. pure coconut extract

¾ cup shredded sweetened coconut

½ cup vegan white chocolate chips, or colored sprinkles (optional)

½ batch White Chocolate Ganache (variation in Chapter 22)

1. Preheat the oven to 350°F. Lightly oil or spray 1 baking sheet with vegetable shortening, or line with parchment paper.

2. In a large bowl, combine unbleached all-purpose flour, aluminum-free baking powder, yellow cornmeal, and salt with a wooden spoon or whisk.

3. In a separate large bowl, and using an electric mixer fitted with the beater attachment on medium speed, beat vegan margarine and unbleached cane sugar for 2 or 3 minutes or until smooth, scraping the bowl as needed with a rubber spatula. Add egg substitute, lime zest, and coconut extract, and beat again for 1 or 2 minutes or until light and fluffy, scraping down the bowl as needed. Cookie dough will be slightly sticky. With a rubber spatula, fold in shredded coconut and vegan white chocolate chips.

4. Turn out cookie dough onto the prepared baking sheet, and with your hands coated in flour, form into 2 logs, each 12 inches long by 1½ inches wide. (Cookie dough will be bumpy.) Leave enough room between logs for dough to spread, about 3 inches apart.

5. Bake logs for 20 to 25 minutes or until logs are lightly golden and springs back slightly when touched. Logs will have flattened and spread out during baking. Remove from the oven and cool for approximately 30 minutes.

6. Transfer logs to a cutting board, and with a serrated knife, cut logs on the diagonal into ¾-inch-thick slices. Place slices cut side down on the baking sheet, and return them to a 350°F oven.

7. Bake for 15 to 20 more minutes or until biscotti are golden brown, fragrant, and firm to the touch. Cool biscotti completely on wire racks before decorating with vegan White Chocolate Ganache. Store cookies in an airtight container.

VEGAN VOCAB

Zest is small slivers of peel, usually from a citrus fruit such as a lemon, lime, or orange. Use a tool called a *zester* (or grater) with small holes to scrape fine zest off a fruit, but avoid getting the white, bitter pith. A small grater also works well.

Chocolate-Chip Biscotti

These biscotti, perfect for dunking in a cup of coffee or hot chocolate, are made with dark cocoa and vegan chocolate chips.

Yield:	Prep time:	Bake time:	Serving size:
30 to 36 cookies	50 to 60 minutes	35 to 40 minutes	1 cookie

1¾ cups unbleached all-purpose flour

¼ cup natural cocoa powder

1 cup Florida Crystals or unbleached cane sugar

¾ tsp. aluminum-free baking powder

¼ tsp. salt

¼ cup nonhydrogenated vegan margarine, cold

1 tsp. pure vanilla extract

Egg substitute for 2 large eggs

1 cup vegan chocolate chips

1. Preheat the oven to 350°F. Lightly oil or spray 1 baking sheet with vegetable shortening, or line with parchment paper.

2. In a food processor fitted with a chopping blade, combine all-purpose flour, natural cocoa powder, Florida Crystals, aluminum-free baking powder, and salt. *Pulse* on and off for 5 to 10 seconds.

3. Add vegan margarine, vanilla extract, and egg substitute, and pulse for 10 to 20 seconds or until mixture resembles coarse cornmeal. Add chocolate chips, and pulse only until dough is mixed and no dry ingredients remain.

4. Turn out cookie dough onto the prepared baking sheet, and with your hands coated in flour, form into 4 equal-size logs, each 6 inches long by 1½ inches wide. Leave enough room between logs for dough to spread, about 3 inches apart.

5. Bake logs for 25 minutes or until logs are lightly golden and spring back slightly when touched. Logs will have flattened and spread out during baking. Remove from the oven and cool for approximately 30 minutes.

6. Transfer logs to a cutting board, and with a serrated knife, cut logs into diagonal ¾-inch-thick slices. Place slices cut side down on the baking sheet, and return them to a 350°F oven.

7. Bake for 10 to 15 more minutes or until biscotti are golden brown and firm to the touch. Cool biscotti completely on wire racks before storing in an airtight container or in zipper-lock bags.

VEGAN VOCAB

To **pulse** in a food processor means to start and stop the motor multiple times, pausing for 1 or 2 seconds between processing. Most processors have a pulse button, so you don't have to push it on and off. Pulsing in this recipe is better than leaving the machine running because it doesn't overwork or overprocess the dough.

Best-Ever Brownies and Bars

In This Chapter

- Chocolate fudgy brownies
- Unbelievable blondies
- Fantastic fruit bars
- Sweet nut and rice treats

A cookbook just isn't a cookbook without brownies and lemon bars! This chapter is full of chocolaty and fudgy brownies, cakey brownies, brownies topped with cream cheese, black bean brownies, and for the chocolate challenged—brownies made with carob, and blond brownies without chocolate. Some recipes are easy-peasy, and some are a little more involved, but all are definitely worth trying. However, not everyone likes chocolate, so ….

The next stop is the bar—the fruit bar, that is. Some of these snacks are made with a bottom crust, fruit filling, and a topping. The Luscious Lemon Bars are tangy and sweet, the Raspberry Shortbread Bars sit on a tender shortbread crust and are topped with coconut streusel, while the Date Nut Squares have a homemade date filling you'll be surprised is so delicious and easy to prepare. Finally, we come to the Crispy Rice Treats, because no matter how old you are, everyone should have these childhood delights in their recipe collection.

For vegans and nonvegans alike, the recipes in this chapter will have you scrambling to the kitchen to get your apron on!

Carob Peanut Butter Brownies

Can't have chocolate? These rich carob brownies with a good dose of peanut butter will make any brownie lover forget chocolate.

Yield:	Prep time:	Bake time:	Serving size:
1 (8×8-inch) pan	20 to 30 minutes	38 to 42 minutes	1 brownie

¼ cup soft silken tofu	⅓ cup carob powder
1 tsp. pure vanilla extract	1 TB. cornstarch
2 TB. ground flaxseed	½ cup canola or vegetable oil
6 TB. water	½ cup creamy or chunky peanut butter
1⅓ cups whole-wheat pastry flour	1½ cups brown rice, agave, or pure maple syrup
½ tsp. aluminum-free baking powder	

1. Preheat the oven to 350°F. Grease and flour an 8×8-inch baking pan with non-hydrogenated shortening, tapping out any excess flour.

2. In a blender, add soft silken tofu, vanilla extract, ground flaxseed, and water, and blend on high speed for 1 minute or until mixture is smooth and thick.

3. Into a large bowl, sift whole-wheat pastry flour, aluminum-free baking powder, carob powder, and cornstarch, or blend with a whisk.

4. In a separate large bowl, and using an electric mixer fitted with a paddle attachment on medium speed, combine canola oil, peanut butter, and brown rice syrup. Reduce speed to low, add ½ of dry ingredients, alternating with tofu mixture, and mix well, scraping the bowl as needed with a rubber spatula. Add remaining dry ingredients, and mix only until batter is incorporated. Do not overmix.

5. Pour batter into the prepared pan, and bake for 38 to 42 minutes or until a toothpick inserted into the center comes out clean. Cool completely in the pan on a wire rack before cutting. Store the pan of brownies at room temperature covered with plastic wrap or in an airtight container for up to 2 days. These brownies can also be frozen for up to 3 months.

BAKER'S BONUS

The standard 8×8-inch and 9×9-inch square baking pans are used for most of the recipes in this chapter. But if you want to double a recipe, you can bake it in a 9×13-inch pan. Doubling the recipe may increase baking time by 5 to 10 minutes.

Chocolate Fudge Brownies

These moist, fudgy brownies contain a secret ingredient to help keep them soft. Black beans puréed with tofu and water yield the most decadent, dark-chocolate brownies ever.

Yield:	Prep time:	Bake time:	Serving size:
1 (9×9-inch) pan	20 to 30 minutes	28 to 32 minutes	1 brownie

½ cup whole-wheat pastry flour

½ cup unbleached all-purpose flour

½ tsp. salt

1 tsp. aluminum-free baking powder

½ cup natural cocoa powder

1 cup unbleached cane sugar

2 (1-oz.) squares unsweetened baking chocolate

2 TB. agave syrup

½ cup canned black beans, rinsed and drained

1 cup water

¼ cup soft tofu

¾ tsp. pure vanilla extract

1. Preheat the oven to 350°F. Grease and flour a 9×9-inch baking pan with nonhydrogenated shortening, tapping out any excess flour.

2. Into a large bowl, sift whole-wheat pastry flour, unbleached all-purpose flour, salt, aluminum-free baking powder, and cocoa powder, or blend with a wire whisk. Add unbleached cane sugar, and stir.

3. In a small microwave-safe bowl, combine unsweetened baking chocolate and agave syrup. Microwave on low power for 1-minute intervals, stirring in between, or until smooth. Be careful to not let chocolate burn.

4. In a blender, add black beans and water, and blend on high speed for 1 minute or until smooth. Add soft tofu and vanilla extract, and blend for 1 or 2 minutes or until mixture is smooth and thick. Reduce speed to low, and slowly add chocolate mixture, blending for 2 or 3 minutes or until smooth. Increase speed to high, and blend again, scraping down the sides of the blender as needed with a rubber spatula.

5. Pour liquid ingredients into dry ingredients, and using a rubber spatula, fold only until ingredients are incorporated and no dry ingredients remain.

6. Pour batter into the prepared pan, and bake for 28 to 32 minutes or until a knife inserted into the center comes out almost clean. Cool completely in the pan on a wire rack before cutting. Store the pan of brownies at room temperature covered with plastic wrap or in an airtight container for up to 2 days. These brownies can also be frozen for up to 3 months.

> **BAKER'S BONUS**
>
> If you don't have any black beans on hand, you can use white cannellini beans, garbanzo beans, or even pinto beans. Most any bean will do, but stay away from refried beans. They contain additional spices that will make your brownies taste like tacos. Whatever bean you use, be sure to purée them in the water and liquid specified in the recipe before adding them to the brownie batter.

Pecan Blondies

A blondie is sort of like a reverse brownie, but while these moist brown sugar bars may be light in color, they're full of flavor. Add a cup of vegan chocolate chips to the batter and top with Penuche Frosting for a unique taste treat.

Yield:	Prep time:	Bake time:	Serving size:
1 (9×9-inch) pan	20 to 30 minutes	28 to 32 minutes	1 blondie

1 cup whole-wheat pastry flour

1 tsp. aluminum-free baking powder

1 tsp. cornstarch

¼ tsp. salt

¼ cup soft silken tofu

1 TB. ground flaxseed

3 TB. water

1 tsp. pure vanilla extract

½ cup nonhydrogenated vegan margarine, softened

1 cup light brown sugar, firmly packed

½ cup toasted, chopped pecans

1. Preheat the oven to 325°F. Lightly oil or spray a 9×9-inch baking pan with canola oil or vegetable shortening spray.

2. Into a large bowl, sift whole-wheat pastry flour, aluminum-free baking powder, cornstarch, and salt, or blend with a wire whisk.

3. In a blender, add soft silken tofu, ground flaxseed, water, and vanilla extract, and blend on high speed for 2 or 3 minutes or until smooth, scraping down the sides of the blender as needed with a rubber spatula.

4. In a separate large bowl, and using an electric mixer fitted with a paddle attachment on medium speed, beat vegan margarine and light brown sugar for 1 or 2 minutes or until light and fluffy. Scrape down the sides of the bowl using a rubber spatula.

5. Reduce speed to low, and add tofu mixture to butter and sugar mixture, and mix well. Add ½ of dry ingredients and mix again, scraping down the sides of the bowl as needed with a rubber spatula. Add remaining dry ingredients and pecans, and mix just until blended.

6. Spread batter into the prepared pan, smoothing top with a spatula. Bake for 28 to 32 minutes or until light brown and a toothpick inserted in the center comes out clean. Do not overbake. Blondies should be moist but baked through. Cool completely before cutting.

Variation: For **Penuche-Frosted Pecan Blondies,** bake as directed, cool completely, and frost with Penuche Frosting (recipe in Chapter 21).

Luscious Lemon Bars

These delicate lemon bars—fresh lemon zest and lemon juice all whipped up and baked on a delicious shortbread crust—are tart yet sweet.

Yield:	Prep time:	Bake time:	Serving size:
1 (8×8-inch) pan	30 to 40 minutes	33 to 43 minutes	1 bar

1 cup unbleached all-purpose flour

½ cup vegan confectioners' sugar

Pinch salt

1 tsp. aluminum-free baking powder

½ cup cold nonhydrogenated vegan margarine, cubed

1 TB. soft tofu

½ cup firm tofu

⅓ cup fresh lemon juice

1 TB. lemon zest

1 TB. *arrowroot* powder

1 cup unbleached cane sugar

1. Preheat the oven to 350°F. Lightly oil or spray a 8×8-inch baking pan with canola oil or vegetable shortening spray.

2. In a food processor fitted with a chopping blade, add unbleached all-purpose flour, ¼ cup vegan confectioners' sugar, salt, and ½ teaspoon aluminum-free baking powder, and pulse 5 to 10 times or until blended. Reduce speed to low, and add vegan margarine a little at a time. Add soft tofu, and blend for about 1 minute or until mixture makes a ball and comes away from the sides of the processor.

3. Press crust into the prepared pan, and bake for 15 to 20 minutes or until light golden.

4. While crust is baking, in a blender, add firm tofu, lemon juice, lemon zest, ½ teaspoon aluminum-free baking powder, and arrowroot powder, and blend on high speed for 2 or 3 minutes or until smooth. Add unbleached cane sugar, and blend on high for 1 or 2 more minutes or until well mixed and smooth.

5. Pour lemon mixture over cooked crust while it's still hot. Bake for 18 to 23 more minutes or until set. Cool completely on a wire rack before sprinkling with remaining ¼ cup vegan confectioners' sugar. Wrap the pan with plastic wrap and store in the refrigerator for up to 3 days. As bars sit, you may need to sprinkle with more confectioners' sugar.

6. Chill bars before cutting. Using a thin, sharp knife, cut through to crust. Use a small metal spatula to gently lift bars out of the pan. If the knife pulls at and/or rips bars, wet the knife in hot water, wipe dry, and try again.

Variation: For **Luscious Lime Bars,** substitute fresh lime zest and juice for the lemon in the recipe.

VEGAN VOCAB

Arrowroot is a starch that comes from the tubers of the arrowroot plant. Virtually tasteless, arrowroot is a snow-white powder used as a thickener much like cornstarch but without the pasty mouthfeel. It thickens at a lower temperature than cornstarch, and doesn't weaken with acidic ingredients.

Raspberry Shortbread Bars

These pretty and sweet fruity bars are made with a tender shortbread crust, topped with raspberry jam, and finished with a coconut and walnut streusel. They're hard to resist!

Yield:	Prep time:	Bake time:	Serving size:
1 (8×8-inch) pan	30 to 40 minutes	40 to 50 minutes	1 bar

1¼ cups unbleached all-purpose flour

¼ cup whole-wheat pastry flour

½ cup vegan confectioners' sugar

½ tsp. aluminum-free baking powder

½ cup cold nonhydrogenated vegan margarine, cubed

2 TB. soft tofu

½ cup unsweetened flaked coconut

½ cup unbleached cane sugar

¼ cup toasted, chopped walnuts

¾ cup raspberry jam

1. Preheat the oven to 350°F. Lightly oil or spray a 8×8-inch baking pan with canola oil or vegetable shortening spray.

2. In a food processor fitted with a cutting blade, add unbleached all-purpose flour, whole-wheat pastry flour, vegan confectioners' sugar, and aluminum-free baking powder, and pulse 5 to 10 times or until blended. Reduce speed to low, and add vegan margarine a little at a time. Add soft tofu, and blend for about 1 minute or until mixture makes a ball and comes away from the sides of the processor.

3. Remove mixture from the processor, and return ⅓ of it back to the food processor. Press remaining ⅔ of mixture into the prepared pan, and bake for 10 minutes.

4. Add flaked coconut, unbleached cane sugar, and walnuts to the food processor, and pulse 10 to 15 times or until mixture resembles streusel.

5. Let cooked crust cool for 15 minutes.

6. Spread raspberry jam over cooled crust, and evenly sprinkle streusel mixture over top, pressing in lightly.

7. Bake for 15 to 25 more minutes or until topping is lightly browned. Cool completely on a wire rack before cutting. Store at room temperature covered with plastic wrap or in an airtight container for up to 24 hours. These bars can also be frozen for up to 3 months.

Variation: For assorted fruit bars, substitute blueberry jam, strawberry jam, apricot jam, or any favorite jam you'd like to try.

BAKER'S BONUS

To toast walnuts, place them in a single layer on an ungreased baking sheet, and bake in a 350°F oven for 8 to 12 minutes or until they start to smell fragrant and turn golden brown. Let cool completely before chopping in a food processor.

Date Nut Squares

In these old-fashioned fruit bars, a rich date filling is sandwiched between a "buttery" crust and sweet coconut streusel. These high-energy snacks are also full of fiber.

Yield:	Prep time:	Bake time:	Serving size:
1 (9×9-inch) pan	30 to 60 minutes	25 to 35 minutes	1 bar

2 cups finely chopped, pitted dates	¼ tsp. aluminum-free baking powder
½ cup water	
¼ cup pure maple syrup	1 tsp. ground cinnamon
¾ cup toasted, chopped walnuts	¼ tsp. ground nutmeg
Pinch salt	½ cup cold nonhydrogenated vegan margarine, cubed
1 cup unbleached all-purpose flour	
¼ cup vegan confectioners' sugar	½ cup unsweetened flaked coconut
¼ cup light brown sugar, firmly packed	½ cup unbleached cane sugar

1. In a small saucepan over medium heat, bring dates, water, maple syrup, walnuts, and salt to a boil, stirring constantly. Reduce heat to low, and continue cooking for 8 to 12 minutes or until mixture is very thick and all liquid is absorbed. Set aside to cool.

2. Preheat the oven to 350°F. Generously coat a 9×9-inch baking pan with cooking oil spray.

3. In a food processor fitted with a chopping blade, add unbleached all-purpose flour, vegan confectioners' sugar, light brown sugar, aluminum-free baking powder, ground cinnamon, and ground nutmeg, and pulse 5 to 10 times or **until** blended. Reduce speed to low, and add vegan margarine a little at a time. **Blend** for about 1 minute or until mixture makes a ball and comes away from the sides of the processor.

4. Remove ⅔ mixture from the processor, and press into the prepared pan. Bake for 10 minutes. Let cooked crust cool for 15 minutes.

5. Add flaked coconut and unbleached cane sugar to remaining ⅓ mixture in the food processor, and pulse 10 to 15 times or until mixture resembles streusel.

6. Spread date filling over cooled crust, and evenly sprinkle streusel over top, pressing in lightly.

7. Bake for 15 to 20 more minutes or until topping is lightly browned. Cool completely on a wire rack before cutting. Store at room temperature covered with plastic wrap or in an airtight container for up to 24 hours. These bars can also be frozen for up to 3 months.

DOUGH-NOT

Be sure you use dried pitted dates in this recipe. If they're not already pitted, you need to remove the pits before chopping and adding the dates to the filling. Medjool dates are the most popular dates and are readily available at most supermarkets.

Crispy Rice Treats

Kids of all ages love crispy bars, especially when peanut butter is added. So indulge and be a kid again!

Yield:	Prep time:	Serving size:
1 (9×9-inch) pan	20 to 30 minutes	1 crispy treat

½ cup nonhydrogenated vegan margarine

1 (10-oz.) tub *vegan marshmallow fluff*

1 cup smooth or crunchy peanut butter

6 cups organic vegan puffed rice cereal

1. Lightly oil or spray a 9×9-inch baking pan with canola oil or vegetable shortening spray.

2. In a large saucepan over medium heat, melt vegan margarine. Add vegan marshmallow fluff and peanut butter, and cook, stirring, for 3 to 5 minutes or until smooth and creamy. Remove from heat, add puffed rice cereal, and stir to coat.

3. Press into the prepared pan with an oiled, heatproof spatula, being careful not to get any on you because it can be hot and sticky. Allow bars to cool and set up before cutting, about 30 minutes to 1 hour. Store at room temperature covered with plastic wrap for up to 3 days. These bars do not freeze well.

Variation: For **Chocolate-Glazed Crispy Rice Treats,** melt 2 tablespoons nonhydrogenated vegan margarine and 1¼ cups vegan semisweet chocolate chips until smooth and runny. Spread over warm (not hot) or cooled Crispy Rice Treats, and let dry before cutting.

VEGAN VOCAB

Vegan marshmallow fluff, sold under the brand name Suzanne's Ricemellow Crème, is an all-natural, vegan, nondairy, and gluten-free marshmallow cream substitute made from brown rice syrup, soy protein, natural gums, and flavors. It might be slightly different from the popular nonvegan variety, but it's so close, you can't tell the difference in these Crispy Rice Treats.

Classic Pies and Desserts

You've baked your way through muffins and coffee cakes, yeast breads and crackers, cookies and brownies, and now you're drooling thinking about the pies and desserts you can make in this part. (This is by far one of the most irresistible parts of the book!) Although these desserts will fool you into thinking you're breaking your vegan oath, you can relax because all the baked goods here are made with 100 percent animal-free ingredients.

In the following chapters, you'll learn many pie-prep tips, including how to make and roll a double-crusted piecrust. I also give you a number of sweet cookie crusts for cheesecakes and single crust pies. Next, you'll jump right into the tasty fruit and nut pies. The classic Grandma's Apple Pie, Pumpkin Pie, and Pecan Pie recipes are all dairy and egg free, and you'll never taste the difference. If you like the natural look, you'll love making simple free-form tarts and galettes that are rustic, yet beautiful in their own unrefined way.

I give you a selection of old-fashioned desserts that are comforting and cozy, with delicious fruit juices that bubble up through the cobbler tops and crisp streusels. Luscious and silky bread puddings will trick your senses and palate and make you believe you're eating eggs and cream.

These desserts will have you coming back for a second helping, because you simply won't believe they're vegan!

Crusts for All Reasons

In This Chapter

- Tips for making perfect piecrusts
- Instructions for rolling a piecrust
- Single and double crusted piecrust help
- Guidance on making a lattice piecrust
- Sweet cookie crusts

Does the thought of making piecrust intimidate you? Maybe you've had a terrible experience with piecrust, or you've just heard all the horror stories. If you're nodding "yes," this chapter is for you! With a good recipe and some handy tricks of the trade, you'll soon be turning out great piecrusts just like a bakery.

Gone are the days when our grandmothers used lard in their piecrusts. (Can you imagine?) For the most part, today's piecrusts are vegan, particularly if they're made with solid vegetable shortening. Nonvegans love their butter crusts and swear by how flaky they are. But you're likely to change their minds with flaky piecrusts you make using nonhydrogenated vegan margarine.

You can use the flour and shortening pie doughs for berry pies, nut pies, pumpkin pies, and all other pies that call for a flaky crust. These recipes are also used for the Blueberry Turnovers (recipe in Chapter 5) and the Rustic Apple Cranberry Galette (recipe in Chapter 15). Shortbread crusts are used in making the Fresh Strawberry Tart (recipe in Chapter 15) and the Raspberry Shortbread Bars (recipe in Chapter 12).

Cookie crusts are easy. You can make them in a snap with store-bought natural vegan cookies, or you can whip up a batch of homemade Soft Molasses Cookie dough (recipe in Chapter 10), and make a Gingersnap Crust for the Pumpkin Cheesecake (recipe in Chapter 19). By the end of this chapter, you'll see that you can have your vegan pie and eat it, too!

Piecrust Tips and Tricks

You don't need a lot of fancy ingredients and equipment to make piecrusts, but some things will yield better results and come in handy.

All-purpose flour works best for plain flaky piecrusts. Whole-wheat flour makes a heartier crust, but it can also turn out heavier. For this reason, adding some whole-wheat pastry flour to the dough lightens it up a bit. Oats, nuts, barley flour, and even bread flour add dimension and a unique taste to piecrust. Some bakers even add cornstarch, baking powder, and vinegar to their recipe.

Just about any solid shortening works in a piecrust. Nonhydrogenated vegan margarine, or a combination of both Crisco Zero Trans Fat Shortening and vegan margarine, is a good way to reduce the trans fats in your diet.

Pie pans can be pretty and practical at the same time. Disposable aluminum, glass Pyrex, Grandma's favorite embossed tin, and stoneware all work well for the recipes in this chapter.

> **DOUGH-NOT**
>
> Do not spray or grease the pie pan unless a recipe specifically directs you to. Some recipes, like the Flaky Piecrust, have enough fat in the dough, so it's not likely to stick to the pan. Other recipes, like the Chocolate Cookie Crust, need a little vegetable spray to make it easier to remove pie slices from the pan after it's baked.

A pastry blender is a handy gadget you'll use often when making pies. Much like using two knives, it is quicker and less messy with the same results.

Use Grandma's favorite wooden rolling pin, or the shiniest stainless-steel pin. You can even roll out pastry piecrusts with a wine bottle (remove the label and wash first, of course)! It doesn't matter as long as you keep it coated with flour as you roll.

Rolled and crimped piecrusts and cookie crusts can be double-wrapped in plastic wrap and frozen before and after baking for longer storage. This is good news when you consider making a large batch of piecrust, rolling them out, baking them (or not), freezing them, and pulling one out whenever you have the urge to make a pie. I don't recommend freezing raw balls of pie dough; they don't thaw out well. Instead, flatten them into disc shapes for faster and easier thawing.

Rolling a Piecrust

If you've never rolled out a piecrust, the thought can be intimidating. But it needn't be! Here's how simple it is:

1. Sprinkle a handful of flour over the countertop, place the ball of chilled dough in the middle of the flour, and coat a rolling pin with flour.

2. Begin by rolling the dough with the pin, turning the dough as you roll to achieve a round shape. This may take several passes over the dough, turning this way and that.

3. Flip the dough over carefully, adding extra flour to the work surface as needed. Finish rolling on the second side to make a circle that's 4 inches larger than the pie pan you're using.

4. Fold the piecrust in half, gently pick it up, and place it in the pie pan, unfolding it to fit. Trim the edges if necessary, but not too much. You need enough overhang to fold the edges under.

5. Fold the edges under, turning the pan and pressing the edges together as you go.

You now have a choice as to how you want to finish the crust. If you're making an open pie, as with a Pumpkin Pie or Pecan Pie (recipes in Chapter 14), press the edges down with the tines of a fork to seal them and give it a nice pattern.

You can also crimp the edges using your thumb and the forefinger of your left hand and the forefinger of your right hand. Go around the edge of the pie making a V-shape pattern, while keeping the edges slightly higher than the pie pan.

Making a Double-Crusted Piecrust

So you want to make an apple pie, but you need a top and a bottom crust. What recipe will you use? Not all piecrust recipes can be used to make a double-crusted pie. Although it sounds delicious, cookie crusts like the Gingersnap Crust won't work for this application. Instead, use the Flaky Piecrust or Whole-Wheat Piecrust recipes, or your favorite pastry piecrust recipe.

After mixing the piecrust dough, place the bottom crust in the pan as directed earlier. Fill the crust with your favorite filling. Then, unfold the top crust and place it over the top of the fruit filling. Fold the edges of the top crust over and under the edges of the bottom crust, and crimp with your fingertips. You can also seal the crust with the tines of a dinner fork.

Brush the piecrust with soy milk, and sprinkle evenly with sugar. Cut small decorative *vent holes* into the top crust using a knife or a very small cookie cutter.

VEGAN VOCAB

Vent holes are cuts made in the top crust of a double-crusted pie to allow steam to escape from the hot bubbling filling. They can be as simple as straight knife cuts or decorative cuts made with small cookie cutter shapes.

Making a Lattice Piecrust

There may be times when you want to serve a really elegant pie with a lattice crust. Southern Peach Pie, Raspberry Pie, and Blueberry Pie will all look stunning with a lattice top, especially if the filling is colorful and sets off the beige piecrust after the juices bubble through. Lattice crusts may look intimidating, but once you get the hang of it, you'll be making beautiful pies just like Grandma did.

After mixing the piecrust dough, place the bottom crust in the pan as directed earlier. Fill the crust with your favorite filling. Then, unfold the top crust. With a ruler and a sharp paring knife, pizza wheel, or crimped pastry wheel, measure and cut the top crust into strips ¾ inch wide. You should have a total of 10 to 12 strips. Some of the pieces may be shorter than others. This is normal and will all even out in the end.

Starting from one side of the pie, lay the smallest strip down over the pie filling, followed by the next size up, and so on, with the longest strip right down the center. Leave an inch between strips. You should have 5 or 6 strips across the pie all equally spaced apart. Lay back every other strip. Fold down, fold in half, and fold over.

Turn the pie 90 degrees. Starting in the middle, lay the longest strip perpendicular and right next to the laid-back strips. Unfold the laid-back strips over the long strip you just placed. Lay back the alternate strips. Place the next-longest strip 1 inch from the first. Unfold more laid-back strips. Fold back the other strips and repeat until all strips are down and you have a lovely lattice pattern.

Trim the edges, leaving enough to fold under, and crimp the edges to seal the crust. Lightly brush nondairy milk over the crust, sprinkle with sugar if desired, and bake as directed.

BAKER'S BONUS

Try this simple trick: make the lattice top on a baking sheet, and freeze it solid. You can then pick it up and place it right on the pie. Let it defrost, crimp the edges, and bake as directed.

Flaky Piecrust

Contrary to popular belief, not all piecrust recipes require ice water and a chilled rolling pin to produce perfect results! This simple crust is flaky and tender, perfect for fruit pies, Pumpkin Pie, Strawberry Rhubarb Pie, and many more.

Yield:	Prep time:
3 or 4 (8- to 9-inch) piecrusts	30 to 45 minutes

3¼ cups unbleached all-purpose flour

1 tsp. salt

1 cup solid vegetable shortening, nonhydrogenated vegan margarine, or a combination of both

¾ cup cool (not cold) water, or as needed

1. In a large bowl, combine unbleached all-purpose flour and salt. Make a well in the middle, and add vegetable shortening to the well.

2. Coat both hands with flour, and being careful not to touch shortening with your warm hands, break it up into chunks. Do not let the heat of your hands melt shortening. The least amount of contact they have with shortening, the better.

3. With both hands, work shortening into flour using a circular, rubbing motion, always keeping contact with flour, not shortening, picking up more flour and shortening as you go. Always keep shortening in middle of flour, until it

resembles small peas. Keep working until shortening is totally incorporated into flour. You can also do this with a pastry blender. Cut in the shortening or nonhydrogenated vegan margarine by pressing the blades of the pastry blender into the flour until mixture resembles small peas.

4. Make another well in middle of flour mixture, pour in water, and gather piecrust together, gently folding—*not* kneading—dough over onto itself 6 to 8 times or until it comes together in a soft ball. Add a little more water if dough is dry. Do not overwork dough; this will make it tough.

5. Divide dough into 3 or 4 equal balls, depending on the size of your pie pan. Use immediately, or wrap in plastic wrap and refrigerate. Or flatten into disc shapes, and freeze for faster, more even defrosting.

BAKER'S BONUS

Baking for the holidays or for a crowd? Save time and energy by multiplying this recipe. You can easily convert it to make 8, 12, 16, or 20 piecrusts. Use what you need now, flatten the rest into disc shapes, wrap in plastic, and freeze for later use.

Whole-Wheat Piecrust

A healthier version of the Flaky Piecrust, this whole-wheat version tastes deliciously nutty when baked. Use it for heavier pies like Pecan Pie, Pumpkin Pie, and Maple Walnut Pie. Keep in mind: the heartier the flour, the heavier the finished piecrust.

Yield:	Prep time:
3 or 4 (8- to 9-inch) piecrusts	30 to 45 minutes

2 cups whole-wheat flour

1 cup plus 2 TB. whole-wheat pastry flour

½ tsp. aluminum-free baking powder

2 TB. wheat germ

1 tsp. salt

1 cup solid vegetable shortening, nonhydrogenated vegan margarine, or a combination of both

¾ cup plus 1 TB. cool (not cold) water, or as needed

1. Into a large bowl, sift whole-wheat flour, whole-wheat pastry flour, and aluminum-free baking powder together. Add wheat germ and salt, and blend well. Make a well in the middle, and add vegetable shortening to the well.

2. Coat both hands with flour, and being careful not to touch shortening with your warm hands, break it up into chunks. Do not let the heat of your hands melt shortening. The least amount of contact they have with shortening, the better.

3. With both hands, work shortening into flour using a circular, rubbing motion, always keeping contact with flour, not shortening, picking up more flour and shortening as you go. Always keep shortening in middle of flour, until it resembles small peas. Keep working until shortening is totally incorporated into flour.

4. Make another well in middle of flour mixture, pour in water, and gather piecrust together, gently folding—*not* kneading—dough over onto itself 6 to 8 times or until it comes together in a soft ball. Add a little more water if dough is dry. Do not overwork dough; this will make it tough.

5. Divide dough into 3 or 4 equal balls, depending on the size of your pie pan. Flatten into disc shapes, wrap in plastic wrap, and chill for at least 4 hours or overnight to allow wheat flour to soften.

6. Remove piecrust from the refrigerator and allow to sit at room temperature for 10 to 15 minutes before you start rolling it. Or you can leave it in the refrigerator, or freeze for later use.

BATTER UP!

If it's especially hot or humid in your kitchen, chilling the flour before making the piecrust helps keep the fat cold. If you're in a hurry, freeze the flour for 30 minutes before using.

Oat Nut Piecrust

This is an easy, no-roll piecrust that also happens to be gluten free for those of you with wheat allergies. Oatmeal and pecans combine to make a delicious nutty crust that goes well with many cream fillings, puddings, or refrigerated fruit pie fillings.

Yield:	Prep time:	Bake time:
1 (9-inch) piecrust	20 to 30 minutes	10 to 15 minutes

1⅔ cups rolled oats

1 cup chopped, toasted pecans, walnuts, or almonds

¼ tsp. ground cinnamon (optional)

Pinch salt

¼ cup light brown sugar, firmly packed

½ cup nonhydrogenated vegan margarine, melted

1. Preheat the oven to 350°F. Lightly coat a 9-inch pie pan with cooking oil spray.

2. In a food processor fitted with a cutting blade, grind rolled oats and pecans for 25 to 35 seconds or until coarsely ground. Add ground cinnamon, salt, and light brown sugar, and pulse 5 to 10 times. Add vegan margarine, and process until crust comes together.

3. Press crust into the bottom of the prepared pie pan and up the sides. Bake for 10 to 15 minutes or until crust begins to brown and smells fragrant.

BATTER UP!

For the best flavor, toast the pecans, walnuts, or almonds first. Preheat the oven to 350°F. Place whole or chopped nuts in a single layer on an ungreased baking pan, and toast, stirring a few times, for 8 to 12 minutes, or until light brown and fragrant. Cool completely before grinding and using in the crust. You can also use this method for toasting pecans in the Pecan Pie recipe found in Chapter 14.

Shortbread Crust

This versatile vegan shortbread crust pairs well with pies, cheesecakes, and bar cookies. It's "buttery" and tender, with whole-wheat pastry flour and vegan confectioners' sugar.

Yield:	Prep time:	Bake time:
1 (9-inch) crust	1 hour, 40 minutes	40 to 45 minutes

1¼ cups unbleached all-purpose flour

¼ cup whole-wheat pastry flour

½ cup vegan confectioners' sugar

Pinch salt

½ cup cold nonhydrogenated vegan margarine, cut in small pieces

2 TB. soft silken tofu

1 TB. water (if necessary)

1. Grease or spray a 9-inch-round fluted tart pan or a springform pan with a removable bottom.

2. In a food processor fitted with a cutting blade, combine unbleached all-purpose flour, whole-wheat pastry flour, confectioners' sugar, and salt for 5 to 10 seconds. With the processor still running, add vegan margarine, and pulse on and off until dough resembles coarse meal.

3. Add soft silken tofu, and pulse only until dough comes together, adding water only if necessary.

4. Turn out dough onto a lightly floured surface, and form dough into a ball, being careful not to knead dough.

5. Using your hands, press dough into the prepared tart pan, making sure to get into all the creases. Chill for at least 1 hour.

6. Preheat the oven to 375°F.

7. Using a fork, prick bottom of crust a few times and line with aluminum foil. Bake for 25 minutes, remove foil, and bake for 15 to 20 more minutes or until fragrant and lightly browned. Cool completely on a wire rack before filling.

BAKER'S BONUS

For small, 3-inch tarts, divide dough into 16 to 18 equal portions. Roll each piece of dough into a ball using the palms of your hands, and place each in a prepared tart pan. With your floured fingers, press dough on the bottom and up against the sides of the pan, all the way to the rim. Chill for 30 minutes, and bake in 350°F oven for 15 to 25 minutes or until light brown.

Gingersnap Crust

This spicy crust, made from Soft Molasses Cookie crumbs or store-bought natural gingersnap cookies, is fantastic for Pumpkin Pie, Pecan Pie, or Pumpkin Cheesecake.

Yield:	Prep time:	Bake time:
1 (9-inch) cookie crust or 1 (9-inch) cheesecake crust	20 to 30 minutes	10 to 12 minutes

1½ cups finely ground Soft Molasses Cookie crumbs (recipe in Chapter 10) or store-bought gingersnap cookies

1 TB. unbleached cane sugar

¼ cup nonhydrogenated vegan margarine, melted

1. Preheat the oven to 350°F. Spray a 9-inch pie pan or a 9-inch springform pan with vegetable spray, or follow directions for your favorite pie that calls for a 9-inch graham cracker crust.

2. If you're making Gingersnap Crust from homemade Soft Molasses Cookies, follow the recipe in Chapter 10, except leave cookies in the oven longer, between 14 to 18 minutes or until firm. Do not overbake. Cookies will continue to dry and get crispy as they cool. Cool completely before grinding into crumbs in the food processor.

3. In a medium bowl, combine cookie crumbs, unbleached cane sugar, and vegan margarine. Depending on the recipe, firmly press crumbs on the bottom and up the sides of the prepared pan.

4. Bake 9-inch piecrust for 10 to 12 minutes. Cool completely before filling.

DOUGH-NOT

If you're using the springform pan version for cheesecake, prebake crust in 350°F oven for 5 minutes.

Graham Cracker Crust

This traditional crust made with homemade Sweet Graham Crackers or store-bought cookies is an excellent crust for Strawberry Cheesecake.

Yield:	Prep time:	Bake time:
1 (9-inch) cookie crust or 1 (9-inch) cheesecake crust	20 to 30 minutes	10 to 12 minutes

1½ cups finely ground Sweet Graham Cracker crumbs (recipe in Chapter 9) or store-bought crackers

¼ cup unbleached cane sugar

¼ cup nonhydrogenated vegan margarine, melted

¼ tsp. ground cinnamon or nutmeg (optional)

1. Preheat the oven to 350°F. Spray a 9-inch pie pan or a 9-inch springform pan with vegetable spray, or follow directions for your favorite pie that calls for a 9-inch graham cracker crust.

2. In a medium bowl, combine Sweet Graham Cracker crumbs, unbleached cane sugar, vegan margarine, and ground cinnamon (if using). Depending on the recipe, firmly press crumbs on the bottom and up the sides of the prepared pan.

3. Bake 9-inch piecrust for 10 to 12 minutes. Cool completely before filling. If using for cheesecake recipes, using the springform pan, prebake crust in a 350°F oven for 5 minutes.

BAKER'S BONUS

Don't have a food processor? Place the cookies in a doubled plastic bag and roll over them with a rolling pin until they're finely ground.

Chocolate Cookie Crust

This delightful chocolaty crust, made with vegan chocolate sandwich or wafer cookies, can be used for Chocolate Cheesecake or piled high with Chocolate Mousse Filling. Chocoholics rejoice!

Yield:	Prep time:	Bake time:
1 (9-inch) cookie crust or 1 (9-inch) cheesecake crust	20 to 30 minutes	10 to 12 minutes

1½ cups finely ground chocolate cookie crumbs

2 TB. unbleached cane sugar

¼ cup nonhydrogenated vegan margarine, melted

1. Preheat the oven to 350°F. Spray a 9-inch pie pan or a 9-inch springform pan with vegetable spray, or follow directions for your favorite pie that calls for a 9-inch chocolate cookie crust.

2. In a medium bowl, combine chocolate cookie crumbs, unbleached cane sugar, and vegan margarine. Depending on the recipe, firmly press crumbs on the bottom and up the sides of the prepared pan.

3. Bake 9-inch piecrust for 10 to 12 minutes. Cool completely before filling. If using for cheesecake recipes, using the springform pan, prebake crust in a 350°F oven for 5 minutes.

DOUGH-NOT

If you're using vegan cream-filled chocolate sandwich cookies, remove the cream filling first. Use only the chocolate wafers for this recipe.

Favorite Fruit and Nutty Pies

In This Chapter

- Pies, pies, and more pies
- Fresh fruit pies
- Fantastic nut pies

Apple pie—the most beloved of all pies—is an indulgence that just can't be beat. After all, it's "as American as apple pie"! Our love affair with pie goes way back to the dark ages, when man (or woman) wrapped a piece of crude dough around a hunk of meat, cooked it, ate it, and called it good. Pie has come a long way since then, eventually evolving into glorious pastries, tarts, and turnovers.

Our grandmothers, and their grandmothers before them, baked everything they could think of into pastry dough. In the best of times, they made apple pie, and when money was tight, they made Ritz mock apple pie with Ritz Crackers in a crust made with lard. Yuck! They made meat pies, pot pies, fruit pies, nut pies, and cream pies, and they lovingly made them by hand for their families. If you're lucky, maybe you even have some of their favorite pie recipes, passed down on small scraps of paper, or in dog-eared journals that were stained and smudged with fruit and chocolate and love.

As a vegan, you're not out of luck when it comes to pie. All you need is a crust, a filling, and a good recipe, and away you go! Simple substitutions and ready-made products can help make your pies vegan-friendly and just as delicious as regular pies.

A Pie for Everyone

With mix-and-match crusts and fillings, pies are so easy to customize until you get your perfect pie.

Some people like their pies in a traditional Flaky Piecrust; others want something a little healthier and go for the Whole-Wheat Piecrust. Some pies do better in a Shortbread Crust, while others are perfect in an Oat Nut Piecrust or Chocolate Cookie Crust. Either way, you'll find plenty of piecrusts in Chapter 13.

Pecan Pie, Pumpkin Pie, Cool Blueberry Pie, and Peanut Butter Pie are simple desserts made with a single crust. Traditional double-crusted pies like Raspberry Pie, Southern Peach Pie, and everyone's favorite—Grandma's Apple Pie—are baked with a second crust on top, cradling a hot and bubbly filling underneath. Covered pies can be as simple as covering the filling with the pie dough and cutting a few holes in the top. Or you can make them as elaborate as you'd like by cutting out decorative shapes in the top crust with cookie cutters—a small apple cookie cutter would make cute vent holes for an apple pie. Or you can get a little more creative and make a lattice top for colorful pies like Blueberry Pie, Very Cherry Pie, and Blackberry Pie.

Most fruit pies can be made with any type of berry or stone fruits you want. Try varying the fruits from what the recipe calls for or mixing two or three fruits together for a mixed berry pie.

DOUGH-NOT

Keep in mind some fruits don't play nicely with each other. Although strawberry and apple pie might sound delicious, the apples will take far longer to bake than the strawberries, and either the apples would be crunchy or the strawberries would end up being mush in the finished pie.

Likewise, experiment with spices in your pies. If you don't care for cinnamon, use nutmeg or ginger. Add nuts, raisins, and dried fruits to fruit pies to make them more interesting and give them extra flavor and texture. If you don't like coconut, leave it out of the streusel.

Vegans will be pleased to discover that dairy-free and egg-free Pumpkin Pie really can taste good. Most people want Pumpkin Pie for Thanksgiving, but you can vary the filling to include yams or sweet potatoes and eat it year round.

Nut pies are another area where you can flex your pie-making skills. Switch them around a bit and make a mixed-nut pie. Add some vegan chocolate chips and bourbon to Pecan Pie for a special holiday treat. Toss some toasted pecans or walnuts in your traditional Pumpkin Pie, or add a crumb topping to make it unique. Mix and match, and have some fun!

To Freeze or Not to Freeze?

With the exception of any lattice-topped pies, the Strawberry Rhubarb Pie (too much moisture), and the Pumpkin Pie, all the fruit pies in this chapter can be frozen before and after baking. Nut pies do not freeze well before baking because they're too gooey and runny. They do however freeze well after they're baked.

To freeze a pie before you bake it, simply double-wrap it in plastic and freeze for up to 3 months.

You have a few options when it comes to baking a frozen pie. One method is to place the frozen pie on a baking sheet (to collect any drips and messes), and bake at 350°F for 50 to 60 minutes. Check the pie, and place an aluminum foil ring around the rim of the crust to prevent it from burning. If the top of the pie is baking too fast, loosely cover the whole pie with foil. Continue to bake for 15-minute intervals, checking each time for doneness. It may take between 1 hour, 15 minutes and 1 hour, 45 minutes to bake your pie, depending on how thick it is.

Another method is to bake the frozen pie at 425°F for 20 minutes, then reduce the oven temperature to 350°F, and continue baking for about 45 minutes or just until the crust is golden brown and the juices begin bubbling out of the vent holes. Baking time may be as many as 10 to 20 minutes shorter or longer, depending on the type of filling, and how thick it is. Keep an eye on it!

If you want to fully bake the pie and then freeze it, you can. After you bake it, allow it to cool completely. Double-wrap it in plastic, and freeze for up to 3 months.

When you're ready to thaw the pie, you can thaw it overnight in the refrigerator. Or you can thaw the frozen, wrapped, baked pie for 30 minutes at room temperature and then place it in a preheated 350°F oven, on a preheated baking sheet, and reheat for no longer than 30 minutes.

BATTER UP!

Don't think you're limited to making large, 9-inch pies. Cute little tarts are perfect individual desserts for a brunch or wedding and can easily be made by cutting piecrust to fit your teeny, tiny pie tins. They bake at the same temperature, but watch the timing. Some are baked longer than others. You'll know they're done when the crusts turn light golden brown and the filling starts to bubble.

A Note on Blind-Baking

Blind-baking, also known as prebaking, is the method of partially or fully baking an empty crust specifically for pies and tarts that are filled with pudding or cream fillings, refrigerated fillings like this chapter's Cool Blueberry Pie, and for piecrusts that need a little more baking time than the filling needs. Partially blind-baking also helps prevent the crust from becoming soggy when baking pumpkin, pecan, or custard pies.

For either completely baked or partially baked piecrusts, chill crust at least 2 hours, or freeze for 30 minutes before baking. Preheat the oven to 375°F. Line crust with parchment paper, or thin aluminum foil, and fill with dried beans (kidney beans, black beans, lentils, dried peas, rice, etc.), or with specially designed pie weights.

To partially blind-bake crust: bake for 15 to 20 minutes or until crust is light brown. Remove the beans or pie weights, cool, and continue with pie recipe.

To fully blind-bake crust: return partially baked crust (beans and parchment removed) to the oven, and continue baking for another 8 to 15 minutes or until golden brown. If the crust begins to pucker, do not prick the crust to allow steam to escape as this will only allow juice or liquid to leak through the holes. Instead, press the crust down with a metal spatula to flatten. Cool crust completely before filling with cream, pudding, or refrigerated fillings.

Grandma's Apple Pie

The apples, cinnamon, nutmeg, and brown sugar are all in perfect harmony in this homey dessert. Baked in a hand-rolled Flaky Piecrust, this all-American pie is so simple, and yet so good—just like Grandma's.

Yield:	Prep time:	Bake time:	Serving size:
1 (9-inch) pie	60 to 70 minutes	50 to 60 minutes	1 slice

2 Flaky Piecrust dough balls (recipe in Chapter 13)

6 cups (about 6 medium to large apples) Granny Smith apples, peeled, cored, and sliced

1 tsp. lemon juice

¾ cup plus 1 TB. unbleached cane sugar

½ cup light brown sugar, firmly packed

½ cup unbleached all-purpose flour

1 tsp. ground cinnamon

½ tsp. ground nutmeg

2 TB. cold nonhydrogenated vegan margarine, cut into small pieces

1 TB. soy, rice, or almond milk

1. Preheat the oven to 375°F.

2. On a lightly floured surface, roll out Flaky Piecrust bottom and top (see Chapter 13 if you need a refresher), leaving enough overhang to fold underneath. Place bottom piecrust evenly in a 9-inch pie pan or ceramic pie dish. Fold top crust in ½ and place a kitchen towel over it so it doesn't dry out.

3. In a large bowl, combine Granny Smith apple slices, lemon juice, ¾ cup unbleached cane sugar, light brown sugar, unbleached all-purpose flour, ¾ teaspoon ground cinnamon, and ground nutmeg, tossing to coat. Arrange into piecrust, and dot with cold vegan margarine.

4. Unfold top crust, and place it over apple filling. Fold edges of top crust over and under bottom edges, and flute with your fingertips. Crusts can also be sealed with the tines of a dinner fork.

5. Brush crust with soy milk, and sprinkle evenly with remaining 1 tablespoon unbleached cane sugar and ¼ teaspoon ground cinnamon. Cut small decorative vent holes in top crust using a knife or a very small cookie cutter.

6. Place the pie pan on a baking sheet, and bake for 50 to 60 minutes or until crust is golden brown and juices are bubbly. Place a piece of aluminum foil around the rim if the edges start to brown too fast. Cool on a wire rack for at least 30 minutes before serving. Let cool completely before wrapping in plastic wrap. Store leftovers—if there are any—in the refrigerator. Double-wrap, and this pie will freeze well for up to 3 months.

BATTER UP!

Hard apples like Granny Smiths are the best apples for apple pie. Other good apples to use: Rome, Pippin, Gala, Cortland, Winesap, and Braeburn varieties. If your recipe calls for apples by the pound, figure on 2½ cups sliced apples to 1 pound.

Apple Crumb Pie

Apples, spices, and brown sugar fill this quick-and-easy pie that's covered with a coconut-walnut streusel crumb topping.

Yield:	Prep time:	Bake time:	Serving size:
1 (9-inch) pie	60 to 70 minutes	45 to 60 minutes	1 slice

1 Flaky Piecrust dough ball or 1 (9-in.) Oat Nut Piecrust prebaked for only 10 minutes (recipes in Chapter 13)

1 (20-oz.) can sliced apples, packed in water, drained

¾ cup unbleached cane sugar

½ cup light brown sugar, firmly packed

¾ cup unbleached all-purpose flour

½ tsp. ground cinnamon

¼ tsp. ground nutmeg

¼ tsp. plus pinch salt

½ cup nonhydrogenated vegan margarine, melted

¼ cup chopped walnuts

⅓ cup sweetened flaked coconut

1. Preheat the oven to 350°F.

2. If using Flaky Piecrust: on a lightly floured surface, roll out piecrust (see Chapter 13 if you need a refresher), leaving enough overhang to fold underneath. Place piecrust evenly in a 9-inch pie pan or ceramic pie dish, and flute the edges with your fingertips. Blind-bake for 15 to 20 minutes or until light brown. Cool before filling.

3. In a large bowl, combine apple slices, ½ cup unbleached cane sugar, light brown sugar, ¼ cup unbleached all-purpose flour, ground cinnamon, ground nutmeg, ¼ teaspoon salt, and ¼ cup melted vegan margarine, tossing to coat. Pour into piecrust.

4. In the same bowl, add remaining ½ cup unbleached all-purpose flour, ¼ cup unbleached cane sugar, pinch salt, and ¼ cup vegan margarine. Using your hands or a pastry blender, mix until crumbly and resembles streusel. Add walnuts and coconut, and mix well. Sprinkle topping evenly over pie.

5. Place the pie pan on a baking sheet, and bake for 50 to 60 minutes or until bubbly and topping is lightly toasted. Cool on a wire rack for 1 hour before serving. Cool completely before wrapping with plastic wrap. Refrigerate any leftovers. Double-wrap, and this pie will freeze well for up to 3 months.

Variation: For **Apple Raisin Crumb Pie,** add ⅓ cup seedless raisins to the apple filling before baking.

DOUGH-NOT

Do not use ready-to-use apple pie filling for this recipe. Be sure to use canned apples packed in water.

Very Cherry Pie

Fresh, ripe cherries are nestled and baked in a flaky, double-crusted pie. This red pie is a perfect candidate for a pretty lattice top. Try it served à la mode with rice or soy ice cream.

Yield:	Prep time:	Bake time:	Serving size:
1 (9-inch) pie	60 to 70 minutes	50 to 60 minutes	1 slice

2 Flaky Piecrust dough balls (recipe in Chapter 13)

4¼ cups fresh cherries, stems removed and pitted

1¼ cups plus 1 TB. unbleached cane sugar

4 TB. quick-cooking *tapioca*, or ½ cup unbleached all-purpose flour

½ tsp. ground cinnamon

1 tsp. pure almond extract or vanilla extract

2 TB. cold nonhydrogenated vegan margarine, cut into small pieces

1 TB. soy, rice, or almond milk

1. Preheat the oven to 375°F.

2. On a lightly floured surface, roll out Flaky Piecrust bottom and top (see Chapter 13 if you need a refresher), leaving enough overhang to fold underneath. Place bottom piecrust evenly in a 9-inch pie pan or ceramic pie dish. Fold top crust in ½ and place a kitchen towel over it so it doesn't dry out.

3. In a large bowl, combine cherries, 1¼ cups unbleached cane sugar, tapioca pearls, ground cinnamon, and almond extract, tossing to coat. Pour into piecrust, and dot with cold vegan margarine.

4. Unfold top crust, and place it over cherry filling. Fold edges of top crust over and under bottom edges, and flute with your fingertips. Crusts can also be sealed with the tines of a dinner fork.

5. Brush crust with soy milk, and sprinkle evenly with remaining 1 tablespoon unbleached cane sugar. Cut small decorative vent holes into top crust using a knife or a very small cookie cutter.

6. Place the pie pan on a baking sheet, and bake for 50 to 60 minutes or until crust is golden brown and juices are bubbly. Place a piece of aluminum foil around the rim if the edges start to brown too fast. For best results, cool on a wire rack for 30 to 60 minutes before serving. Cool completely before wrapping with plastic wrap. Store leftovers in the refrigerator. Double-wrap, and this pie will freeze well for up to 3 months.

VEGAN VOCAB

Tapioca is a starch extracted from the cassava root and is used as a thickener in puddings, pies, and jellies. Quick-cooking or minute tapioca works well in binding the cherry pie. No prep is needed; just add it right in with the cherries. Tapioca is sold in most supermarkets in the baking section. Flour helps bind the pie; you can even use a combination of both flour and tapioca.

Southern Peach Pie

Ripe, juicy peaches baked with a hint of cinnamon and piled high in a flaky crust is a summertime favorite. Try it served with vegan peach ice cream or sorbet for a real treat.

Yield:	Prep time:	Bake time:	Serving size:
1 (9-inch) pie	60 to 70 minutes	50 to 60 minutes	1 slice

2 Flaky Piecrust dough balls (recipe in Chapter 13)

5 cups fresh or frozen peaches, peeled, pitted, and sliced

1 tsp. fresh lemon juice

1¼ cups plus 1 TB. unbleached cane sugar

½ cup unbleached all-purpose flour

¾ tsp. ground cinnamon or nutmeg

2 TB. cold nonhydrogenated vegan margarine, cut into small pieces

1 TB. soy, rice, or almond milk

1. Preheat the oven to 375°F.

2. On a lightly floured surface, roll out Flaky Piecrust bottom and top (see Chapter 13 if you need a refresher), leaving enough overhang to fold underneath. Place bottom piecrust evenly in a 9-inch pie pan or ceramic pie dish. Fold top crust in ½ and place a kitchen towel over it so it doesn't dry out.

3. In a large bowl, combine peaches, lemon juice, 1¼ cups unbleached cane sugar, unbleached all-purpose flour, and ground cinnamon, tossing to coat. Pour into piecrust, and dot with cold vegan margarine.

4. Unfold top crust, and place it over peach filling. Fold edges of top crust over and under bottom edges, and flute with your fingertips. Crusts can also be sealed with the tines of a dinner fork.

5. Brush crust with soy milk, and sprinkle evenly with remaining 1 tablespoon unbleached cane sugar. Cut small decorative vent holes into top crust using a knife or a very small cookie cutter.

6. Place the pie pan on a baking sheet, and bake for 50 to 60 minutes or until crust is golden brown and juices are bubbly. Place a piece of aluminum foil around the rim if the edges start to brown too fast. For best results, cool on a wire rack for 30 to 60 minutes before serving. Cool completely before wrapping with plastic wrap. Store leftovers in the refrigerator. Double-wrap, and this pie will freeze well for up to 3 months.

BAKER'S BONUS

Frozen peaches are an excellent choice for peach desserts during the winter when fresh peaches are hard to come by. Most supermarkets stock IQF (individually quick frozen) peaches in their freezer section. Use frozen peaches right from the bag, or thaw out and drain completely before using them in this pie. Add an extra 2 tablespoons unbleached all-purpose flour to the frozen peaches to soak up the extra juice.

Blueberry Pie

This traditional double-crusted pie is bursting with fresh fruit flavor. The antioxidant-rich blueberries make this pie not only good for you, but delicious, too!

Yield:	Prep time:	Bake time:	Serving size:
1 (9-inch) pie	60 to 70 minutes	50 to 60 minutes	1 slice

2 Flaky Piecrust dough balls (recipe in Chapter 13)

4¼ cups fresh blueberries

1 TB. lemon zest

1 tsp. fresh lemon juice

1 cup plus 1 TB. unbleached cane sugar

3 TB. cornstarch or quick-cooking tapioca

¼ tsp. ground nutmeg

2 TB. cold nonhydrogenated vegan margarine, cut into small pieces

1 TB. soy, rice, or almond milk

1. Preheat the oven to 375°F.

2. On a lightly floured surface, roll out Flaky Piecrust bottom and top (see Chapter 13 if you need a refresher), leaving enough overhang to fold underneath. Place bottom piecrust evenly in a 9-inch pie pan or ceramic pie dish. Fold top crust in ½ and place a kitchen towel over it so it doesn't dry out.

3. In a large bowl, combine blueberries, lemon zest, lemon juice, 1 cup unbleached cane sugar, cornstarch, and ground nutmeg, tossing to coat. Pour into piecrust, and dot with cold vegan margarine.

4. Unfold top crust, and place over blueberry filling. Fold edges of top crust over and under bottom edges, and flute with your fingertips. Crusts can also be sealed with the tines of a dinner fork.

5. Brush crust with soy milk, and sprinkle evenly with remaining 1 tablespoon unbleached cane sugar. Cut small decorative vent holes into top crust using a knife or a very small cookie cutter.

6. Place the pie pan on a baking sheet, and bake for 50 to 60 minutes or until crust is golden brown and juices are bubbly. Place a piece of aluminum foil around the rim if the edges start to brown too fast. For best results, cool on a wire rack for 30 to 60 minutes before serving. Cool completely before wrapping with plastic wrap. Store leftovers in the refrigerator. Double-wrap, and this pie will freeze well for up to 3 months.

> **BAKER'S BONUS**
>
> Can you make a Blueberry Pie with frozen blueberries? Yes, just be sure to use frozen IQF (individually quick frozen) blueberries straight from the freezer. Do not thaw them, or you'll have a soupy pie. Adjust the cornstarch or quick-cooking tapioca to 5 tablespoons when using frozen blueberries.

Blackberry Pie

Fresh blackberries are only available for a short time, so why not enjoy the summer by baking this yummy pie in a double-crusted Flaky Piecrust? This goes great with vegan ice cream.

Yield:	Prep time:	Bake time:	Serving size:
1 (9-inch) pie	60 to 70 minutes	50 to 60 minutes	1 slice

2 Flaky Piecrust dough balls (recipe in Chapter 13)

5 cups fresh or frozen blackberries

1 tsp. lime zest

1 cup plus 1 TB. unbleached cane sugar

¼ cup light brown sugar, firmly packed

¼ cup unbleached all-purpose flour

¼ cup quick-cooking tapioca

½ tsp. ground nutmeg (optional)

2 TB. cold nonhydrogenated vegan margarine, cut into small pieces

1 TB. soy, rice, or almond milk

1. Preheat the oven to 375°F.

2. On a lightly floured surface, roll out Flaky Piecrust bottom and top (see Chapter 13 if you need a refresher), leaving enough overhang to fold underneath. Place bottom piecrust evenly in a 9-inch pie pan or ceramic pie dish. Fold top crust in ½ and place a kitchen towel over it so it doesn't dry out.

3. In a large bowl, combine blackberries, lime zest, 1 cup unbleached cane sugar, light brown sugar, unbleached all-purpose flour, quick-cooking tapioca, and ground nutmeg (if using), tossing to coat. Pour into prepared piecrust, and dot with cold vegan margarine.

4. Unfold top crust, and place over blackberry filling. Fold edges of top crust over and under bottom edges, and flute with your fingertips. Crusts can also be sealed with the tines of a dinner fork.

5. Brush crust with soy milk, and sprinkle evenly with remaining 1 tablespoon unbleached cane sugar. Cut small decorative vent holes into top crust using a knife or a very small cookie cutter.

6. Place the pie pan on a baking sheet, and bake for 50 to 60 minutes or until crust is golden brown and juices are bubbly. Place a piece of aluminum foil around the rim if the edges start to brown too fast. For best results, cool on a wire rack for 30 to 60 minutes before serving. Cool completely before wrapping with plastic wrap. Store leftovers in the refrigerator. Double-wrap, and this pie will freeze well for up to 3 months.

Variation: For **Mixed-Berry Pie,** substitute 2 cups fresh blackberries, 1 cup blueberries, and 2 cups raspberries for all the blackberries.

> **BAKER'S BONUS**
>
> Although blackberries are best used fresh right off the vine, you can use them frozen in pie. Large grocery stores sell frozen IQF (individually quick frozen) blackberries in 1-pound bags. To make a blackberry pie with frozen blackberries, do not thaw the blackberries first. Add an additional ¼ cup unbleached all-purpose flour or quick-cooking tapioca pearls to the berry mixture before baking.

Raspberry Pie

Beautiful, plump red raspberries are cradled in a tender crust and baked to perfection. This vegan fruit pie would look striking in a lattice crust as the red raspberry juices bubble up from the pie vents!

Yield:	Prep time:	Bake time:	Serving size:
1 (9-inch) pie	60 to 70 minutes	50 to 60 minutes	1 slice

2 Flaky Piecrust dough balls (recipe in Chapter 13)

5 cups fresh raspberries

1 to 1¼ cups plus 1 TB. unbleached cane sugar

½ cup unbleached all-purpose flour, or 4 TB. tapioca pearls or quick-cooking tapioca

¼ tsp. ground nutmeg

1 tsp. pure vanilla extract

2 TB. cold nonhydrogenated vegan margarine, cut into small pieces

1 TB. soy, rice, or almond milk

1. Preheat the oven to 375°F.

2. On a lightly floured surface, roll out Flaky Piecrust bottom and top (see Chapter 13 if you need a refresher), leaving enough overhang to fold underneath. Place bottom piecrust evenly in a 9-inch pie pan or ceramic pie dish. Fold top crust in ½ and place a kitchen towel over it so it doesn't dry out.

3. In a large bowl, combine raspberries, 1 cup unbleached cane sugar (use up to 1¼ cups if raspberries are especially tart), unbleached all-purpose flour, ground nutmeg, and vanilla extract, tossing to coat. Pour into piecrust, and dot with cold vegan margarine.

4. Unfold top crust, and place over raspberry filling. Fold edges of top crust over and under bottom edges, and flute with your fingertips. Crusts can also be sealed with the tines of a dinner fork.

5. Brush crust with soy milk, and sprinkle evenly with remaining 1 tablespoon unbleached cane sugar. Cut small decorative vent holes into top crust using a knife or a very small cookie cutter.

6. Place the pie pan on a baking sheet, and bake for 50 to 60 minutes or until crust is golden brown and juices are bubbly. Place a piece of aluminum foil around the rim if the edges start to brown too fast. For best results, cool on a wire rack for 30 to 60 minutes before serving. Cool completely before wrapping with plastic wrap. Store leftovers in the refrigerator. Double-wrap, and this pie will freeze well for up to 3 months.

DOUGH-NOT

Frozen raspberries can also be used for this pie, but thaw them out first, and drain them well. Frozen raspberries give off lots of juice, which would make the pie very mushy. Add an additional ¼ cup unbleached all-purpose flour to the fruit mixture before baking.

Cool Blueberry Pie

This chilled pie is refreshingly delicious. Fresh blueberries are folded into a home-made filling made by cooking half the blueberries with sugar and thickener.

Yield:	Prep time:	Bake time:	Serving size:
1 (9-inch) pie	60 to 70 minutes	23 to 35 minutes	1 slice

1 Flaky Piecrust dough ball, 1 (9-in.) Graham Cracker Crust, or 1 (9-in.) Shortbread Crust (recipes in Chapter 13)

1¼ cups unbleached cane sugar

⅓ cup cornstarch

¼ tsp. ground nutmeg (optional)

5 cups fresh blueberries

1 TB. fresh lemon juice

1 tsp. lemon zest

1. Preheat the oven to 375°F.

2. If using Flaky Piecrust: on a lightly floured surface, roll out piecrust (see Chapter 13 if you need a refresher), leaving enough overhang to fold underneath. Place piecrust evenly in a 9-inch pie pan or ceramic pie dish, and flute the edges with your fingertips. Blind-bake for a total of 23 to 35 minutes, or until golden brown. If using a Shortbread Crust, press dough into a prepared 9-inch fluted tart pan (see Chapter 13), and bake according to directions. If using a Graham Cracker Crust, bake at 350°F for 10 to 12 minutes or until golden brown and fragrant. Cool before filling.

3. In a large saucepan over medium heat, combine unbleached cane sugar, cornstarch, and ground nutmeg (if using). Stir in 2½ cups blueberries, and bring to a boil, stirring constantly. Turn heat to low, and simmer for 3 to 5 minutes or until mixture is thick. Remove from heat, and stir in remaining 2½ cups blueberries, lemon juice, and lemon zest. Cool for 30 minutes before filling baked crust.

4. Pour filling into piecrust, and chill at least 4 hours before serving. Cover left-over pie with plastic wrap, and keep refrigerated. This pie does not freeze well.

Variation: For **Cool Raspberry Pie,** substitute raspberries for the blueberries.

BATTER UP!

This shimmering blue pie is delicious when topped with vegan whipped topping or ice cream.

Strawberry Rhubarb Pie

Sweet, juicy strawberries and tart rhubarb join with ground cardamom and sugar in this tasty pie.

Yield:	Prep time:	Bake time:	Serving size:
1 (9-inch) pie	60 to 70 minutes	50 to 65 minutes	1 slice

2 Flaky Piecrust dough balls (recipe in Chapter 13)

1 pt. (2 cups) fresh strawberries, hulled and halved

2 cups (about 2 medium stalks) rhubarb, cut into 1-in. pieces

1⅓ cups plus 1 TB. unbleached cane sugar

¼ cup unbleached all-purpose flour

2 TB. quick-cooking tapioca

½ tsp. ground cardamom or cinnamon

2 TB. cold nonhydrogenated vegan margarine, cut into small pieces

1 TB. soy, rice, or almond milk

1. Preheat the oven to 375°F.

2. On a lightly floured surface, roll out Flaky Piecrust bottom and top (see Chapter 13 if you need a refresher), leaving enough overhang to fold underneath. Place bottom piecrust evenly in a 9-inch pie pan or ceramic pie dish. Fold top crust in ½ and place a kitchen towel over it so it doesn't dry out.

3. In a large bowl, combine strawberries, rhubarb, 1⅓ cups unbleached cane sugar, unbleached all-purpose flour, tapioca, and ground cardamom, tossing to coat. Pour into piecrust, and dot with cold vegan margarine.

4. Unfold top crust, and place it over top of filling. Fold edges of top crust over and under bottom edges, and flute with your fingertips. Crusts can also be sealed with the tines of a dinner fork.

5. Brush crust with soy milk, and sprinkle evenly with remaining 1 tablespoon unbleached cane sugar. Cut small decorative vent holes into top crust using a knife or a very small cookie cutter.

6. Place the pie pan on a baking sheet, and bake for 50 to 65 minutes or until crust is golden brown and juices are bubbly. Place a piece of aluminum foil around the rim if the edges start to brown too fast. For best results, cool on a wire rack for 30 to 60 minutes before serving. Cool completely before wrapping with plastic wrap. Store leftovers in the refrigerator.

BATTER UP!

When buying or picking rhubarb, look for clean, bright fruit. Wilted rhubarb that's old and woody tastes horrible and bitter and should not be used for this pie. Remove the leaves and discard, wash the rhubarb, pat it dry, cut off the ends, and cut into 1-inch chunks. There's no need to cut off the strings if the pieces are cut small and baked in a pie.

Pumpkin Pie

No Thanksgiving or holiday dinner is complete without Pumpkin Pie. You can feel good about chowing down on this vegan pie. It's just as good as the real thing, but without the dairy and eggs.

Yield:	Prep time:	Bake time:	Serving size:
1 (9-inch) pie	60 to 70 minutes	60 to 80 minutes	1 slice

1 Flaky Piecrust dough ball, 1 Whole-Wheat Piecrust dough ball, or 1 (9-in.) Oat Nut Piecrust prebaked for only 10 minutes (recipes in Chapter 13)

1 (15-oz.) can pumpkin purée, solid pack (not pumpkin pie filling)

1 cup soy milk

1 tsp. pure vanilla extract

½ cup soft tofu, drained

Egg substitute for 2 large eggs (Ener-G is best)

½ cup unbleached cane sugar

⅓ cup light brown sugar, firmly packed

1 TB. ground flaxseed

1½ tsp. ground cinnamon

½ tsp. ground ginger

⅛ tsp. ground nutmeg

⅛ tsp. ground cloves

⅛ tsp. salt

⅓ cup cornstarch

1. Preheat the oven to 375°F.

2. If using Flaky Piecrust or Whole-Wheat Piecrust: on a lightly floured surface, roll out piecrust (see Chapter 13 if you need a refresher), leaving enough over-hang to fold underneath. Place piecrust evenly in a 9-inch pie pan or ceramic pie dish, and flute the edges with your fingertips. Blind-bake crust for 15 to 20 minutes or until light brown. Cool on a wire rack while making pumpkin filling.

3. In a blender, add pumpkin purée, soy milk, vanilla extract, and soft tofu, and blend on high speed for 1 to 3 minutes or until smooth and creamy.

4. Add egg substitute, unbleached cane sugar, light brown sugar, ground flaxseed, ground cinnamon, ground ginger, ground nutmeg, ground cloves, salt, and cornstarch, and blend on high for 1 to 3 minutes or until well mixed and smooth, scraping down the sides of the blender as needed with a rubber spatula. Pour into piecrust.

5. Place the pie pan on a baking sheet, and bake for 60 to 80 minutes or until a knife inserted into the center comes out clean. Cool completely on a wire rack, and refrigerate at least 4 hours before serving. Cover any leftovers with plastic wrap, and keep refrigerated for up to 3 days. This pie does not freeze well.

Variation: For **Sweet Potato** or **Squash Pie,** substitute equal amounts of canned puréed sweet potatoes, yams, or squash for pumpkin (about 1¾ cups). If using water- or syrup-packed fruit in cans, be sure to drain them well before using. If not already puréed, drain and mash well with a fork or a potato masher before adding them to the blender to mix with the other ingredients. Follow the rest of the Pumpkin Pie recipe.

BAKER'S BONUS

If you decide to use fresh, whole squash for this recipe, bake it first. You'll need 1 medium to large butternut squash, or 2 small to medium acorn squash to yield 1¾ cups cooked fruit purée. Preheat the oven to 400°F. Lightly oil, or spray with vegetable spray, a baking sheet lined with foil or parchment paper. Remove the stem, scoop out seeds and discard, and cut squash in half lengthwise. Place cut side down on baking sheet, cover with foil, and bake for 40 to 55 minutes or until you can pierce the squash through with a fork or knife and flesh is tender. Remove from the oven, and cool completely on the baking sheet. Peel squash and discard peel. Mash or purée fruit in a food processor or blender before using.

Pecan Pie

This classic pie showcases beautiful toasted pecans that magically float to the top. Vegan butter and pure maple syrup give it a rich but mellow taste.

Yield:	Prep time:	Bake time:	Serving size:
1 (9-inch) pie	70 to 80 minutes	50 to 60 minutes	1 slice

1 Flaky Piecrust dough ball (recipe in Chapter 13)

1½ cups toasted pecans

⅓ cup nonhydrogenated vegan margarine, melted

¾ cup light corn syrup or brown rice syrup

¾ cup pure maple syrup

1½ tsp. pure vanilla extract

Egg substitute for 2 large eggs (Ener-G or Bob's Red Mill)

2 TB. ground flaxseed

⅛ tsp. salt

2 TB. cornstarch

½ cup soy milk

1. Preheat the oven to 350°F.

2. On a lightly floured surface, roll out Flaky Piecrust (see Chapter 13 if you need a refresher), leaving enough overhang to fold underneath. Place piecrust evenly in a 9-inch pie pan or ceramic pie dish, and flute the edges with your fingertips.

3. Arrange pecans evenly on bottom of piecrust.

4. In a blender, add light corn syrup, maple syrup, vanilla extract, egg substitute, ground flaxseed, salt, cornstarch, and soy milk, and blend on high speed. Add melted vegan margarine, and blend on high for 2 to 4 minutes or until incorporated and batter is smooth, scraping down the sides of the blender as needed with a rubber spatula. Carefully pour batter over pecans, being careful not to disturb nuts.

5. Place the pie pan on a baking sheet, and bake for 50 to 60 minutes or until top is slightly browned and puffy. This will fall as it cools. Cool completely on a wire rack. Chill for at least 4 hours before slicing. Wrap with plastic wrap, and store at room temperature for 1 day, or refrigerate for longer storage. Double-wrap, and this pie will freeze well for up to 3 months.

Variation: For **Chocolate Bourbon Pecan Pie,** layer ¾ cup vegan semisweet chocolate chips on top of pecans. Add 2 tablespoons good-quality bourbon to the liquid ingredients, and mix well.

> **BATTER UP!**
>
> Any good bourbon or whiskey will do in this pie, but don't use cheap liquor. Jim Beam, or Woodford Reserve Bourbon, Jack Daniels Whiskey (black label), and Jameson Irish Whiskey also work. Whatever you use, be sure it's vegan-friendly because some alcohol has been processed using animal-based methods. Although most people assume that baking at high temperatures burns the alcohol out of baked goods, the taste is still there. Use your own judgment when serving children or teetotalers.

Maple Walnut Pie

This rich, flavorful pie, made with pure maple syrup and studded with toasted walnuts, is similar to pecan pie with its "buttery" brown sugar goodness.

Yield:	Prep time:	Bake time:	Serving size:
1 (9-inch) pie	70 to 80 minutes	50 to 70 minutes	1 slice

1 Flaky Piecrust dough ball or 1 Whole-Wheat Piecrust dough ball (recipes in Chapter 13)	½ cup light corn syrup or brown rice syrup
1½ cups toasted walnut halves	½ cup pure maple syrup
6 TB. nonhydrogenated vegan margarine	2 tsp. pure maple extract
½ cup light brown sugar, firmly packed	Egg substitute for 2 large eggs
	2 TB. ground flaxseed
	2 TB. cornstarch
	½ cup soft tofu

1. Preheat oven to 350°F.

2. On a lightly floured surface, roll out Flaky Piecrust or Whole-Wheat Piecrust (see Chapter 13 if you need a refresher), leaving enough overhang to fold underneath. Place piecrust evenly in a 9-inch pie pan or ceramic pie dish, and flute the edges with your fingertips.

3. Arrange walnuts evenly on bottom of piecrust.

4. In a medium saucepan over medium heat, melt vegan margarine. Add light brown sugar, and stir.

5. In a blender, add corn syrup, maple syrup, maple extract, egg substitute, ground flaxseed, cornstarch, and soft tofu, and blend on high speed. Add vegan margarine and brown sugar mixture, and blend on high for 1 to 3 minutes or until incorporated and batter is smooth, scraping down the sides of the blender as needed with a rubber spatula. Carefully pour batter over walnuts, being careful not to disturb nuts.

6. Place the pie pan on a baking sheet, and bake for 50 to 60 minutes or until top is slightly browned and puffy. It will fall as it cools. Cool completely on a wire rack and then chill for at least 4 hours before slicing. Wrap with plastic wrap, and store at room temperature for 1 day, or refrigerate for longer storage. Double-wrap, and this pie will freeze well for up to 3 months.

BAKER'S BONUS

Use only pure maple syrup for this pie. Dark amber or Grade B baking grade maple syrup is the darkest in color and has the richest flavor. Do not use fancy light maple syrup because it's not strong enough to stand up to baking.

Peanut Butter Pie

This pie features a fluffy peanut butter filling atop a Chocolate Cookie Crust, decorated with chopped peanuts and vegan peanut butter cups.

Yield:	Prep time:	Bake time:	Serving size:
1 (9-inch) pie	30 to 40 minutes	4 to 8 hours or overnight	1 slice

1¾ cups vegan soy cream cheese

1 cup creamy or chunky peanut butter

1 cup vegan confectioners' sugar

1½ tsp. pure vanilla extract

1 cup vegan Whipped Topping (recipe in Chapter 22), or store-bought nondairy whipped topping

1 (9-in.) Chocolate Cookie Crust (recipe in Chapter 13), cooled

1 cup Chocolate Ganache (recipe in Chapter 22), or store-bought vegan chocolate sauce

¼ cup roasted peanuts (optional)

2 vegan peanut butter cups, each chopped into 8 pieces

1. In a large bowl, and using an electric mixer fitted with a paddle attachment on high speed, beat vegan soy cream cheese and peanut butter until creamy. Add vegan confectioners' sugar and vanilla extract, and beat again, scraping the bowl as needed with a rubber spatula. Fold in Whipped Topping, and pour ½ of filling into cooled Chocolate Cookie Crust.

2. Drizzle ½ of Chocolate Ganache over top, and sprinkle with roasted peanuts (if using). Gently spread remaining filling on top and smooth down. Drizzle with remaining Chocolate Ganache, and top with chopped vegan peanut butter cups.

3. Chill for 4 to 8 hours before slicing.

Variation: For **Peanut Butter Parfaits,** in a tall parfait glass, layer peanut butter filling, Chocolate Ganache, and peanuts. Repeat and top with chopped vegan peanut butter cups.

BATTER UP!

This pie needs 4 to 8 hours (or overnight) to firm up enough to slice. It does not freeze well, but it does keep for a number of days in the refrigerator.

Rustic Tarts and Galettes

In This Chapter

- Fresh berry tarts
- Free-form galettes
- Getting creative with ingredients and baking pans

Vegan tarts and galettes? You bet! These fancy-looking desserts are far easier to make than they appear—and they're over-the-top rich and delicious! Best of all, they can be whipped up with little more effort than making a piecrust and slicing fruit. Speaking of crusts, if you don't have the time to make them from scratch, don't feel guilty about purchasing all-natural piecrusts or frozen vegan puff pastry dough. They're good to have in the freezer if you're ever in a pinch.

Most of the fruit desserts in this chapter are open to variation. Use your imagination and get creative when it comes to the fruits you choose. If apples are in season right now, use apples to make a Rustic Apple Cranberry Galette. If you found a good sale on strawberries at your local grocery store, make a Fresh Strawberry Tart for dessert. Got a good deal on walnuts? Substitute them for pecans in the Chocolate Pecan Tart. Easy!

Most serious bakers have all the bells, whistles, and toys in their arsenal to make just about any recipe that comes their way. You may be just starting out and don't have some of those shiny and pricey pans. What do you do when you don't have a 9-inch fluted tart pan? Use a springform pan. If you don't have that, a 9-inch pie plate will do just fine for most recipes.

Having a party and need individual desserts? With a little reconfiguring, most recipes can be made in mini tart pans, or even pastry lined muffin tins. The sky's the limit!

Fresh Strawberry Tart

Fresh, juicy strawberries and plump blueberries star with a "buttery" shortbread crust that's spread with strawberry jam—beautiful and delicious!

Yield:	Prep time:	Bake time:	Serving size:
1 (9-inch) tart	30 to 40 minutes	40 to 45 minutes	1 slice

1¼ cups unbleached all-purpose flour

¼ cup whole-wheat pastry flour

½ cup vegan confectioners' sugar

Pinch salt

½ cup nonhydrogenated vegan margarine, cold, cut in small pieces

2 TB. soft silken tofu

1 qt. fresh strawberries

2 TB. pure maple syrup

1 pt. fresh blueberries

½ tsp. grated lime zest

1½ cups strawberry jam

1 batch Whipped Topping (recipe in Chapter 22) or store-bought nondairy whipped topping (optional)

1. Lightly coat a 9-inch round fluted tart pan with a removable bottom with cooking oil spray.

2. In a large-capacity food processor fitted with a cutting blade, combine unbleached all-purpose flour, whole-wheat pastry flour, confectioners' sugar, and salt. Pulse for 5 to 10 seconds to blend. With the processor running, add vegan margarine a little at a time and process until dough resembles coarse meal. Add tofu, and pulse only until dough comes together. Do not overprocess dough or it will become tough. Turn out onto floured surface, and form dough into a ball, being careful not to knead dough. Using your hands, press dough into the prepared tart pan, making sure to get into all the creases. Freeze crust for at least 1 hour.

3. Place on a baking sheet, and blind-bake in a preheated 375°F oven for 15 to 18 minutes or until light brown. Remove and cool completely on a wire rack before filling.

4. Using a fork, prick bottom of crust a few times, and line with aluminum foil. Bake for 25 minutes, remove foil, and bake for 15 to 20 more minutes or until fragrant and lightly browned. Let cool completely on a wire rack before filling.

5. Rinse, hull, and halve strawberries (and slice strawberries if they're too large). In a medium bowl, toss strawberries with maple syrup, and let sit for 5 to 10 minutes.

6. Rinse blueberries. In a small bowl, toss blueberries with lime zest.

7. Place crust on a serving platter. Spread jam over the bottom of baked crust. Arrange strawberries in layers, packing them in tight, and sprinkle blueberries over the top. Chill for 30 minutes before serving.

8. With a sharp knife, cut into serving size slices, and top each with Whipped Topping (if using). The Fresh Strawberry Tart is best eaten within a few hours as the strawberries will begin to soak through the crust. Keep leftovers covered in plastic wrap and refrigerated. This dessert does not freeze well.

Variation: For **Raspberry Tart,** bake the crust as directed, and cool. Spread 1½ cups seedless raspberry jam over bottom, and substitute fresh raspberries for strawberries. Add 2 cups fresh blueberries if desired. Drizzle ½ to ¾ cup Chocolate Ganache (recipe in Chapter 22) over the top.

DOUGH-NOT

The fresh fruit and jam will quickly soak through this crust, so plan on eating this the day you make it. That shouldn't be a problem once your diners see how delicious it looks!

Puff Pastry Fruit Tart

A light, flaky puff pastry shell, filled with vegan white chocolate mousse, topped with fresh fruit, and drizzled with Raspberry Coulis—it really doesn't get much better than this!

Yield:	Prep time:	Bake time:	Serving size:
1 (9×13-inch) tart	2 hours, 30 minutes, to 3 hours	20 to 30 minutes	1 slice

2 cups vegan white chocolate chips, or 1 (10-oz.) vegan white chocolate bar, chopped into very small pieces

3 TB. agave syrup, or brown rice syrup

1 (12-oz.) pkg. soft silken tofu, drained

½ tsp. almond extract, or 1 tsp. pure vanilla extract

¼ tsp. ground nutmeg (optional)

1 (9×13-in.) sheet puff pastry, or frozen puff pastry, thawed

2 TB. soy milk

1 pt. fresh raspberries

1 pt. fresh blueberries

½ cup Raspberry Coulis (recipe in Chapter 22; optional), or 2 TB. apple juice mixed with 4 TB. seedless raspberry jelly

¼ cup vegan confectioners' sugar (optional)

1. In a microwavable bowl, melt white chocolate chips and agave syrup in the microwave for 30-second intervals, checking and stirring each time. Alternately, you could melt them in a bowl over hot water, stirring until smooth. Watch white chocolate carefully because it scorches and burns quickly. Do not let any water come in contact with white chocolate or it will seize up and clump and be ruined. Let cool slightly while continuing with recipe.

2. In a blender, combine soft silken tofu, almond extract, and ground nutmeg (if using). Blend on high speed for 1 minute or until nice and smooth.

3. Slowly add melted chocolate mixture to tofu, and blend on high for 1 or 2 more minutes or until well blended and no lumps remain, scraping down the sides of the blender with a rubber spatula if needed. Pour into a medium bowl, cover loosely with plastic wrap, and refrigerate for 2 hours or until firm. Keep refrigerated until ready to use in tart.

4. Line a large baking sheet with parchment paper.

5. On a lightly floured surface, and using a rolling pin, roll out puff pastry sheet to 9×13 inches. With a sharp knife, or pizza wheel, slice a thin, ½-inch strip from each side of pastry dough. This will become the sides, or borders. Using your fingers or a pastry brush, "glue" down strips of dough along the edges with soy milk, pressing to adhere. Brush remaining soy milk lightly over entire pastry shell. Prick the bottom of shell thoroughly with a fork. Transfer to the prepared baking sheet, and refrigerate for 20 minutes.

6. Preheat the oven to 375°F.

7. Bake puff pastry shell for 20 to 30 minutes or until puffy and golden brown. Cool completely on a wire rack before filling.

8. When pastry shell is cool, spread vegan white chocolate mousse evenly over the bottom. Arrange raspberries and blueberries on top, and refrigerate until ready to serve. Drizzle Raspberry Coulis over top, or gently brush fruit with apple juice and jelly mixture. Sprinkle with confectioners' sugar (if using), and serve.

Variation: For **Assorted Fruit Tart,** substitute equal amounts of fruit for the raspberries and blueberries. Glaze as desired.

BATTER UP!

Pepperidge Farms Puff Pastry Dough is vegan, although it does contain partially hydrogenated vegetable shortening containing soybean and cottonseed oils. You can find it in the supermarket freezer section. Be sure to thaw it before using. Separate the sheets, cover with plastic wrap, and thaw at room temperature for about 30 minutes. Alternatively, you can thaw the whole package in the refrigerator for 4 hours or longer.

Chocolate Pecan Tart

Chocolate lovers rejoice in this "buttery" Shortbread Crust layered with vegan chocolate and toasted pecans, baked with an extra-rich layer of brown sugar and maple syrup filling, and drizzled with vegan Chocolate Ganache Icing.

Yield:	Prep time:	Bake time:	Serving size:
1 (9-inch) tart	40 to 50 minutes	50 to 60 minutes	1 slice

1½ cups toasted pecans

1 (9-in.) fluted Shortbread Crust (recipe in Chapter 13), frozen for at least 30 minutes, blind-baked for 15 to 20 minutes or until light brown, and cooled completely

¾ cup vegan semisweet chocolate chips, or shaved vegan dark chocolate

2 TB. finely ground flaxseed

6 TB. water

⅓ cup nonhydrogenated vegan margarine

¾ cup light brown sugar, firmly packed

¾ cup pure maple syrup or light corn syrup

1½ tsp. pure vanilla extract

2 TB. bourbon whisky (optional)

¼ cup vegan Chocolate Ganache Icing (recipe in Chapter 22)

1. Preheat the oven to 375°F.

2. Arrange toasted pecans in bottom of baked Shortbread Crust, and layer vegan chocolate chips over pecans. Place crust on a baking sheet to prevent drips.

3. In a blender, or using an immersion blender on medium to high speed, blend together ground flaxseed and water until completely blended. Let sit for 15 minutes to thicken.

4. In medium saucepan over medium heat, melt vegan margarine. Reduce heat to low, add light brown sugar, and stir until dissolved. Pour into a large bowl, and using an electric mixer fitted with the whisk attachment on high speed, beat mixture for 1 minute. Add maple syrup, flaxseed mixture, vanilla extract, and bourbon whisky (if using), and whip for 1 or 2 minutes or until light and fluffy, scraping the bowl as needed with a rubber spatula.

5. Carefully pour batter over vegan chocolate chips and pecans in crust, being careful not to disturb them. Bake for 50 to 60 minutes or until top is slightly browned and puffed up. Cool completely before drizzling with vegan Chocolate Ganache Icing.

> **BAKER'S BONUS**
>
> Ground flaxseed acts as a binder, taking the place of eggs in certain recipes, at the same time adding a good deal of fiber.

Rustic Apple Cranberry Galette

A basic flaky crust is the shell for this free-form pie filled with fresh apples and cranberries, a touch of cinnamon, and optional "custard" filling for the perfect fall dessert.

Yield:	Prep time:	Bake time:	Serving size:
1 (9-inch) galette	40 to 50 minutes	40 to 50 minutes	1 slice

1 double Flaky Piecrust (recipe in Chapter 13)

4 TB. apple butter, or jam

3 large Cortland, Baldwin, or Granny Smith apples, peeled, cored, and sliced

4 TB. unbleached cane sugar

2 TB. light brown sugar, firmly packed

1½ tsp. ground cinnamon

1½ cups fresh or frozen cranberries

2 TB. chopped pecans (optional)

½ tsp. cornstarch (optional)

¼ cup plus 2 TB. soy or almond milk (optional)

¼ cup soft silken tofu (optional)

½ tsp. pure vanilla extract, or almond extract (optional)

1 TB. nonhydrogenated vegan margarine, melted (optional)

1. Preheat the oven to 350°F. Line a baking sheet with parchment paper, or with aluminum foil.

2. On a floured surface, and with a rolling pin, roll piecrust to approximately 14 inches in diameter. Leave edges ragged, or trim as desired. Carefully transfer piecrust to the prepared baking sheet. Edges should fall over the sides of the baking sheet.

3. Using a 9-inch inverted bowl or pan lid, lightly mark inside of piecrust (this will be a guide for apple butter), being careful not to cut through dough. Spread apple butter evenly over piecrust within the circle.

4. In a medium bowl, toss apple slices with 2 tablespoons unbleached cane sugar, light brown sugar, and 1 teaspoon ground cinnamon.

5. Layer sliced apples and ½ of cranberries inside and around apple butter–topped circle until it's full, poking in remaining ½ of cranberries to fit. Sprinkle pecans (if using) on top.

6. Using a pastry brush or your fingers, moisten edges of piecrust with a small amount of water, and carefully fold up, pressing, folding, and pinching edges in a rustic pattern. Bake for 30 minutes.

7. In a small cup, mix 1 tablespoon unbleached cane sugar and remaining ½ teaspoon ground cinnamon.

8. Meanwhile, for "custard" (if using): in a small bowl, dissolve cornstarch in ¼ cup plus 1 tablespoon soy milk.

9. In a blender, combine soft silken tofu, remaining 1 tablespoon unbleached cane sugar, and vanilla extract, and blend until smooth. Add melted vegan margarine and cornstarch mixture, and blend on high speed for 1 minute or until smooth.

10. Remove galette from the oven after 30 minutes, and carefully pour "custard" into the center. With a pastry brush, paint outside of crust with remaining 1 tablespoon soy milk, and sprinkle with cinnamon sugar. Return galette to the oven, and bake for 10 to 20 more minutes or until fruit is tender and "custard" is set. Remove galette from the oven, and let sit for 10 to 15 minutes before transferring to a wire rack to cool completely. This galette is best eaten within a day, but will keep in the refrigerator loosely covered for up to 3 days. It does not freeze well.

DOUGH-NOT

Depending on the amount of fruit juice the tart has produced while baking, some of it may need to be spooned out to make room for the "custard" filling. Don't worry if it doesn't all fit. Some is better than none.

Free-Form Peach Galette

Juicy yellow peaches, combined with red cherries and a touch of spice and baked in a rustic flaky pastry crust, make this one of the prettiest—and tastiest!—galettes around.

Yield:	Prep time:	Bake time:	Serving size:
1 (9-inch) galette	40 to 50 minutes	40 to 50 minutes	1 slice

1 double Flaky Piecrust (recipe in Chapter 13)

4 TB. peach butter or peach jam

4 large ripe peaches, peeled, pitted, and sliced

6 TB. unbleached cane sugar

1 tsp. ground cinnamon

1 cup fresh cherries, pitted and cut in ½

2 TB. toasted, sliced almonds or pecans (optional)

½ tsp. cornstarch (optional)

¼ cup plus 2 TB. soy or almond milk (optional)

¼ cup soft silken tofu (optional)

½ tsp. pure almond extract (optional)

1 TB. nonhydrogenated vegan margarine, melted (optional)

1. Preheat the oven to 350°F. Line a baking sheet with parchment paper, or with aluminum foil.

2. On a floured surface, and with a rolling pin, roll piecrust to approximately 14 inches in diameter. Leave edges ragged, or trim as desired. Carefully transfer piecrust to the prepared baking sheet. Edges should fall over the sides of the baking sheet.

3. Using a 9-inch inverted bowl or pan lid, lightly mark inside of piecrust (this will be a guide for peach butter), being careful not to cut through dough. Spread peach butter evenly over piecrust within the circle.

4. In a medium bowl, toss peaches with 4 tablespoons unbleached cane sugar and ½ teaspoon ground cinnamon.

5. Layer peaches and ½ of cherries inside and around peach butter–topped circle until it's full, poking in remaining ½ of cherries to fit. Sprinkle almonds (if using) on top.

6. Using a pastry brush or your fingers, moisten edges of piecrust with a small amount of water, and carefully fold up, pressing, folding, and pinching the edges in a rustic pattern. Bake for 30 minutes.

7. In a small cup, mix 1 tablespoon cane sugar and remaining ½ teaspoon ground cinnamon.

8. Meanwhile, for "custard" (if using): in a small bowl, dissolve cornstarch in ¼ cup plus 1 tablespoon soy milk.

9. In a blender, combine soft silken tofu, remaining 1 tablespoon cane sugar, and almond extract, and blend until smooth. Add melted vegan margarine and cornstarch mixture, and blend on high speed for 1 minute or until smooth.

10. Remove galette from the oven after 30 minutes, and carefully pour "custard" into the center. With a pastry brush, paint outside of crust with remaining 1 tablespoon soy milk, and sprinkle with cinnamon sugar. Return galette to the oven, and bake for 10 to 20 more minutes or until fruit is tender and "custard" is set. Remove galette from the oven, and let sit for 10 to 15 minutes before transferring to a wire rack to cool completely. This galette is best eaten within a day, but will keep in the refrigerator loosely covered for up to 3 days. It does not freeze well.

Variation: For **Mixed Fruit Galette,** experiment with different berries, fruits, jams, and spices.

BAKER'S BONUS

Instead of one big galette, you could create mini galettes. Divide piecrust into 4 balls, and roll out each individually. Arrange fruit in them as you would the large galette. Continue with the recipe directions, decreasing the baking time by approximately 15 minutes or until galettes are golden brown and bubbly.

Cobblers and Crisps

In This Chapter

- Cobblers and crisps—comfort-food favorites
- Fresh fruit cobblers with soft biscuit toppings
- Crumbly fresh fruit crisps

Old-fashioned desserts such as fruit cobblers and crisps have been around for a very long time. Recipes from cookbooks printed in the 1800s reference these delicious seasonal and regional specialties. Many years later, we still rely on fresh seasonal fruit for their awesome flavor in baked goods.

Although traditional cobblers, crisps, and fruit dessert recipes were originally written with gobs of butter and cream, they are super easy for today's vegans to adapt. With a few substitutions and ingredient replacements, dairy-free and egg-free cobblers and crisps are just a few minutes away!

Cobblers Versus Crisps

Depending on where you live, *cobbler* can mean different things to different bakers. The only thing regional bakers can agree on is that everyone has their own interpretation of how a cobbler is made. Some argue that a cobbler has to have a piecrustlike cover, while others say a solid biscuit topping with decorative vents cut out is best. Still others claim the only way a dessert can be called a cobbler is if it's baked with individual sweet dough biscuits on top. They say this cobbler topping most resembles the cobblestone streets cobblers were named after way back when.

Crisps, on the other hand, are more straightforward. A crisp is a crisp because it's crispy! Baked crisps consist of two parts: a layer of fresh fruit on the bottom and a streusel-like crumble layer on top. Although the crisp is less likely to be open to debate, some bakers still like it the way they like it. Some say a crisp has to contain rolled oats, brown sugar, flour, and spices and that it has to have the right "crisp" texture. Others like it without oats, preferring a less-crumbly, sweeter topping.

There are also many options when it comes to the fruit used. Go beyond the standard Apple or Blueberry Crisp, and try experimenting with unusual fruits for your crisps. Try apricots, pears, plums, and cranberries. For cobblers, mix and match the fruits according to the season. Choose from basic fruits like peaches, apples, strawberries, rhubarb, and cherries, or try some of the seasonal options available where you live.

And dare to venture away from the same-old fruits sometimes, with options like red currants, loganberries and lingonberries, huckleberries, gooseberries, cranberries, or boysenberries!

Peach Cobbler

This homey cobbler features ripe, juicy peaches with a touch of cinnamon, baked until bubbling hot under a full sweet biscuit dough topping.

Yield:	Prep time:	Bake time:	Serving size:
1 (2-quart) round cobbler	40 to 50 minutes	40 to 50 minutes	1 piece

6 cups (about 10 to 12 medium, or 8 large) peeled, pitted, and sliced peaches, fresh or frozen

½ cup plus ⅓ cup plus 1 TB. unbleached cane sugar

½ cup light brown sugar, firmly packed

¼ cup cornstarch

¾ tsp. plus ⅛ tsp. ground cinnamon or ground nutmeg

2 cups unbleached all-purpose flour

2 tsp. aluminum-free baking powder

¼ tsp. salt

6 TB. nonhydrogenated vegan margarine, cold and cut in small pieces

Egg substitute for 1 large egg (Ener-G or Bob's Red Mill works best)

¾ cup plus 2 TB. soy, rice, or almond milk

1. Preheat the oven to 375°F. Lightly coat a 2-quart round baking dish with cooking oil spray.

2. In a large bowl, and with a large spoon or your hands, combine peaches, ½ cup unbleached cane sugar, light brown sugar, cornstarch, and ¾ teaspoon ground cinnamon, tossing ingredients together to coat. Pour into the prepared baking dish.

3. Into a separate large bowl, sift unbleached all-purpose flour, aluminum-free baking powder, and salt, or blend with a wire whisk. Add ⅓ cup unbleached cane sugar, and whisk to combine. Using a pastry blender or 2 dinner knives, cut in cold vegan margarine until mixture resembles coarse meal.

4. In a small bowl, whisk together egg substitute and ¾ cup soy milk until foamy. Add to dough, and mix only until dough is moistened and comes together in a ball. Do not overwork dough.

5. Turn out dough onto a floured surface, and pat with your hands into a round circle big enough to cover the baking dish.

6. Carefully lift dough onto fruit, gently patting into place. With a sharp knife, cut a few decorative vent holes on top. Brush remaining 2 tablespoons soy milk over dough, and sprinkle remaining 1 tablespoon unbleached cane sugar and $\frac{1}{8}$ teaspoon ground cinnamon over top.

7. Bake for 40 to 50 minutes or until cobbler dough is light golden brown and juices begin to bubble through vents and around edges. Remove from the oven, and cool on a wire rack for at least 30 minutes or until ready to serve.

Variation: For **Apple Cobbler,** substitute 6 cups peeled, cored, and sliced apples for the peaches. If you're using firm apples, increase the baking time by 5 to 10 minutes if necessary. Hard, crisp apples like Cortland, Granny Smith, Empire, and Gravenstein are best for recipes that require long baking times.

BATTER UP!

To peel fresh peaches, first wash or rinse ripe peaches. Boil a pan of water deep enough to cover 2 peaches at a time. Turn heat to low, just enough to keep a low boil. Using a slotted spoon, dip peaches into boiling water for 30 to 40 seconds. Remove peaches with the spoon, and plunge peaches into a bowl of very cold water for about 2 or 3 minutes. Peel skin off peaches with a small paring knife (the skin should slip off easily), and discard peels. Place peaches on a paper towel to dry slightly. With a sharp knife, cut peach in half right down to the pit. The peach should come away easily from the pit without much effort. Discard the pit. Slice, dice, or halve the peaches depending on the recipe.

Very Berry Cobbler

Farm fresh berries, mixed with sugar and spices, are baked under individual sweet vegan biscuits in this hot and bubbly cobbler.

Yield:	Prep time:	Bake time:	Serving size:
1 (9×13-inch) cobbler	40 to 50 minutes	55 to 60 minutes	1 piece

6 cups mixed berries (blueberries, raspberries, blackberries, strawberries, etc.), fresh or frozen

1 cup unbleached cane sugar

3 TB. cornstarch

½ tsp. plus ¼ tsp. ground nutmeg

½ tsp. ground cinnamon

Grated zest of ½ lemon or lime

3 cups unbleached all-purpose flour

2 TB. aluminum-free baking powder

½ tsp. salt

1½ TB. light brown sugar, firmly packed

½ cup nonhydrogenated vegan margarine, cold and cut in small pieces

¾ to 1 cup soy, rice, or almond milk

1. Preheat the oven to 375°F. Lightly coat a 9×13-inch baking dish with cooking oil spray.

2. In a large bowl, and with a large spoon or your hands, combine mixed berries, ¾ cup unbleached cane sugar, cornstarch, ½ teaspoon ground nutmeg, ground cinnamon, and lemon zest, tossing ingredients together to coat. Pour into the prepared baking dish.

3. Into a separate large bowl, sift unbleached all-purpose flour, aluminum-free baking powder, remaining ¼ teaspoon ground nutmeg, and salt, or blend with a wire whisk. Add light brown sugar and remaining ¼ cup unbleached cane sugar, and whisk to combine. Using a pastry blender or 2 dinner knives, cut in cold vegan margarine until mixture resembles crumbs the size of oatmeal or small peas.

4. Add soy milk, and mix only until dough is moistened and comes together in a ball. Do not overwork dough; it will be soft and sticky. Divide biscuit dough into 15 equal balls. Flatten each ball slightly, and arrange evenly over top of berries.

5. Bake for 55 to 60 minutes or until biscuits are light golden brown and juices begin to bubble around biscuits. Remove from the oven, and cool on a wire rack for at least 30 minutes or until ready to serve.

BATTER UP!

Fresh juicy berries are always the best, especially when they're ripe and in season. But there's no excuse to miss out on luscious fruit cobblers during the cold bleak winter when frozen organic berries are available in the supermarket's freezer section. Look for unsweetened frozen berries with nothing added. For best results, use the frozen berries right out of the bag. If they do happen to thaw, drain them completely before adding to the rest of the ingredients. Excess moisture can ruin recipes that were created for use with fresh, dry berries.

Mixed Fruit Cobbler

In this delicious and colorful cobbler, fresh peaches, blueberries, and cherries bake together under a soft whole-wheat biscuit topping.

Yield:	Prep time:	Bake time:	Serving size:
1 (9×13-inch) cobbler	40 to 50 minutes	40 to 50 minutes	1 piece

2 cups fresh cherries, pitted and cut in ½

2 cups fresh blueberries

2 cups (about 4 medium, or 3 large) fresh peeled, pitted, and sliced peaches

¾ cup plus ⅓ cup plus 1 TB. unbleached cane sugar

¼ cup light brown sugar, firmly packed

¼ cup cornstarch

¾ tsp. plus ⅛ tsp. ground cinnamon

½ tsp. lemon zest

1 cup unbleached all-purpose flour

1 cup whole-wheat pastry flour

2 tsp. aluminum-free baking powder

¼ tsp. ground nutmeg

¼ tsp. salt

6 TB. nonhydrogenated vegan margarine, cold and cut in small pieces

Egg substitute for 1 large egg (Ener-G or Bob's Red Mill works best)

¾ cup plus 2 TB. soy, rice, or almond milk

1. Preheat the oven to 375°F. Lightly coat a 9×13-inch baking dish with cooking oil spray.

2. In a large bowl, with a large spoon or your hands, combine cherries, blueberries, peaches, ¾ cup unbleached cane sugar, light brown sugar, cornstarch, ¾ teaspoon ground cinnamon, and lemon zest, tossing ingredients together to coat. Pour into the prepared baking dish.

3. Into a separate large bowl, sift unbleached all-purpose flour, whole-wheat pastry flour, aluminum-free baking powder, ground nutmeg, and salt, or blend with a wire whisk. Add ⅓ cup unbleached cane sugar, and whisk to combine. Using a pastry blender or 2 dinner knives, cut in cold vegan margarine until mixture resembles coarse meal.

4. In a small bowl, whisk together egg substitute and ¾ cup soy milk until foamy. Add to dough, and mix only until dough is moistened and comes together in a ball. Do not overwork dough.

5. Turn out dough onto a floured surface, and pat with your hands into a round circle big enough to cover the baking dish.

6. Carefully lift dough onto fruit, gently patting into place. With a sharp knife, cut a few decorative vent holes on top. Brush remaining 2 tablespoons soy milk over dough, and sprinkle remaining 1 tablespoon unbleached cane sugar and ⅛ teaspoon ground cinnamon over top.

7. Bake for 40 to 50 minutes or until cobbler dough is light golden brown and juices begin to bubble through the vents and around the edges. Remove from the oven, and cool on a wire rack for at least 30 minutes or until ready to serve.

BAKER'S BONUS

Many vegan egg substitutes are available, but this biscuit dough works best using Ener-G or Bob's Red Mill Egg Replacer. Experiment with other egg substitutes (see Chapter 2) until you find the one you like best.

Apple Crisp

Fresh-from-the-orchard apples, tossed with cinnamon and brown sugar, bake under a crispy topping made of oats, whole-wheat flour, and more brown sugar and spices in this quick and easy crisp.

Yield:	Prep time:	Bake time:	Serving size:
1 (9×13-inch) crisp	30 to 40 minutes	45 to 55 minutes	1 piece

7 cups (about 6 or 7 large) peeled, cored, and sliced apples (your choice)

¼ cup unbleached all-purpose flour

1¼ cups light brown sugar, firmly packed

¼ cup pure maple syrup

5 tsp. ground cinnamon

¾ cup whole-wheat pastry flour

1 cup rolled oats

¾ cup nonhydrogenated vegan margarine, cold and cut into small pieces

½ cup chopped walnuts (optional)

1. Preheat the oven to 350°F. Lightly coat a 9×13-inch baking dish with cooking oil spray.

2. In a large bowl, with a large spoon or your hands, combine apples, unbleached all-purpose flour, ¼ cup light brown sugar, maple syrup, and 3 teaspoons ground cinnamon, tossing ingredients together to coat. Pour into the prepared baking dish.

3. In a separate large bowl, with a large spoon, combine whole-wheat flour, rolled oats, remaining 1 cup light brown sugar, and remaining 2 teaspoons ground cinnamon. Using a pastry blender or 2 dinner knives, cut in vegan margarine until mixture resembles crumbs. Add walnuts (if using), and spread evenly over apples.

4. Bake for 45 to 55 minutes or until crisp is nicely browned and apples are tender and bubbly. Cool on a wire rack for at least 30 minutes before serving.

Variation: For **Apple Cranberry Crisp,** reduce the apples to 4½ cups (about 4 large apples), and add 2 cups fresh or frozen whole or sliced cranberries.

BATTER UP!

Harder apples such as Granny Smith, Gala, Pippin, Rhode Island Greening, Braeburn, Rome, Northern Spy, Gravenstein, and Cortland are good choices for this crisp because they stand up to baking.

Strawberry Rhubarb Crisp

Fresh, ripe strawberries and tart rhubarb pair perfectly with a touch of cinnamon and cardamom in this crisp. A crumbly top nicely finishes off this classic dessert.

Yield:	Prep time:	Bake time:	Serving size:
1 (9×13-inch) crisp	30 to 40 minutes	30 to 40 minutes	1 piece

3 cups fresh strawberries, cut in ½

3 cups (about 3 medium stalks) rhubarb, cut into 1-in. pieces

½ cup plus ¾ cup light brown sugar, firmly packed

1 cup unbleached cane sugar

3 TB. cornstarch

1½ tsp. ground cinnamon

½ tsp. ground cardamom

1 TB. fresh lemon juice

1¼ cups unbleached all-purpose flour

¾ cup nonhydrogenated vegan margarine, cold and cut into small pieces

1. Preheat the oven to 350°F. Lightly coat a 9×13-inch baking dish with cooking oil spray.

2. In a large bowl, with a large spoon or your hands, combine strawberries, rhubarb, ½ cup light brown sugar, ¼ cup unbleached cane sugar, cornstarch, ½ teaspoon ground cinnamon, ground cardamom, and lemon juice, tossing ingredients together to coat. Pour into the prepared baking dish.

3. In a separate large bowl, with a large spoon, combine unbleached all-purpose flour, remaining ¾ cup brown sugar, remaining ¾ cup unbleached cane sugar, and remaining 1 teaspoon ground cinnamon. Using a pastry blender or 2 dinner knives, cut in vegan margarine until mixture resembles crumbs, and spread evenly over fruit mixture.

4. Bake for 30 to 40 minutes or until crisp is beginning to brown and fruit filling is bubbly. Cool on a wire rack for at least 30 minutes before serving.

BAKER'S BONUS

In the winter off-season, when fresh strawberries and rhubarb aren't available, frozen fruit will work in this recipe. Leave it frozen, and use it right from the bag. Do not thaw it first.

Blueberry Crisp

Just try to resist this crisp—made with fresh blueberries and a brown sugar–lime filling, bubbling under a crispy topping of rolled oats, brown sugar, and cinnamon.

Yield:	Prep time:	Bake time:	Serving size:
1 (9×13-inch) crisp	20 to 30 minutes	30 to 40 minutes	1 piece

6 cups (about 3 pt.) fresh or frozen blueberries, rinsed and picked over for stems if fresh

¼ cup plus ¾ cup light brown sugar, firmly packed

½ cup unbleached cane sugar

2 TB. plus 1 cup unbleached all-purpose flour

1 TB. cornstarch

1¾ tsp. ground cinnamon

1 TB. fresh lime or lemon juice

1 tsp. grated lime zest

¾ cup rolled oats

½ cup nonhydrogenated vegan margarine, cold and cut in small pieces

1. Preheat the oven to 350°F. Lightly coat a 9×13-inch baking dish with cooking oil spray.

2. In a large bowl, with a large spoon or your hands, combine blueberries, ¼ cup light brown sugar, unbleached cane sugar, 2 tablespoons unbleached all-purpose flour, cornstarch, ¾ teaspoon ground cinnamon, lime juice, and lime zest, tossing ingredients together to coat. Pour into the prepared baking dish.

3. In a separate large bowl, with a large spoon, combine remaining ¾ cup light brown sugar, remaining 1 cup flour, rolled oats, and remaining 1 teaspoon ground cinnamon. Using a pastry blender or 2 dinner knives, cut in vegan margarine until mixture is crumbly, and spread evenly over fruit mixture.

4. Bake for 30 to 40 minutes or until crisp is beginning to brown and fruit filling is bubbly. Cool on a wire rack for at least 30 minutes before serving.

Variation: For **Mixed Fruit Crisp,** reduce blueberries to 2 cups, and add 2 cups (about 4 medium) sliced peaches and 2 cups pitted Bing cherries. Substitute lemon juice for lime juice and lemon zest for lime zest.

BAKER'S BONUS

If you use frozen blueberries, add 2 extra tablespoons unbleached all-purpose flour when tossing frozen blueberries to account for the additional juice.

Puddings and Such

In This Chapter

- Bread puddings = comfort food
- Sweet fruity clafoutis
- The perfect brown Betty

I could have titled this chapter "The Comfort Food Chapter." The puddings and such recipes in the following pages are comfort food to many people, possibly because they remind us of curling up in a big armchair by the fireplace. That's what these desserts are all about—comfort and coziness.

So dig in! All the desserts in this chapter are just waiting for a bowl, a spoon, and a scoop of vegan ice cream to make your day.

Getting Comfy with Desserts

Bread pudding is an old-fashioned dessert. Most often made with stale or leftover bread, bread puddings rely on a custardlike mixture—usually made with cream and eggs—to hold together the bread filling. Vegan bakers are especially challenged when it comes to custard-type desserts. How do you make bread pudding without cream and eggs? Simple. By using products like nondairy milk, tofu, arrowroot powder, cornstarch, and egg substitutes, vegan bread pudding can be just as delicious as its nonvegan counterpart—without all the animal products. By varying additional ingredients, you could be enjoying Chocolate Bread Pudding, Bourbon Bread Pudding with a tasty whiskey sauce, Apple Cider Bread Pudding, or a luscious Pumpkin Bread Pudding for tonight's dessert.

> **BATTER UP!**
>
> The water bath technique is essential to achieving the texture desired in all bread puddings. Use any pan that is larger and a little deeper than the pudding dish, place the pudding in the larger pan, filling the pan halfway with hot water, and bake.

Next up, clafoutis. Clafoutis (pronounced *kla-fu-ti*) is a French dessert, generally made with fresh cherries swimming in a baked custard filling. While the cherry dessert is called clafoutis, it can be made with most any fresh fruit, at which time it's a *flaugnarde*. The recipes that follow have a great-tasting flan filling made with tofu, nondairy milk, and egg substitutes. All you need to dress them up is a little sprinkle of vegan confectioners' sugar.

Another old-fashioned comfort dessert, the Apple Brown Betty is like a cobbler, crisp, and bread pudding all rolled into one. It contains fruit and bread like a bread pudding and a crispy topping like a crisp. However, in this chapter's recipe, the bread is in the form of toasted breadcrumbs, both in the fruit filling and the spicy topping.

Apple Cider Bread Pudding

Made with fresh apples, apple cider, pure maple syrup, and your favorite bread, this bread pudding will knock your socks off. Go ahead: close your eyes and think of fall foliage in Vermont.

Yield:	Prep time:	Bake time:	Serving size:
1 (9×9-inch) pan	55 to 60 minutes	50 to 60 minutes	1 portion

½ loaf (about 6 cups, packed) Cinnamon Raisin Bread, Whole-Wheat Bread, or Basic White Bread (recipes in Chapter 7)

1½ cups soy, rice, or almond milk

Ener-G Egg Replacer for 2 large eggs

2 tsp. pure vanilla extract

½ cup pure maple syrup

⅓ cup apple cider, or thawed or frozen apple juice concentrate, not diluted

2½ tsp. ground cinnamon

1 cup (about 1 large) Cortland, Granny Smith, Empire, Gravenstein, or other hard crisp apple, peeled, cored, and finely chopped

¼ cup seedless raisins (optional)

¼ cup chopped walnuts (optional)

1. Lightly coat a 9×9-inch baking dish with cooking oil spray.

2. Into a large bowl, break Cinnamon Raisin Bread into 1½-inch cubes.

3. In a separate large bowl, combine soy milk, egg substitute, vanilla extract, maple syrup, apple cider, and ground cinnamon. Add chopped apple, raisins (if using), and walnuts (if using). Pour mixture over bread, and gently fold in, coating evenly.

4. Pour bread pudding into the prepared baking dish. Place a layer of plastic wrap over the top, and press down. Let sit for 30 minutes for bread to absorb liquid.

5. Preheat the oven to 350°F.

6. Carefully place the baking dish in a larger and deeper dish, and fill the larger dish half full of hot water. Bake for 50 to 60 minutes or until pudding is set and a knife inserted into the center comes out clean. Cool on a wire rack for at least 30 minutes before serving.

BATTER UP!

If you can't get your hands on fresh apple cider, unsweetened apple juice concentrate is a good substitute. It has a natural sweetness and adds the apple flavor necessary in this recipe. Do not dilute it though. Use it straight from the can, frozen or thawed.

Chocolate Bread Pudding

This sinfully rich bread pudding is made with homemade bread, real vanilla bean, and a touch of cinnamon; soaked in a vegan chocolate custard; and baked until perfectly delicious.

Yield:	Prep time:	Bake time:	Serving size:
1 (9×9-inch) pan	80 to 90 minutes	40 to 50 minutes	1 portion

2 cups soy milk

½ vanilla bean, split down the middle and opened

1 (4-in.) cinnamon stick, food grade (optional)

½ loaf (about 6 cups, packed) Basic White Bread (recipe in Chapter 7), sliced

¾ cup vegan semisweet chocolate chips

½ cup soft silken tofu

⅓ cup unbleached cane sugar

1 tsp. arrowroot powder

1 tsp. pure vanilla extract

¼ cup vegan confectioners' sugar (optional)

1. In a medium saucepan over medium heat, bring soy milk and vanilla bean to a *scald*. Turn heat off, add cinnamon stick (if using), and set aside to cool for 30 minutes.

2. Remove vanilla bean from the pan, open pod, and scrape out seeds, returning them to soy milk. Discard pod and cinnamon stick.

3. Lightly coat a 9×9-inch baking dish with cooking oil spray.

4. Layer Basic White Bread slices in the prepared baking dish.

5. Reheat soy milk almost to a scald. Add vegan chocolate chips, and whisk until smooth and chocolate chips are melted. Let cool for 15 minutes.

6. In a blender, add soft silken tofu, unbleached cane sugar, and arrowroot powder, and blend on high speed for 2 or 3 minutes or until smooth, scraping down the sides of the blender as needed with a rubber spatula.

7. With the blender on low, slowly add chocolate mixture and vanilla extract, and blend until well mixed. Pour chocolate mixture over bread, lifting bread to be sure custard coats all bread evenly.

8. Place a layer of plastic wrap over the bread pudding and press down. Let sit for 30 to 40 minutes for bread to absorb the custard.

9. Preheat the oven to 325°F.

10. Carefully place the baking dish in a larger and deeper dish, and fill the larger dish half full of hot water. Bake for 40 to 50 minutes or until pudding is set and a knife inserted into the center comes out clean.

11. Cool on a wire rack for at least 30 minutes before sprinkling with vegan confectioners' sugar (if using) and serving.

VEGAN VOCAB

Scalding is a method by which milk, or in this case vegan nondairy milk, is heated to just below the boiling point (185°F or more). In the days before pasteurization, dairy milk was scalded to destroy potentially harmful bacteria in the milk. We're using vegan nondairy milk, so there's really no need to scald milk for safety reasons. Instead, the vegan milk is scalded simply to speed up the process of melting the vegan chocolate chips quickly.

Bourbon Bread Pudding

You'll get a taste of New Orleans in this bourbon-infused bread pudding. Toasted pecans, pure maple syrup, vanilla, raisins, and spices are soaked and baked with homemade bread—it's a vegan's dream come true.

Yield:	Prep time:	Bake time:	Serving size:
1 (8×8-inch) pan	70 to 80 minutes	45 to 60 minutes	1 portion

½ loaf (about 6 cups, packed) Cinnamon Raisin Bread, Whole-Wheat Bread, or Basic White Bread (recipes in Chapter 7)

½ cup seedless raisins

½ cup pure maple syrup

⅓ cup bourbon or apple juice

2 tsp. pure vanilla extract

1½ cups soy, rice, or almond milk

Ener-G Egg Replacer for 2 large eggs

2 tsp. ground cinnamon

½ tsp. ground nutmeg

¼ cup toasted chopped pecans (optional)

1. Lightly coat a 9×9-inch baking dish with cooking oil spray.

2. Into a large bowl, break Cinnamon Raisin Bread into 1½-inch cubes.

3. In a medium bowl, combine raisins, maple syrup, bourbon, and vanilla extract. Set aside to soak.

4. In a separate large bowl, and using a hand whisk, combine soy milk, egg substitute, ground cinnamon, and ground nutmeg. Stir in raisin mixture with a rubber spatula. Pour mixture over bread, add pecans (if using), and gently fold in, coating evenly.

5. Pour bread pudding into the prepared baking dish. Place a layer of plastic wrap over the top, and press down. Let sit for 30 minutes for bread to absorb liquid.

6. Preheat the oven to 350°F.

7. Carefully place the baking dish in a larger and deeper dish, and fill the larger dish half full of hot water. Bake for 45 to 60 minutes or until a knife inserted in the middle comes out clean. Cool on a wire rack for at least 30 minutes before serving. Serve with Bourbon Sauce (recipe in Chapter 22).

BATTER UP!

Use good-quality Kentucky bourbon, or whiskey, for this pudding. If you don't want to use alcohol, substitute an equal amount of apple juice.

Pumpkin Bread Pudding

This beautiful bread pudding, a cross between pumpkin pie and pumpkin pound cake, gets its good looks and taste from pumpkin purée, brown sugar, and spices. It would make a yummy edible holiday centerpiece.

Yield:	Prep time:	Bake time:	Serving size:
1 (8×8-inch) pan	50 to 60 minutes	45 to 60 minutes	1 portion

½ loaf (about 6 cups packed) Whole-Wheat Bread or Basic White Bread (recipes in Chapter 7)

1½ cups soy milk

1 cup fresh or canned pumpkin purée

1 cup soft silken tofu

1 tsp. pure vanilla extract

½ cup light brown sugar, firmly packed

1 tsp. ground cinnamon

¼ tsp. ground nutmeg

¼ tsp. ground ginger

1 tsp. cornstarch

Pinch salt

1. Lightly coat a 9×9-inch baking dish with cooking oil spray.

2. Into a large bowl, break Whole-Wheat Bread into 1½-inch cubes.

3. In a blender, add soy milk, pumpkin purée, soft silken tofu, and vanilla extract, and blend on high speed for 2 or 3 minutes or until smooth. Add light brown sugar, ground cinnamon, ground nutmeg, ground ginger, cornstarch, and salt, and blend on high speed for another 2 or 3 minutes or until creamy and free of lumps, scraping down the sides of the blender as needed with a rubber spatula. Pour pumpkin mixture over bread, and gently fold in, coating evenly.

4. Pour bread pudding into prepared baking dish. Place a layer of plastic wrap over the top, and press down. Let sit for 30 minutes for bread to absorb liquid.

5. Preheat the oven to 350°F.

6. Carefully place the baking dish in a larger and deeper dish, and fill the larger dish half full of hot water. Bake for 45 to 60 minutes or until a knife inserted in the middle comes out clean. Cool on a wire rack for at least 30 minutes before serving.

BAKER'S BONUS

Fresh homemade bread makes great bread puddings, but if you have some dry, leftover bread hanging out in your freezer, even better.

Cherry Clafoutis

A classic French flanlike pudding, this baked casserole is full of fresh cherries and toasted almonds and topped with a sweet brown sugar streusel. The custard filling is smooth and silky with a touch of almond flavoring.

Yield:	Prep time:	Bake time:	Serving size:
1 (9×9-inch) pan	30 to 45 minutes	45 to 50 minutes	1 portion

2 cups pitted and halved fresh cherries

½ cup toasted slivered or sliced almonds

½ vanilla bean

½ cup soft silken tofu

Ener-G Egg Substitute for 2 large eggs

1 cup soy, rice, or almond milk

½ tsp. pure almond extract

1 tsp. pure vanilla extract

¾ cup unbleached cane sugar

¼ cup plus 2 TB. light brown sugar, firmly packed

⅔ cup plus 1 TB. unbleached all-purpose flour

Pinch salt

1 TB. nonhydrogenated vegan margarine, softened

2 TB. vegan confectioners' sugar (optional)

1. Preheat the oven to 350°F. Lightly coat a 9×9-inch baking dish, or a similar-size casserole dish, with cooking oil spray.

2. In a small bowl, combine cherries and almonds. Sprinkle on the bottom of the prepared baking dish.

3. Scrape seeds out of vanilla bean, and discard pod. Set seeds aside.

4. In a blender, add soft silken tofu, egg substitute, soy milk, almond extract, and vanilla extract, and blend on high speed for 1 or 2 minutes or until mixture is smooth and frothy. Add unbleached cane sugar, ¼ cup light brown sugar, ⅔ cup unbleached all-purpose flour, salt, and vanilla bean seeds, and blend for 1 or 2 minutes or until smooth with no lumps.

5. Pour custard gently over cherries and almonds, being careful not to disturb fruit. Bake for 30 minutes.

6. In a small bowl, using a fork, or your fingers, combine remaining 2 tablespoons light brown sugar, 1 tablespoon unbleached all-purpose flour, and vegan margarine.

7. Remove clafoutis from the oven, and sprinkle streusel on top. Return to the oven, and bake for 15 to 20 more minutes or until light brown and slightly puffed and a knife inserted into the center comes out clean. Clafoutis will fall during cooling time; this is normal.

8. Cool on a wire rack for 30 minutes. Dust with vegan confectioners' sugar (if using), and serve warm.

Variation: For **Blueberry Clafoutis,** substitute 2½ cups of fresh (not frozen) blueberries for the cherries.

> **BATTER UP!**
>
> To cut open a vanilla bean, lay it flat on a cutting board. Slice the bean open lengthwise from one end to the other being careful not to slice through it. This will expose thousands of tiny seeds you can scrape out and into pot. Don't waste the pod! Soak it in the soy milk, too. Discard the bean when you're done.

Apple Brown Betty

This Apple Brown Betty has a crispy, crunchy breadcrumb topping inside the apple filling and outside in the streusel-like topping.

Yield:	Prep time:	Bake time:	Serving size:
1 (9×9-inch) pan	30 minutes	48 to 60 minutes	1 portion

3 slices Basic White Bread or Whole-Wheat Bread (recipes in Chapter 7)

4 Cortland, Granny Smith, Empire, Gravenstein, or other hard crisp apples, peeled, cored, and sliced

1 tsp. ground cinnamon

½ cup light brown sugar, firmly packed

¼ cup thawed or frozen apple juice concentrate, not diluted

4 TB. nonhydrogenated vegan margarine, melted

½ tsp. grated lemon zest

¼ cup unbleached cane sugar

¼ tsp. ground nutmeg

¼ tsp. ground ginger

1. Preheat the oven to 350°F. Lightly coat a 9×9-inch baking dish, or a similar-size casserole pan, with cooking oil spray.

2. In a food processor fitted with a cutting blade, grind Basic White Bread until you have fine breadcrumbs. Spread out on a baking sheet, and bake for 8 to 10 minutes or until golden brown.

3. In a large bowl, combine apples, ¼ teaspoon ground cinnamon, ¼ cup light brown sugar, ¾ cup breadcrumbs, and apple juice concentrate. Pour into the prepared pan.

4. In the same bowl, combine melted vegan margarine, grated lemon zest, remaining ¾ cup breadcrumbs, remaining ¾ teaspoon ground cinnamon, remaining ¼ cup light brown sugar, unbleached cane sugar, ground nutmeg, and ground ginger. Using a wooden spoon or spatula, mix until streusel is crumbly. Sprinkle evenly on top of Brown Betty.

5. Bake for 40 to 50 minutes or until filling begins to bubble up around the edges. Cool on a wire rack for at least 30 minutes before serving.

BATTER UP!

Homemade breadcrumbs always taste better, but store-bought bread or breadcrumbs also work in this recipe. Always toast them first to not only crisp them, but also give them a toasty taste.

Cakes and Cupcakes

You can't leave yet! You've come to the sweetest chapters in the book. Pull up a chair and have a slice of the most decadent vegan "cheesecakes" you'll ever taste. The Pumpkin Cheesecake, Chocolate Cheesecake, and New York–style Strawberry Cheesecake recipes are to die for. One bite, and you'll think you're in cheesecake heaven.

Or how about a piece of moist Carrot Cake with "cream cheese" frosting? You know you want to. Strawberry Shortcake, upside-down cakes, and Black Bottom Cupcakes—oh my goodness! And believe it or not, these desserts are all made without butter, eggs, cream cheese, or honey.

And to top it all off, you'll be whipping up a lot of finger-licking-good frostings and icings for all the cakes and cupcakes you're going to be topping. In Part 6, you also learn how to make and decorate simple cupcakes and double-layer cakes.

There's no need to deprive yourself any longer. Have your way with these vegan dessert recipes, and enjoy! After all, life is uncertain, eat vegan dessert first!

Have Your Vegan Cake and Eat It, Too

In This Chapter

- Tips for freezing cakes
- Doing double duty, from cakes to cupcakes
- Quick-and-easy single-layer sheet cakes
- Multi-layer cakes

Just because you're vegan, doesn't mean you can't enjoy baking and eating delicious cake. On the contrary, you can turn just about any cake recipe into a thing of beauty, but it has to taste good, too. There's nothing worse than drooling over a gorgeous three-tier chocolate cake with buttercream frosting, only to bite into a heavy piece of bland cardboard with gritty brown icing.

Substituting vegan ingredients for the butter and egg in recipes can be a snap, but you need to be mindful of the necessary chemical reactions that have to take place to produce a cake with the right texture and taste. The recipes in this chapter have that covered. Plus, they're healthier than store-bought baked goods, or recipes that come out of traditional cookbooks using animal-based products for leavening and flavor.

Freezing Layer Cakes

Most cakes freeze and thaw successfully. However, a few cakes should not be frozen. Cream-, custard-, and pudding-filled cakes are not freezer-friendly. Basic cakes frosted with buttercream, cream cheese frosting, or chocolate icing generally freeze well, provided you take the appropriate steps beforehand.

The best way to freeze cake layers is to leave them unfrosted, plain, and undecorated. After baking, let the cake layers cool completely. Double-wrap the layers with plastic wrap, and place in large zipper-lock bags. You can then store the layers in the freezer for up to 3 to 6 months and decorate them straight out of the freezer.

When wrapping a beautifully decorated cake, take extra care so you don't disturb the icing and decorations. It's a good idea to stick toothpicks in the cake to keep the wrap from messing it up. After loosely wrapping the cake, return it to the freezer for no longer than 3 months.

Individually decorated cake slices take between 20 to 30 minutes to thaw and need no special treatment while thawing. Simply leave slices on a plate to thaw on the counter.

Whole or partially decorated cakes, however, need extra care, especially if the cake is frosted with cream cheese frosting. Thaw it overnight in the refrigerator until you're ready to serve it. Depending on the size of the cake, it could take several hours to completely thaw.

BAKER'S BONUS

For instant satisfaction later, slice the cake and freeze it in individual servings. This way, you can remove a piece from the freezer, defrost it, and enjoy it whenever the urge for birthday cake hits!

Yummy Vegan Cupcakes

Cupcakes are the best thing that ever happened to cake batter! Most of the following vegan cake recipes can be made into cupcakes without much fuss. The only additional equipment you need is cupcake pans and paper cupcake liners to bake them in. Cupcakes take less time in the oven, so be sure to read the directions carefully.

Mix and match the frostings, and decorate them any way you wish. Or eat them plain! They're *that* good!

Spice Cake

Deliciously moist, this classy, quick-and-easy cake gets its spiciness from allspice, cinnamon, and cloves.

Yield:	Prep time:	Bake time:	Serving size:
1 (9×13-inch) cake, 2 (9×2-inch) round cakes, or 24 to 30 cup- cakes	30 to 40 minutes	20 to 50 minutes	1 slice cake, or 1 cupcake

2½ cups unbleached all-purpose flour	1 tsp. salt
½ cup *cornstarch*	2 cups light brown sugar, firmly packed
2 tsp. baking soda	⅔ cup canola or vegetable oil
2 tsp. ground allspice	2 TB. white or apple cider vinegar
2 tsp. ground cinnamon	2 cups lukewarm water
1 tsp. ground cloves	

1. Preheat the oven to 350°F. Lightly coat a 9×13-inch baking pan with cooking oil spray, or line 24 to 30 muffin cups with paper cupcake liners. If using 9×2-inch round cake pans, oil 2 pans and line the bottoms with parchment paper.

2. Into a medium bowl, sift together unbleached all-purpose flour, cornstarch, baking soda, ground allspice, ground cinnamon, ground cloves, and salt, or blend with a wire whisk. Add light brown sugar, and blend with a wooden spoon or a whisk, breaking up lumps as needed.

3. In a large bowl, and using an electric mixer fitted with a paddle attachment on medium speed, mix canola oil, white vinegar, and lukewarm water. Reduce speed to low, add ½ of dry ingredients, and mix well, scraping the bowl as needed with a rubber spatula. Add remaining dry ingredients, and mix for 1 or 2 more minutes, scraping the bowl as needed, or until batter is nice and smooth with no lumps.

4. Pour batter into the prepared pans, or divide evenly among the cupcake tins, filling each cup about ¾ full. Bake 9×13-inch cake for 40 to 50 minutes or until a toothpick inserted into the center comes out clean. Bake round cake layers for 25 to 35 minutes. Bake cupcakes for 20 to 30 minutes or until tops spring back when lightly touched.

5. Cool 9×13-inch cake and cupcakes completely on wire racks before frosting or freezing. Cool round layers and cupcakes 10 minutes before loosening from the pans. Gently remove round layers and cupcakes from the pans, and cool completely on wire racks. Cool 9×13-inch cake in its pan.

6. Frost with your choice of frosting (try Penuche Frosting or Buttercream Frosting, recipes in Chapter 21), or double-wrap in plastic and freeze.

VEGAN VOCAB

Most commonly used as a thickener in gravies, soups, and puddings, **cornstarch** is sometimes blended with flour in cookies, cakes, and pastries to produce more tender—and some bakers swear—moister baked goods. Cornstarch, also called cornflour, is tasteless, imparting no flavor in anything you use it in.

Carrot Cake

This classic carrot cake is nice and spicy with cinnamon and vegan buttermilk. It's a solid, sturdy cake, so it can handle some extra-delicious ingredients like raisins, coconut, or chopped nuts.

Yield:	Prep time:	Bake time:	Serving size:
1 (9×13-inch) cake, 2 (9×2-inch) round cakes, or 24 to 30 cupcakes	40 minutes	20 to 60 minutes	1 slice cake, or 1 cupcake

2⅓ cups unbleached all-purpose flour

1½ tsp. ground cinnamon

1½ tsp. baking soda

½ tsp. salt

½ cup canola or vegetable oil

½ cup Vegan Buttermilk (recipe in Chapter 2)

1 cup Florida Crystals or unbleached cane sugar

Egg substitute for 3 large eggs (Ener-G or Bob's Red Mill works best)

1 tsp. pure vanilla extract

2⅓ cups (about 5 medium to large) grated carrots

½ cup raisins (optional)

¼ cup unsweetened shredded coconut (optional)

1 cup walnuts or toasted pecans, finely chopped (optional)

1. Preheat the oven to 350°F. Grease and flour 1 (9×13-inch) baking pan or 2 (9×2-inch) round cake pans with nonhydrogenated shortening, tapping out excess flour. Or line 24 to 30 muffin cups with paper cupcake liners.

2. Into a medium bowl, sift together unbleached all-purpose flour, ground cinnamon, baking soda, and salt, or blend with a wire whisk.

3. In a large bowl, and using an electric mixer fitted with a paddle attachment on medium speed, beat canola oil, Vegan Buttermilk, Florida Crystals, egg substitute, and vanilla extract for 1 or 2 minutes or until light and fluffy. Scrape down the sides of the bowl using a rubber spatula.

4. Add grated carrots, and mix for 1 or 2 minutes or until well blended. Reduce speed to low, add ½ of dry ingredients, and mix well, scraping the bowl as needed. Add remaining dry ingredients, and mix for 1 or 2 more minutes until batter is nice and smooth with no lumps. Be careful not to overmix. *Fold* in raisins (if using) and shredded coconut (if using).

5. Pour batter into the prepared pans, or divide evenly among the cupcake tins, filling each cup ¾ full. Bake 9×13-inch cake for 50 to 60 minutes or until a toothpick inserted into the center comes out clean. Bake round cake layers for 35 to 45 minutes. Bake cupcakes for 20 to 30 minutes or until tops spring back when lightly touched.

6. Cool 9×13-inch cake and cupcakes completely on wire racks before frosting or freezing. Cool round layers and cupcakes 10 minutes before loosening from the pans. Gently remove round layers and cupcakes from the pans, and cool completely on wire racks. Cool 9×13-inch cake in its pan.

7. Frost with your choice of frosting (try Vegan Cream Cheese Frosting or Penuche Frosting, recipes in Chapter 21), and decorate the sides of round cake or top of 9×13-inch cake with chopped walnuts (if using). Or double-wrap in plastic and freeze.

VEGAN VOCAB

To **fold** is to combine a dense mixture with a light mixture using a circular action from the middle of the bowl. Don't overmix; the idea is to keep some of the air in the batter so the cake isn't heavy and tough.

Basic Yellow Cake

This soft, moist, and "buttery" yellow cake might be called "basic," but you can consider it a blank canvas for extra-special desserts like Boston Cream Pie, or a refreshing Strawberry Cream Cake. Let the culinary artist in you emerge and create something delicious!

Yield:	Prep time:	Bake time:	Serving size:
1 (9×13-inch) cake, 2 (9×2-inch) round cakes, or 24 to 30 cupcakes	40 minutes	20 to 45 minutes	1 slice cake, or 1 cupcake

3 cups cake flour

2 TB. cornstarch

1½ tsp. aluminum-free baking powder

1 tsp. baking soda

½ tsp. salt

¾ cup nonhydrogenated vegan margarine, softened

1½ cups unbleached cane sugar

Egg substitute for 3 large eggs (Ener-G Egg Replacer or Bob's Red Mill works best)

2 tsp. pure vanilla extract

1½ cup Vegan Buttermilk (recipe in Chapter 2)

1. Preheat the oven to 350°F. Grease and flour 1 (9×13-inch) baking pan or 2 (9×2-inch) round cake pans with nonhydrogenated shortening, tapping out excess flour. Or line 24 to 30 muffin cups with paper cupcake liners.

2. Into a large bowl, sift together cake flour, cornstarch, aluminum-free baking powder, baking soda, and salt, or blend with a wire whisk.

3. In a separate large bowl, and using an electric mixer fitted with a paddle attachment on medium speed, beat vegan margarine and unbleached cane sugar for 1 or 2 minutes or until light and fluffy. Scrape down the sides of the bowl using a rubber spatula. Add egg substitute a little at a time, beating after each addition. Add vanilla extract, and mix well, scraping the bowl once more.

4. Reduce speed to low, and add dry ingredients 1 cup at a time, alternating with Vegan Buttermilk, until well blended and free of lumps. Do not overmix.

5. Pour batter into the prepared pans, or divide evenly among the cupcake tins, filling each cup ¾ full. Bake 9×13-inch cake for 35 to 45 minutes or until a toothpick inserted into the center comes out clean. Bake round cake layers for 30 to 40 minutes. Bake cupcakes for 20 to 30 minutes or until tops spring back when lightly touched.

6. Cool 9×13-inch cake and cupcakes completely on wire racks before frosting or freezing. Cool round layers and cupcakes 10 minutes before loosening from the pans. Gently remove round layers and cupcakes from the pans, and cool completely on wire racks. Cool 9×13-inch cake in its pan.

7. Fill and frost round layers with your choice of frosting (try Vanilla Bean Buttercream Frosting, variation in Chapter 21; or Chocolate Ganache Icing, recipe in Chapter 22), or double-wrap in plastic and freeze.

Variations: For **Strawberry Cream Cake,** omit the frosting, and spread a thin layer of seedless strawberry preserves on the bottom of a 9×2-inch round cake layer. Arrange a layer of lightly sweetened sliced fresh strawberries on top. Place another 9×2-inch round cake layer on top, and decorate it with nondairy whipped topping and more strawberries. For **Boston Cream Pie,** spread about 2 cups vegan custard filling between 2 (9×2-inch) round yellow cake layers. Chill for 2 hours. Pour or spread Chocolate Ganache Icing (recipe in Chapter 22) or Chocolate Frosting (recipe in Chapter 21) on the top of the cold cake. Top with a perfect fresh whole strawberry.

Devil's Food Chocolate Cake

Dark, moist cake layers taste heavenly when filled and frosted. Decorate this death-by-chocolate devil's food cake with chocolate shavings, chopped walnuts, and a cherry on top!

Yield:	Prep time:	Bake time:	Serving size:
1 (9×13-inch) cake, 2 (9×2-inch) round cakes, or 24 to 30 cupcakes	40 minutes	20 to 55 minutes	1 slice cake, or 1 cupcake

2 cups unbleached all-purpose flour

1 cup *natural cocoa powder*

1½ tsp. baking soda

½ tsp. salt

½ cup nonhydrogenated vegan margarine, softened

1 cup light brown sugar, firmly packed

1 cup Florida Crystals or unbleached cane sugar

Egg substitute for 3 large eggs (Ener-G Egg Replacer or Bob's Red Mill works best)

1½ tsp. pure vanilla extract

1½ cup Vegan Buttermilk (recipe in Chapter 2)

1. Preheat the oven to 350°F. Grease and flour 1 (9×13-inch) baking pan or 2 (9×2-inch) round cake pans with nonhydrogenated shortening, tapping out excess flour. Or line 24 to 30 muffin cups with paper cupcake liners.

2. Into a large bowl, sift together unbleached all-purpose flour, natural cocoa powder, baking soda, and salt, or blend with a wire whisk.

3. In a separate large bowl, and using an electric mixer fitted with a paddle attachment on medium speed, beat vegan margarine with light brown sugar and Florida Crystals for 1 or 2 minutes or until light. Scrape down the sides of the bowl using a rubber spatula. Add egg substitute a little at a time. Add vanilla extract, and beat again until light and fluffy, scraping the bowl as needed.

4. Reduce speed to low, and add ½ of dry ingredients to batter, alternating with ½ of vegan buttermilk, until well blended. Add remaining dry ingredients and Vegan Buttermilk, and mix for 1 minute or only until cake batter is nice and smooth and free of lumps. Do not overmix.

5. Pour batter into the prepared pans, or divide evenly among the cupcake tins, filling each cup ¾ full.

6. Bake 9×13-inch cake for 45 to 55 minutes or until a toothpick inserted into the center comes out clean. Bake the 2 (9×2-inch) round cake layers for 25 to 35 minutes. Bake cupcakes for 20 to 30 minutes or until tops spring back when lightly touched.

7. Cool 9×13-inch cake and cupcakes completely on wire racks before frosting or freezing. Cool round layers and cupcakes 10 minutes before loosening from the pans. Gently remove round layers and cupcakes from the pans, and cool completely on wire racks. Cool 9×13-inch cake in its pan.

8. Frost with your choice of frosting (try Chocolate Frosting or Peanut Butter Frosting, recipes in Chapter 21), or double-wrap in plastic and freeze.

VEGAN VOCAB

Natural cocoa powder has a stronger, more pronounced chocolate flavor—which is good when using in recipes where intensity is desired. Dutch process cocoa has been treated to neutralize the acidity, resulting in a milder chocolate flavor. Either cocoa is fine for this recipe, although some studies say natural cocoa contains more antioxidants.

Peanut Butter Cake

This rich, moist cake is made with smooth peanut butter, and decorated with vegan peanut butter cups and chopped peanuts.

Yield:	Prep time:	Bake time:	Serving size:
1 (9×13-inch) cake, 2 (9×2-inch) round cakes, or 24 to 30 cupcakes	40 minutes	20 to 50 minutes	1 slice cake, or 1 cupcake

2 cups unbleached all-purpose flour or whole-wheat flour

1 TB. aluminum-free baking powder

1 TB. cornstarch

1 tsp. salt

½ cup nonhydrogenated vegan margarine, softened

1½ cups Florida Crystals or unbleached cane sugar

¼ cup all-natural smooth peanut butter

½ cup soft silken tofu

1 tsp. pure vanilla extract

Egg substitute for 2 large eggs (Ener-G Egg Replacer or Bob's Red Mill works best)

1 cup soy or rice milk

12 to 14 mini vegan peanut butter cups

¼ cup chopped peanuts (optional)

1. Preheat the oven to 350°F. Grease and flour 1 (9×13-inch) baking pan or 2 (9×2-inch) round cake pans with nonhydrogenated shortening, tapping out excess flour. Or line 24 to 30 muffin cups with paper cupcake liners.

2. Into a medium bowl, sift together unbleached all-purpose flour, aluminum-free baking powder, cornstarch, and salt, or blend with a wire whisk.

3. In a large bowl, and using an electric mixer fitted with a paddle attachment on medium speed, beat vegan margarine and Florida Crystals for 1 or 2 minutes or until creamy. Scrape down the sides of the bowl using a rubber spatula. Add soft silken tofu, smooth peanut butter and vanilla extract, and beat again. Add egg substitute a little at a time, and beat for 1 or 2 minutes or until light and fluffy, scraping the bowl as needed using a rubber spatula.

4. Reduce speed to low, and add ½ of dry ingredients to batter, alternating with ½ of soy milk, until well blended. Add remaining dry ingredients and soy milk, and mix for 1 minute or only until cake batter is nice and smooth with no lumps. Be careful not to overmix. Scrape down the sides of the bowl.

5. Pour batter into the prepared pans, or divide evenly among the cupcake tins, filling each cup about ¾ full. Bake 9×13-inch cake for 40 to 50 minutes or until a toothpick inserted into the center comes out clean. Bake round cake layers for 35 to 45 minutes. Bake cupcakes for 20 to 30 minutes or until tops spring back when lightly touched. Do not overbake.

6. Cool 9×13-inch cake and cupcakes completely on wire racks before frosting or freezing. Cool round layers and cupcakes 10 minutes before loosening from the pans. Gently remove round layers and cupcakes from the pans, and cool completely on wire racks. Cool 9×13-inch cake in its pan.

7. Fill and frost cake with your choice of frosting (try Peanut Butter Frosting, recipe in Chapter 21; Vanilla Bean Buttercream Frosting, variation in Chapter 21; or Chocolate Ganache Icing, recipe in Chapter 22). Decorate with mini vegan peanut butter cups and chopped peanuts (if using). Or double-wrap in plastic and freeze.

BATTER UP!

Check your natural food store or the organic section in your local supermarket for vegan peanut butter cups. They'll dress up this Peanut Butter Cake, and you'll get lots of compliments!

Coconut Cake

Snow-white cake layers frosted with coconut-infused buttercream icing and decorated with fragrant toasted coconut, this cake is a real show-stopper and is especially pretty when decorated for spring and summer parties.

Yield:	Prep time:	Bake time:	Serving size:
1 (9×13-inch) cake, 2 (9×2-inch) round cakes, or 24 to 30 cup-cakes	40 to 50 minutes	20 to 45 minutes	1 slice cake, or 1 cupcake

2¼ cups cake flour

1 TB. aluminum-free baking powder

1 TB. cornstarch

½ tsp. salt

½ cup nonhydrogenated vegan margarine, softened

1½ cups unbleached cane sugar

Egg substitute for 2 large eggs (Ener-G Egg Replacer or Bob's Red Mill works best)

2 tsp. pure coconut extract

¾ cup nondairy vanilla rice milk

1 cup shredded unsweetened coconut, toasted (optional)

1. Preheat the oven to 350°F. Grease and flour 1 (9×13-inch) baking pan or 2 (9×2-inch) round cake pans with nonhydrogenated shortening, tapping out excess flour. Or line 24 to 30 muffin cups with paper cupcake liners.

2. Into a medium bowl, sift together cake flour, aluminum-free baking powder, cornstarch, and salt, or blend with a wire whisk.

3. In a large bowl, and using an electric mixer fitted with a paddle attachment on medium speed, beat vegan margarine and unbleached cane sugar for 1 or 2 minutes or until creamy. Scrape down the sides of the bowl using a rubber spatula. Add egg substitute a little at a time, and beat for 1 or 2 minutes or until light and fluffy, scraping the bowl as needed using a rubber spatula. Add coconut extract, and beat again.

4. Reduce speed to low, and add ½ of dry ingredients to batter, alternating with ½ of vanilla rice milk, until well blended. Add remaining dry ingredients and rice milk, and mix for 1 minute or only until cake batter is nice and smooth with no lumps. Be careful not to overmix. Scrape down the sides of the bowl.

5. Pour batter into the prepared pans, or divide evenly among the cupcake tins, filling each cup about ¾ full. Bake 9×13-inch cake for 35 to 45 minutes or until a toothpick inserted into the center comes out clean. Bake round cake layers for 25 to 35 minutes. Bake cupcakes for 20 to 30 minutes or until tops spring back when lightly touched. Do not overbake.

6. Cool 9×13-inch cake and cupcakes completely on wire racks before frosting or freezing. Cool round layers and cupcakes 10 minutes before loosening from the pans. Gently remove round layers and cupcakes from the pans, and cool completely on wire racks. Cool 9×13-inch cake in its pan.

7. Fill and frost cake with your choice of frosting (try Coconut Frosting, recipe in Chapter 21; or Vanilla Bean Buttercream Frosting, variation in Chapter 21). Pat toasted coconut all around the sides, pressing lightly to adhere. Save a small amount to garnish top of cake. Or double-wrap in plastic and freeze.

DOUGH-NOT

To toast coconut, place on a baking sheet, and bake in a 350°F oven for 8 to 12 minutes, stirring every 3 or 4 minutes, or until golden brown and fragrant. Keep an eye on the coconut because it can burn very quickly. Let the coconut cool before adding to the cake.

Mocha Cake

With this cake, you can have your chocolate cake and a cup of coffee in one. The best of both worlds come together in a delicious mocha chocolate cake with a mellow coffee flavor.

Yield:	Prep time:	Bake time:	Serving size:
1 (9×13-inch) cake, 2 (9×2-inch) round cakes, or 24 to 30 cupcakes	40 to 50 minutes	20 to 55 minutes	1 slice cake, or 1 cupcake

2½ cups unbleached all-purpose flour

½ cup cornstarch

6 TB. Dutch cocoa powder

2 tsp. baking soda

1 tsp. salt

2 cups light brown sugar, firmly packed

⅔ cup canola or vegetable oil

2 tsp. dry instant coffee

2 TB. white or apple cider vinegar

1 tsp. pure vanilla extract

2 cups water, at room temperature

Chocolate shavings

1. Preheat the oven to 350°F. Grease and flour 1 (9×13-inch) baking pan or 2 (9×2-inch) round cake pans with nonhydrogenated shortening, tapping out excess flour. Or line 24 to 30 muffin cups with paper cupcake liners.

2. Into a medium bowl, sift unbleached all-purpose flour, cornstarch, Dutch cocoa powder, baking soda, and salt, or blend with a wire whisk. Add light brown sugar, and blend with a wooden spoon or a whisk, breaking up lumps as needed.

3. In a large bowl, and using an electric mixer fitted with a paddle attachment on medium speed, mix canola oil, dry instant coffee, white vinegar, vanilla extract, and water for 1 or 2 minutes or until well blended. Scrape down the sides of the bowl using a rubber spatula.

4. Reduce speed to low, add ½ of dry ingredients to liquid ingredients, and mix to combine, scraping the bowl as needed with a rubber spatula. Add remaining dry ingredients, and mix for 1 or 2 minutes, scraping down the bowl, until batter is nice and smooth with no lumps.

5. Pour batter into the prepared pans, or divide evenly among the cupcake tins, filling each cup about ¾ full. Bake 9×13-inch cake for 45 to 55 minutes or until a toothpick inserted into the center comes out clean. Bake round cake layers for 25 to 35 minutes. Bake cupcakes for 20 to 30 minutes or until tops spring back when lightly touched. Do not overbake.

6. Cool 9×13-inch cake and cupcakes completely on wire racks before frosting or freezing. Cool round layers and cupcakes 10 minutes before loosening from the pans. Gently remove round layers and cupcakes from the pans, and cool completely on wire racks. Cool 9×13-inch cake in its pan.

7. Frost with your choice of frosting (try Chocolate Frosting, recipe in Chapter 21; Vanilla Bean Buttercream Frosting, variation in Chapter 21; or Chocolate Ganache Icing, recipe in Chapter 22), and sprinkle with chocolate shavings. Or double-wrap in plastic and freeze.

Variations: For **Macho Mocha Cake,** add 1 or 2 teaspoons instant coffee to a batch of Chocolate Frosting (recipe in Chapter 21) and decorate. For **Mexican Chocolate Cake,** add ½ teaspoon ground cinnamon and ¼ teaspoon ground chili powder to the cake batter.

BAKER'S BONUS

Using dry instant coffee is an easy way to add a strong coffee flavor without adding extra liquid to a recipe. Crush the coffee crystals, and add them to the liquid in the recipe before using so they dissolve faster.

Red Velvet Cake

This deep red cake with a hint of cocoa and cinnamon makes for a very striking cake when decorated with creamy white frosting. This is the perfect party cake for Valentine's Day or Christmas.

Yield:	Prep time:	Bake time:	Serving size:
1 (8×2-inch) cake, 1 (8×8-inch) round cakes, or 12 cupcakes	40 minutes	20 to 45 minutes	1 slice cake, or 1 cupcake

1 tsp. pure vanilla extract

¾ cup Vegan Buttermilk (recipe in Chapter 2)

2 cups unbleached all-purpose flour, or ½ unbleached all-purpose flour and ½ whole-wheat pastry flour

2 TB. Dutch cocoa powder

½ tsp. salt

1¼ cups Florida Crystals or unbleached cane sugar

¾ cup canola or vegetable oil

Egg substitute for 2 large eggs (Ener-G Egg Replacer or Bob's Red Mill works best)

1 tsp. all-natural red food coloring

1 tsp. baking soda

1 tsp. white or cider vinegar

1. Preheat the oven to 350°F. Grease and flour 1 (8×2-inch) round cake pan, or 1 (8×8-inch) baking pan with nonhydrogenated shortening, tapping out excess flour. Or line 12 muffin cups with paper cupcake liners.

2. In a small bowl, whisk together vanilla extract and Vegan Buttermilk.

3. Into a medium bowl, sift together unbleached all-purpose flour, Dutch cocoa powder, and salt, or blend with a wire whisk.

4. In a large bowl, and using an electric mixer fitted with a paddle attachment on medium speed, mix Florida Crystals and canola oil for 1 or 2 minutes or until light. Add egg substitute and all-natural food coloring, and whisk again until well blended and smooth, scraping the bowl as needed using a rubber spatula.

5. Reduce speed to low, and add ½ of dry ingredients to batter, alternating with ½ of vegan vanilla buttermilk mixture, until well blended. Add remaining dry ingredients and remaining vegan vanilla buttermilk, and mix 1 or 2 minutes or only until cake batter is nice and smooth with no lumps.

6. In a small cup, mix baking soda and white vinegar. With a rubber spatula, gently fold mixture into batter, blending well, but be careful not to overmix. Scrape down the sides of the bowl.

7. Pour batter into the prepared pan, or divide evenly among the cupcake tins, filling each cup about ¾ full. Bake 8×2-inch round cake layer for 25 to 35 minutes. Bake 8×8-inch cake for 30 to 45 minutes or until a toothpick inserted in the center comes out clean. Bake cupcakes for 20 to 30 minutes or until tops spring back when lightly touched.

8. Cool square cake and cupcakes completely on wire racks before frosting or freezing. Cool round layer and cupcakes 10 minutes before loosening from the pans. Gently remove round layer and cupcakes from the pans, and cool completely on wire racks. Cool square cake in its pan.

9. Frost with your choice of frosting (try Vegan Cream Cheese Frosting, recipe in Chapter 21; or Vanilla Bean Buttercream Frosting, variation in Chapter 21), or double-wrap in plastic and freeze.

BAKER'S BONUS

You can double this recipe to make a 9×13-inch cake, 24 cupcakes, or a 9-inch double layer cake.

German Apple Cake

This old-fashioned "butter" brown sugar cake has chunks of apples baked on top of the batter that's seasoned with cinnamon and nutmeg and topped with cinnamon sugar and confectioners' sugar.

Yield:	Prep time:	Bake time:	Serving size:
1 (8×8-inch) cake	20 to 30 minutes	35 to 45 minutes	1 piece

1 cup unbleached all-purpose flour

½ cup whole-wheat pastry flour

2½ tsp. aluminum-free baking powder

¼ tsp. salt

¾ tsp. ground cinnamon

¼ tsp. ground nutmeg

¼ cup nonhydrogenated vegan margarine, softened

¾ cup light brown sugar, firmly packed

Egg substitute for 2 large eggs

¼ cup canola oil

1 tsp. pure vanilla extract

3 medium Cortland, Granny Smith, Empire, Gravenstein, or other hard crisp apples, peeled, cored, and quartered lengthwise

1 TB. unbleached cane sugar

2 TB. vegan confectioners' sugar (optional)

1. Preheat the oven to 350°F. Grease and flour 1 (8×8-inch) baking pan with nonhydrogenated shortening, tapping out excess flour.

2. Into a medium bowl, sift together unbleached all-purpose flour, whole-wheat pastry flour, aluminum-free baking powder, salt, ½ teaspoon ground cinnamon, and ground nutmeg, or blend with a wire whisk.

3. In a large bowl, and using an electric mixer fitted with a paddle attachment on medium speed, beat vegan margarine and light brown sugar for 1 or 2 minutes or until creamy. Scrape down the sides of the bowl using a rubber spatula. Add egg substitute a little at a time, and beat for 1 or 2 minutes or until light and fluffy, scraping the bowl as needed using a rubber spatula. Add canola oil and vanilla extract, and beat again.

4. Reduce speed to low, and add dry ingredients, mixing for 1 minute, or only until cake batter is nice and smooth. Be careful not to overmix. Scrape down the sides of the bowl.

5. Pour cake batter into the prepared pan, smoothing top if necessary.

6. With a sharp knife, slice vertically into quartered apples almost all the way through. Place apples on top of cake batter, leaving room between apples to fan out during baking. Press lightly into batter.

7. In a small bowl, mix unbleached cane sugar with remaining ¼ teaspoon ground cinnamon. Sprinkle cinnamon sugar evenly over top of cake.

8. Bake for 35 to 45 minutes or until golden brown and a toothpick inserted into the center comes out clean. Cool completely on a wire rack before sprinkling with confectioners' sugar (if using) or frosting with your choice of frosting (try Confectioners' Sugar Drizzle, recipe in Chapter 22).

DOUGH-NOT

When slicing through the apples, be careful not to cut all the way through. The cake looks pretty when the apples fan out naturally during baking.

Maple Walnut Cake

Pure maple syrup and maple extract give this cake a delicious mellow flavor. Decorated with chopped walnuts, this cake is a winner!

Yield:	Prep time:	Bake time:	Serving size:
1 (9×13-inch) cake, 2 (9×2-inch) round cakes, or 24 to 30 cupcakes	40 to 45 minutes	20 to 45 minutes	1 slice cake, or 1 cupcake

2½ cups unbleached all-purpose flour

½ cup cornstarch

2 tsp. baking soda

1 TB. ground cinnamon

1 tsp. salt

2 cups light brown sugar, firmly packed

⅓ cup canola or vegetable oil

⅓ cup pure maple syrup, dark amber or Grade B

2 tsp. pure maple extract

2 TB. white or apple cider vinegar

2 cups lukewarm water

1 cup walnuts, finely chopped (optional)

1. Preheat the oven to 325°F. Lightly coat a 9×13-inch baking pan with cooking oil spray, or line 24 to 30 muffin cups with paper cupcake liners. If using 9×2-inch round cake pans, oil 2 pans and line the bottoms with parchment paper.

2. Into a medium bowl, sift together unbleached all-purpose flour, cornstarch, baking soda, ground cinnamon, and salt, or blend with a wire whisk. Add light brown sugar, and blend with a wooden spoon or a whisk, breaking up lumps as needed.

3. In a large bowl, and using an electric mixer fitted with a paddle attachment on medium speed, mix canola oil, maple syrup, maple extract, white vinegar, and lukewarm water. Reduce speed to low, add ½ of dry ingredients to liquid ingredients, and mix to combine, scraping the bowl as needed with a rubber spatula. Add remaining dry ingredients, and mix for 1 or 2 more minutes, scraping down the bowl, until batter is nice and smooth with no lumps.

4. Pour batter into the prepared pans, or divide evenly among the cupcake tins, filling each cup about ¾ full. Bake 9×13-inch cake for 40 to 45 minutes or until a toothpick inserted into the center comes out clean. Bake round cake layers for 25 to 35 minutes. Bake cupcakes for 20 to 30 minutes or until tops spring back when lightly touched.

5. Cool 9×13-inch cake and cupcakes completely on wire racks before frosting or freezing. Cool round layers and cupcakes 10 minutes before loosening from the pans. Gently remove round layers and cupcakes from the pans, and cool completely on wire racks. Cool 9×13-inch cake in its pan.

6. Frost with your choice of frosting (try Maple Walnut Frosting, variation in Chapter 21), and sprinkle chopped walnuts (if using), over top of cake. Or double-wrap in plastic and freeze.

BATTER UP!

Don't skimp and get the cheap maple syrup for this recipe. Go for the real stuff!

Lemon Bundt Cake

This moist "sour cream" pound cake, flavored with fresh-squeezed lemon juice and lemon zest, is baked in a Bundt pan, and drizzled with lemon powdered sugar glaze. It's sweet and tart and very pretty.

Yield:	Prep time:	Bake time:	Serving size:
1 (12-cup) Bundt cake	40 minutes	50 to 60 minutes	1 slice

3 TB. plain vegan breadcrumbs, homemade or store-bought, finely crushed

3 cups unbleached all-purpose flour

2 tsp. cornstarch

½ tsp. baking soda

¼ tsp. salt

¾ cup nonhydrogenated vegan margarine, softened

2½ cups unbleached cane sugar

Egg substitute for 3 large eggs

2 tsp. pure lemon extract

1½ TB. grated lemon zest

1 cup *vegan sour cream*

1 cup vegan confectioners' sugar

2 TB. fresh lemon juice

1. Preheat the oven to 350°F. Grease and flour 1 large (12-cup) Bundt cake pan with nonhydrogenated shortening, tapping out excess flour. Sprinkle the inside of the pan with breadcrumbs.

2. Into a medium bowl, sift together unbleached all-purpose flour, cornstarch, baking soda, and salt, or blend with a wire whisk.

3. In a large bowl, with an electric mixer fitted with a paddle attachment on medium-high speed, beat softened vegan margarine until creamy. Add unbleached cane sugar ½ cup at a time, and beat until light, scraping down the sides of the bowl with a rubber spatula as necessary. Add egg substitute a little at a time, beating after each addition. Add lemon extract and lemon zest, and scrape the bowl once more.

4. Reduce speed to low, and add ½ of dry ingredients to batter until well blended. Add remaining dry ingredients, and mix for 1 minute or only until cake batter is nice and smooth with no lumps. Scrape down the sides of the bowl again.

5. Fold in vegan sour cream with a rubber spatula, making sure to incorporate well. Be careful not to overmix.

6. Pour batter into the prepared pan, and bake for 50 to 60 minutes or until a toothpick inserted into center comes out clean. Let cool in the pan for about 10 minutes, and gently turn out onto a wire rack to cool completely.

7. In a small bowl, mix vegan confectioners' sugar and lemon juice with a spoon until smooth. Drizzle icing over cake, and let dry before serving.

VEGAN VOCAB

Vegan sour cream is a unique blend of tofu, lemon juice, oil, vinegar, and salt that, when blended together, makes a product very similar to regular dairy yogurt. It can be substituted in most recipes that call for sour cream with good results.

Hot Fudge Pudding Cake

Dark cocoa, brown sugar, and soy milk combined with hot water produces a gooey pudding that makes this chocolaty dessert simply irresistible!

Yield:	Prep time:	Bake time:	Serving size:
1 (8×8-inch) cake	15 to 20 minutes	45 to 50 minutes	1 piece

1 cup unbleached all-purpose flour	2 TB. canola oil
2 tsp. aluminum-free baking powder	1 cup walnuts, finely chopped (optional)
¼ tsp. salt	1 cup light brown sugar, firmly packed
¾ cup unbleached cane sugar	
2 TB. plus ¼ cup natural cocoa powder	1¾ cups hot water
½ cup soy milk	

1. Preheat the oven to 350°F. Lightly coat 1 (8×8-inch) baking pan or casserole dish with cooking oil spray.

2. In a medium bowl, and with a wooden spoon, mix together unbleached all-purpose flour, baking powder, salt, unbleached cane sugar, and 2 tablespoons natural cocoa powder. Add soy milk, canola oil, and walnuts (if using), and mix well. Spread cake batter in the baking dish. Batter will be very thick, and you might need a spatula to spread it.

3. In the same bowl, mix light brown sugar and remaining ¼ cup natural cocoa powder, and sprinkle it evenly over cake batter.

4. Pour hot water over batter very slowly, being careful not to disturb batter. Do not stir in water. Let water sit on top in a puddle.

5. Bake for 45 to 50 minutes. Do not overbake. Pudding will be jiggly but will set up as it cools.

6. Cool for 10 minutes on a wire rack. Serve warm or cool with vegan whipped topping or vanilla rice ice cream.

BATTER UP!

This cake magically makes its own pudding as it bakes. The preparation is a little strange, in that the hot water sits on top of the batter in a messy, gooey puddle. Do not be tempted to stir it in. This is not a mistake. As the pudding bakes, the water mixes with the batter and forms its own rich, chocolate pudding, just like magic!

Cheesecakes and Shortcakes

In This Chapter

- Perfect vegan cheesecakes
- Sweet and satisfying shortcakes
- Unbelievable upside-down cakes

Ahhh, cheesecake! One of the basic food groups for sure. But what do vegans eat when the craving for cheesecake hits? How do they get their cheesecake fix without straying from their diet?

Well, cheesecakes can be made vegan, but generally speaking, most vegan cheesecakes are gummy and tasteless. No more! Whether you're a vegan or not, this chapter will change your mind and make a vegan cheesecake-lover out of you!

Making the Perfect Vegan Cheesecake

Have you ever made cheesecake before? If you have, you've more than likely lamented, "Why did my cheesecake crack?!" Followed by, "Now how do I fix it?" You're not alone. This is one of the most common cheesecake complaints—and a reason some bakers can't be bothered to make cheesecakes. But if you follow the tips and tricks I share with you in the following pages, you'll soon be making the best vegan cheesecakes ever.

The vegan cheesecake recipes in this chapter rely on alternative products to mimic the taste and texture of full-fat dairy cream cheese and sour cream. With the addition of soy-based cream cheese, real-tasting cheesecake is now possible. Thank goodness for tofu!

But what about a binder to hold the cheesecake together when eggs are off the list? That's where cornstarch and egg replacements come in. The Strawberry Cheesecake and Pumpkin Cheesecake recipes use Ener-G Egg Replacer, which you can find at most supermarkets and health food stores.

Experimenting with other egg substitutes can yield varying results; however, some good replacements are available, such as Ener-G Egg Replacer, and Bob's Red Mill All Natural Egg Replacer. I don't recommend using the Flaxseed Egg Substitute (recipe in Chapter 2) in these cheesecake recipes because it adds graininess to the cheesecake as well as changes its color.

Up till now, we've used unbleached cane sugar in these vegan recipes. While this is the preferred product for most recipes in this book, it is darker than its cousin, white granulated sugar. For the sake of a beautiful cheesecake, you can use granulated vegan cane sugar. Look for it at the health food store. Be sure the package says it's vegan and not processed with animal-based bone char. There are some good vegan sugar products available, you just have to hunt them down. The vegan cane sugar is nice and white, and suitable for the cheesecake recipes in this chapter.

BATTER UP!

The Chocolate Cheesecake doesn't require any egglike product because the vegan chocolate holds it together.

Other than the Chocolate Cheesecake, which uses a 9-inch pie pan, springform pans are the preferred pans for making cheesecakes. Using the spring hinge, take the pan apart, line the bottom plate with aluminum foil, and reassemble the pan. Pull the excess foil up and around the pan to prevent any batter from leaking into the oven, and spray the sides and bottom with vegetable shortening spray.

When it comes to mixing, a heavy-duty stand mixer or handheld electric mixer can take on heavy cheesecake batter with ease, but be careful not to overmix. Too much air in the batter causes bubbles that can lead to cracks. Mix just until creamy and all lumps are gone.

Cheesecakes benefit from baking with a pan of hot water in the bottom of the oven. As the oven heats, the water in the pan evaporates and adds moisture to the oven.

Fluctuations in oven temperature can result in unsightly cracks, so resist the urge to open and close the oven door while baking. The cheesecake is generally done when the sides are set and a little puffy and the very center is slightly wiggly.

Cool the cheesecake slowly on a wire rack away from drafts and at an even temperature for 2 or 3 hours. Lay a piece of paper towel over the pan to hold in the moisture. Resist the urge to remove the cheesecake from the pan right away. Run a sharp knife around the sides, but *leave the cheesecake in the pan.* Refrigerate for at least 4 hours or overnight, and run the knife around the pan once more before releasing the sides.

When all else fails, and you get a crack down the center of your cheesecake, there is still hope. Fresh fruit and pie fillings, frosting, glaze, cookie crumbs, and chocolate ganache can always cover a multitude of sins. Your guests will never know the difference!

To slice, dip a large, sharp knife into hot water, and dry it off. Slice the cheesecake by cutting through it all the way to the plate. Do not saw through the cheesecake. Rinse off the knife in hot water, dry it, and cut another slice. Repeat and enjoy!

Strawberry Cheesecake

This rich and creamy New York–style cheesecake with Graham Cracker Crust and strawberry topping is the ultimate dessert. The delicious "cream cheese" filling is made with soy cream cheese and tofu, with a fresh zesty lemon flavor. You won't believe it's not cheesecake.

Yield:	Prep time:	Bake time:	Serving size:
1 (9-inch) cheesecake	7 to 12 hours	65 to 75 minutes	1 slice

1 (9-in.) Graham Cracker Crust (recipe in Chapter 13)

3 (8-oz.) pkgs. soy cream cheese

1 cup soft tofu

2½ cups vegan cane sugar

¼ cup cornstarch

Egg substitute for 2 large eggs (Ener-G or Bob's Red Mill works best)

1 TB. pure vanilla extract

1 tsp. grated lemon zest

1 qt. fresh hulled strawberries

1. Preheat the oven to 350°F. Place a pan of hot water in the bottom of the oven.

2. Spray the bottom and sides of a springform pan with vegetable spray. Pat Graham Cracker Crust mixture on the bottom and halfway up the sides of the pan. Prebake or blind-bake crust for 5 minutes. Remove from the oven, and let cool while making cheesecake filling.

3. In a large bowl, and using an electric mixer fitted with a paddle attachment on high speed, beat soy cream cheese and soft tofu for 2 or 3 minutes or until creamy. Add 1½ cups unbleached cane sugar and cornstarch, and beat again for 1 or 2 minutes, scraping the bowl as needed with a rubber spatula. Add egg substitute, vanilla extract, and lemon zest, and beat for 1 or 2 more minutes or until light and fluffy. Scrape down the bowl once more, and pour into the prepared crust.

4. Bake for 60 to 70 minutes or until sides are set and cheesecake is a little puffy. The very center will be slightly wiggly.

5. Cool slowly on a wire rack away from drafts and at an even temperature for 2 or 3 hours. Continue cooling in the refrigerator for at least 4 hours or overnight. Remove the sides of the springform pan, and transfer cheesecake to a serving platter. At this point, you can store cheesecake wrapped in plastic and refrigerated for up to 3 days. Double-wrapped, this cheesecake can be frozen for up to 2 months, although the texture will be slightly different after thawing.

6. Before serving, make strawberry topping. In a food processor fitted with a cutting blade, add ½ of strawberries and remaining 1 cup unbleached cane sugar, and purée. Remove to a medium bowl, and add remaining 1 cup whole strawberries. Stir and let sit for 30 minutes. Spoon strawberry topping over cheesecake slices before serving.

Variation: For **Fruit Cheesecake,** top plain cheesecake with a variety of fresh fruit or canned fruit pie fillings like blueberries or cherries.

BAKER'S BONUS

Leftover cheesecake? Vegan cheesecakes freeze great for 2 or 3 months, provided they're double-wrapped with plastic wrap and kept away from strong-smelling items.

Chocolate Cheesecake

This ultra-creamy vegan Chocolate Cheesecake in a Chocolate Cookie Crust is made with vegan chocolate chips, vegan cream cheese, and tofu. Decorate with Chocolate Ganache, and it will quickly become your favorite dessert.

Yield:	Prep time:	Bake time:	Serving size:
1 (9-inch) cheesecake	7 to 12 hours	45 to 55 minutes	1 slice

1 (8-oz.) pkg. soy cream cheese

1 cup soft silken tofu

¾ cup unbleached cane sugar

¼ cup cornstarch

1½ tsp. pure vanilla extract

1 cup vegan semisweet chocolate chips, melted

¼ cup soy milk

1 (9-in.) Chocolate Cookie Crust (recipe in Chapter 13) in a pie pan, prebaked for 5 minutes and cooled

½ cup Chocolate Ganache (recipe in Chapter 22; optional)

1. Preheat the oven to 350°F. Place a pan of hot water in the bottom of the oven.

2. In a large bowl, and using an electric mixer fitted with a paddle attachment on high speed, beat soy cream cheese and soft silken tofu until creamy. Add unbleached cane sugar and cornstarch, and beat again, scraping the bowl as needed with a rubber spatula.

3. Reduce speed to medium, add vanilla extract, and slowly add melted vegan chocolate chips. Beat for 1 minute, add soy milk, and continue beating for 1 more minute or until light and fluffy. Scrape down the bowl once more. Pour into unbaked Chocolate Cookie Crust.

4. Bake for 40 to 50 minutes or until sides are set and cheesecake is a little puffy. The very center will be slightly wiggly.

5. Cool slowly on a wire rack away from drafts and at an even temperature for 2 or 3 hours. Continue cooling in the refrigerator for at least 4 hours or overnight. At this point, you can store cheesecake wrapped in plastic and refrigerated for up to 3 days. Double-wrapped, this cheesecake can be frozen for up to 2 months, although the texture will be slightly different after thawing.

6. Before serving, decorate with Chocolate Ganache (if using) before serving.

Variation: For **Chocolate, Chocolate-Chip Cheesecake,** add ¾ cup vegan semisweet chocolate chips (mini chips if you can find them) to the batter before baking.

BATTER UP!

Melting vegan chocolate chips isn't difficult, but you should keep a few considerations in mind. Melt chocolate in a metal bowl over a pan of simmering water, stirring occasionally until smooth. Or melt in the microwave at half power. Microwave for 30 seconds, stir, and microwave for an additional 30 seconds. It should be smooth and flowing. Be sure no water comes into contact with the chocolate, or it will seize up.

Pumpkin Cheesecake

Baked in a Gingersnap Crust, this luscious vegan cheesecake is flavored with cinnamon, nutmeg, and ginger—all your favorite autumn spices.

Yield:	Prep time:	Bake time:	Serving size:
1 (9-inch) cheesecake	7 to 12 hours	60 to 75 minutes	1 slice

1 (9-in.) unbaked Gingersnap Crust (recipe in Chapter 13)

3 (8-oz.) pkgs. soy cream cheese

1 cup vegan cane sugar

¼ cup cornstarch

Ener-G Egg Replacer for 2 large eggs

1 tsp. pure vanilla extract

1¾ cups pumpkin purée, not pumpkin pie filling

1¼ tsp. ground cinnamon

½ tsp. ground nutmeg

¼ tsp. ground ginger

1. Preheat the oven to 350°F. Place a pan of hot water in the bottom of the oven.

2. Spray the bottom and sides of a springform pan with vegetable spray. Pat Gingersnap Crust mixture on the bottom and halfway up the sides of the pan. Prebake or blind-bake crust for 5 minutes. Remove from the oven, and let cool while making cheesecake filling.

3. In a large bowl, and using an electric mixer fitted with a paddle attachment on high speed, beat soy cream cheese for 1 or 2 minutes or until creamy. Add vegan cane sugar and cornstarch, and beat again for 2 or 3 minutes, scraping the bowl as needed with a rubber spatula. Add egg substitute and vanilla extract, and beat for 1 more minute. Add pumpkin purée, ground cinnamon, ground nutmeg, and ground ginger, and beat for 1 more minute or until light and fluffy. Scrape down the bowl once more, and pour into the prepared crust.

4. Bake for 55 to 70 minutes, or until sides are set and cheesecake is a little puffy. The very center will be slightly wiggly.

5. Cool slowly on a wire rack away from drafts and at an even temperature for 2 or 3 hours. Continue cooling in the refrigerator for at least 4 hours or overnight. Remove the sides of the springform pan, and transfer cheesecake to a serving platter. At this point, you can store cheesecake wrapped in plastic and refrigerated for up to 3 days. Double-wrapped, this cheesecake can be frozen for up to 2 months, although the texture will be slightly different after thawing.

Strawberry Shortcake

Not your typical Strawberry Shortcake, this giant vanilla cake is layered with vegan whipped topping and ripe, juicy strawberries.

Yield:	Prep time:	Bake time:	Serving size:
1 (9-inch) round layer cake	1 hour 10 minutes to 2 hours	25 to 35 minutes	1 slice

½ vanilla bean	⅔ cup canola or vegetable oil
2½ cups unbleached all-purpose flour	2 TB. white or apple cider vinegar
½ cup cornstarch	2 cups lukewarm water
2 tsp. baking soda	1½ tsp. pure vanilla extract
½ tsp. salt	1 qt. fresh hulled strawberries
1¾ cups unbleached cane sugar	1 batch vegan Whipped Topping (recipe in Chapter 22), or non-dairy whipped topping
½ cup light brown sugar, firmly packed	

1. Preheat the oven to 325°F. Lightly oil or spray 2 (9×2-inch) round cake pans, and line the bottoms with parchment paper.

2. Scrape seeds out of vanilla bean, and discard pod.

3. Into a medium bowl, sift unbleached all-purpose flour, cornstarch, baking soda, and salt, or blend with a wire whisk. Add vanilla bean seeds, 1½ cups unbleached cane sugar, and light brown sugar, and blend with a wooden spoon or a whisk.

4. In a large bowl, and using an electric mixer fitted with a paddle attachment on medium speed, combine canola oil, white vinegar, lukewarm water, and vanilla extract. Reduce speed to low, add ½ of dry ingredients to liquid ingredients, and mix to combine, scraping the bowl as needed with a rubber spatula. Add remaining dry ingredients, and mix for 1 or 2 more minutes, scraping down the bowl, until batter is nice and smooth with no lumps. Pour into the prepared pans.

5. Bake for 25 to 35 minutes or until a toothpick inserted into center comes out clean. Cool layers for 10 minutes before loosening. Gently remove cake layers from the pans, and cool completely.

6. In a medium bowl, combine strawberries and remaining ¼ cup unbleached cane sugar. Let sit for 20 minutes for flavors to meld and sugar to dissolve.

7. To assemble Strawberry Shortcake, place 1 cake layer on a serving platter. Top with ½ of Whipped Topping and ½ of strawberries. Place remaining cake layer on top and repeat with remaining Whipped Topping and remaining strawberries. Refrigerate until ready to serve.

DOUGH-NOT

This cake is best served the same day because the juicy strawberries will begin to soak through and break down the cake.

Peach Shortcake

Individual cinnamon-spiced baking powder biscuits, layered with ripe juicy peaches and vegan Whipped Topping—you'll love this dessert!

Yield:	Prep time:	Bake time:	Serving size:
12 shortcakes	1 hour 20 minutes to 1 hour 40 minutes	10 to 12 minutes	1 shortcake

2 cups unbleached all-purpose flour

½ tsp. salt

2 tsp. aluminum-free baking powder

½ tsp. baking soda

2 tsp. ground cinnamon

4 TB. nonhydrogenated vegan margarine

3 TB. solid vegetable shortening

⅔ to ¾ cup Vegan Buttermilk (recipe in Chapter 2)

3 large peaches

¾ cup unbleached cane sugar

Whipped Topping (recipe in Chapter 22)

12 to 24 fresh mint leaves (optional)

1. Preheat the oven to 400°F. Line a baking sheet with parchment paper, or spray with vegetable shortening spray.

2. Into a large bowl, sift unbleached all-purpose flour, salt, aluminum-free baking powder, baking soda, and 1 teaspoon ground cinnamon, or blend with a wire whisk. Add vegan margarine and vegetable shortening, and using a pastry blender, cut in until mixture resembles small peas.

3. Make a well in middle of dough, and pour in ⅔ cup Vegan Buttermilk. Using your hands or a rubber spatula, mix gently, making sure all dry ingredients are incorporated. Add more Vegan Buttermilk if needed until dough comes together and is soft but not sticky.

4. Turn out dough onto a well-floured surface. Using a rolling pin, roll dough to approximately ¾ inch thick. Using a 3-inch biscuit cutter, cut out as many biscuits as possible. Gather up any extra dough, roll it or pat it, and cut out remaining biscuits. Place biscuits on the prepared baking sheet.

5. Bake for 10 to 12 minutes or until nicely risen and light brown. Cool on a wire rack.

6. Peel, pit, and slice peaches, and place in a large bowl. Add unbleached cane sugar and remaining 1 teaspoon ground cinnamon. Let sit for 15 to 30 minutes for sugar to dissolve. Refrigerate until ready to use.

7. To assemble Peach Shortcakes, split biscuits in ½. Spoon some peaches and juice on 1 half. Place 1 dollop Whipped Topping on top of peaches. Place top half of biscuit on top; repeat with remaining biscuits, peaches, and Whipped Topping. Sprinkle a little ground cinnamon on top, and add a fresh mint sprig for decoration.

Variation: For **Fruit Shortcakes,** use a variety of fresh berries, fruits, and stone fruits like blueberries, blackberries, raspberries, strawberries, and pears. Some fruits like peaches take more preparation than others with peeling, pitting, and slicing. Others such as blueberries and raspberries need only a quick rinse and pat dry before adding them to the recipe.

BAKER'S BONUS

Although fresh peaches are always better, you can also use canned cling peaches in light syrup. Look for better-quality peaches. Many upscale grocery stores have cling peaches in glass jars that are more natural than commercial varieties. Drain off some of the juice before assembling shortcakes.

Pineapple Upside-Down Cake

An old-fashioned dessert, this Pineapple Upside-Down Cake is not only tasty but striking as well. With brown sugar syrup cradling the pineapple rings and topped with cherries, this yellow cake is bursting with flavor.

Yield:	Prep time:	Bake time:	Serving size:
1 (9×2-inch) round cake	40 to 50 minutes	63 to 80 minutes	1 slice

10 TB. nonhydrogenated vegan margarine, softened

½ cup light brown sugar, firmly packed

1 (20-oz.) can pineapple rings, drained

7 or 8 maraschino cherries, stems removed

1½ cups unbleached all-purpose flour

¾ tsp. aluminum-free baking powder

½ tsp. baking soda

¼ tsp. salt

¾ cup unbleached cane sugar

Egg substitute for 2 large eggs

1 tsp. pure vanilla extract

¾ cup Vegan Buttermilk (recipe in Chapter 2)

1. Preheat the oven to 350°F. Generously coat a 9×2-inch-round cake pan with cooking oil spray.

2. In a medium saucepan over medium heat, combine 4 tablespoons vegan margarine with light brown sugar, and cook, stirring for 3 to 5 minutes or until margarine is melted and brown sugar is no longer gritty. Pour into the prepared cake pan.

3. Arrange 7 or 8 pineapple slices on top, and place 1 cherry inside each pineapple ring.

4. Into a large bowl, sift unbleached all-purpose flour, aluminum-free baking powder, baking soda, and salt, or blend with a wire whisk.

5. In a separate large bowl, and using an electric mixer fitted with a paddle attachment on medium speed, beat remaining 6 tablespoons vegan margarine and unbleached cane sugar for 1 minute or until light and fluffy. Scrape down the sides of the bowl as needed using a rubber spatula.

6. Add egg substitute a little at a time, beating after each addition. Add vanilla extract, and scrape the bowl once more.

7. Reduce speed to low, and add ½ of dry ingredients, alternating with Vegan Buttermilk, until well blended. Do not overmix batter, just remove any lumps. Gently pour cake batter over pineapple.

8. Bake for 60 to 75 minutes or until golden brown and brown sugar syrup is bubbly. Cool cake in the pan for 5 to 10 minutes.

9. Lay a serving plate over the top of the cake pan, and with one swift motion, flip the cake pan upside down and place the platter on the counter. Carefully remove the cake pan, and scrape any remaining syrup over cake. Cool on a wire rack, or serve warm.

BATTER UP!

If you have a nice fresh sweet pineapple on hand, use that instead. Figure on using ½ fresh pineapple, cored, peeled, cut into slices, and blotted dry for this Pineapple Upside-Down Cake. If using canned pineapple slices, look for pineapple in its own juices, and be sure to drain and blot pineapple rings dry before arranging them in the pan.

Cranberry Upside-Down Cake

An ooey, gooey bottom of plump cranberries and chopped pecans become the topping when this impressive cinnamon and nutmeg–flavored cake is flipped over.

Yield:	Prep time:	Bake time:	Serving size:
1 (10×2-inch) round cake	40 to 50 minutes	63 to 80 minutes	1 slice

10 TB. nonhydrogenated vegan margarine, softened

½ cup light brown sugar

1½ cups fresh cranberries

½ cup toasted, chopped pecans

1½ cups whole-wheat pastry flour

¾ tsp. aluminum-free baking powder

½ tsp. baking soda

¼ tsp. salt

¾ tsp. ground cinnamon

¼ tsp. ground nutmeg

¾ cup unbleached cane sugar

Egg substitute for 2 large eggs

1 tsp. pure vanilla extract

¾ cup Vegan Buttermilk (recipe in Chapter 2)

1. Preheat the oven to 350°F. Generously coat 1 (10×2-inch-round) cake pan with cooking oil spray.

2. In a medium saucepan over medium heat, combine 4 tablespoons vegan margarine and light brown sugar. Bring to a boil, and cook, stirring, for 3 to 5 minutes or until margarine is melted and brown sugar is no longer gritty. Pour into the prepared pan.

3. Arrange cranberries and pecans over the bottom of the pan.

4. Into a large bowl, sift whole-wheat pastry flour, aluminum-free baking powder, baking soda, salt, ground cinnamon, and ground nutmeg, or blend with a wire whisk.

5. In a separate large bowl, and using an electric mixer fitted with a paddle attachment on medium speed, beat remaining 6 tablespoons vegan margarine and unbleached cane sugar for 1 minute or until light. Scrape down the sides of the bowl as needed using a rubber spatula.

6. Add egg substitute a little at a time, beating after each addition. Add vanilla extract, and scrape the bowl once more.

7. Reduce speed to low, and add ½ of dry ingredients, alternating with Vegan Buttermilk, until well blended. Do not overmix batter, just remove any lumps. Gently pour cake batter over cranberries.

8. Bake for 60 to 75 minutes or until light brown and brown sugar syrup is bubbly. A toothpick inserted into the center should come out clean. Cool cake in the pan for 5 to 10 minutes.

9. Lay a serving plate over the top of the cake pan, and with one swift motion, flip the cake pan upside down and place the platter on the counter. Carefully remove the cake pan, and scrape any remaining syrup over cake. Cool on a wire rack, or serve warm.

BAKER'S BONUS

Frozen cranberries will also work in this recipe. Do not thaw, but use straight from the bag. Substitute walnuts or almonds for the pecans if you want, too.

Gourmet Cupcakes

In This Chapter

- Cupcake decorating tips
- Freezing cupcakes
- Yummy specialty cupcakes

Have you noticed lately that the world is in love with cupcakes? In the past 10 years, shops selling designer cupcakes have sprung up in every major city. Cupcake cookbooks line bookstore shelves, and hundreds of websites and blogs are dedicated to promoting "cupcake love." In fact, many businesses have made millions selling cupcakes and cupcake paraphernalia to the cupcake obsessed. Cupcakes are so popular, they've reached cult status, as witnessed on the Food Network's recently launched show, *Cupcake Wars*. There's no doubt about it, cupcakes are here to stay.

In this chapter, I give you specialty cupcakes that are so much more fun than the average cake-mix-brand cupcakes. Confetti Cupcakes baked with brightly colored sprinkles inside are sure to bring out the kid in you. And some are so tasty—like the Black Bottom Cupcakes—they don't need any frosting at all, but seriously, doesn't just about everything taste better with frosting on it? You'll also find cupcake decorating tips and tricks that will make your "baby cakes" the hit of your next party. And the best thing of all? They're vegan!

Dressing Up Your Cupcakes

Part of the fun of cupcakes is decorating them! And with the tips in this section, you're sure to have the best-looking cupcakes in town.

Before anything else, be sure your cupcakes are completely cool before frosting them. You'll need a spatula or a knife to decorate the most basic cupcake. Simply spoon some frosting on the top of the cupcake and with a metal spatula, spread it to the edges and then up with a slight twist of the wrist to form a swirl.

Colored sprinkles and jimmies are the quickest and easiest decorations for cupcakes and will bring smiles to all who eat them.

For more advanced decorating, spoon some frosting into a large pastry bag fitted with a large star or rosette tip. Starting close to the cupcake's outside edge, firmly squeeze the bag and frosting through the tip in a round circular motion, finally swirling the frosting into a peak in the center.

Edible flowers like pansies, rose petals, and colorful nasturtiums make an easy but elegant finishing touch for cupcakes.

The Big Chill

Naturally, you'll want to eat those cute little cupcakes right away, but if you can't finish them within a few days, you should plan to freeze them. Cupcakes can be frozen with or without frosting. Place completely cooled cupcakes in zipper-lock bags, and freeze for up to 3 to 6 months. Thaw overnight in the refrigerator or for 30 minutes on the counter if you're in a hurry.

Vanilla Bean Cupcakes

These delicious, intensely flavorful cupcakes rely on the addition of natural vanilla seeds to the tasty yellow cake batter.

Yield:	Prep time:	Bake time:	Serving size:
22 to 26 cupcakes	1 hour 15 minutes to 2 hours	20 to 25 minutes	1 cupcake

¾ cup soy or rice milk

1 vanilla bean

2 cups unbleached all-purpose flour

2 tsp. aluminum-free baking powder

½ tsp. baking soda

1 tsp. salt

½ cup nonhydrogenated vegan margarine, softened

1 cup unbleached cane sugar

Egg substitute for 1 large egg

1 tsp. white or cider vinegar

1. In a medium saucepan over medium heat, bring soy milk and vanilla bean to a boil. Turn off heat, and let cool for 45 to 60 minutes. Remove vanilla bean from the pan, open pod, and scoop out seeds, returning them to soy milk. Discard pod.

2. Preheat the oven to 350°F. Line 22 to 26 muffin cups with paper cupcake liners.

3. Into a large bowl, sift together unbleached all-purpose flour, aluminum-free baking powder, baking soda, and salt, or blend with a wire whisk.

4. In a separate large bowl, and using an electric mixer fitted with a paddle attachment on medium speed, beat vegan margarine and unbleached cane sugar for 1 or 2 minutes or until light. Scrape down the sides of the bowl using a rubber spatula. Add egg substitute and white vinegar, and beat again.

5. Reduce speed to low, and add ½ of dry ingredients, alternating with ½ vanilla bean soy milk, until well blended. Add remaining dry ingredients and soy milk, and mix for 1 minute or only until cake batter is nice and smooth with no lumps, scraping down the sides of the bowl as needed. Be careful not to overmix.

6. Pour batter into the prepared cupcake tins, filling each cup about ¾ full. Bake for 20 to 25 minutes, or until tops spring back when lightly touched and a toothpick inserted into the center comes out clean.

7. Cool cupcakes for 10 minutes in the pans. Remove to a wire rack, and cool completely before frosting.

8. Frost with your choice of frosting (try Vanilla Buttercream Frosting, recipe in Chapter 21), or double-wrap in plastic, and freeze.

> **BAKER'S BONUS**
>
> Natural vanilla beans are also known as pods. To cut open a vanilla bean, lay it flat on a cutting board. Slice open the bean lengthwise from one end to the other, being careful not to slice through it. This exposes thousands of tiny seeds you can scrape out and use in recipes.

Black Bottom Cupcakes

Gooey chocolate cupcakes baked with a vegan cream cheese center and loaded with chocolate chips are a chocoholic's dream come true! These cupcakes are so moist and yummy, they don't need frosting.

Yield:	Prep time:	Bake time:	Serving size:
12 to 16 cupcakes	30 minutes	23 to 28 minutes	1 cupcake

1 (8-oz.) pkg. vegan cream cheese, at room temperature

1½ cups Florida Crystals or unbleached cane sugar

¼ cup soft silken tofu or soy yogurt

1½ tsp. pure vanilla extract

½ cup vegan semisweet chocolate chips

1½ cups unbleached all-purpose flour

½ cup natural cocoa powder

1 tsp. baking soda

¼ tsp. salt

1 cup water

⅓ cup canola or vegetable oil

1 TB. white vinegar or apple cider vinegar

1. Preheat the oven to 350°F. Line 12 to 16 muffin cups with paper cupcake liners.

2. In a medium bowl, and using an electric mixer on high speed, beat vegan cream cheese and ½ cup Florida Crystals for 1 minute. Add soft silken tofu and ½ teaspoon vanilla extract, and beat for 1 more minute or until creamy. Scrape down the sides of the bowl as needed with a rubber spatula. Stir in vegan chocolate chips.

3. Into a medium bowl, sift together unbleached all-purpose flour, natural cocoa powder, baking soda, and salt, or blend with a wire whisk.

4. In a large bowl, and using an electric mixer fitted with a paddle attachment on medium speed, mix water, canola oil, remaining 1 teaspoon vanilla extract, white vinegar, and remaining 1 cup Florida Crystals for 1 minute or until well blended, scraping the bowl as needed.

5. Reduce speed to low, add ½ of dry ingredients, and mix to combine. Add remaining dry ingredients, and mix for 1 minute, scraping down the sides of the bowl, until batter is well blended.

6. Pour batter into the prepared cupcake tins, filling each cup about ¾ full. Gently spoon vegan cream cheese filling on top of each batter-filled tin, evenly dividing among cupcakes. Bake for 23 to 28 minutes or until cheesecake is lightly browned and tops spring back when lightly touched.

7. Cool cupcakes for 10 minutes in the pans. Remove to a wire rack, and cool completely before serving.

BATTER UP!

Vegan cream cheese is a real treat for vegans. Natural food stores carry brands that are nonhydrogenated and dairy free—and actually taste good! It can be used interchangeably in most any recipe calling for cream cheese.

Chocolate-Chip Banana Cupcakes

Bananas and chocolate taste so good together, especially when cinnamon is added to the batter.

Yield:	Prep time:	Bake time:	Serving size:
12 to 16 cupcakes	30 minutes	23 to 28 minutes	1 cupcake

1½ cups unbleached all-purpose flour

1½ tsp. ground cinnamon

½ tsp. salt

½ tsp. baking soda

¼ tsp. aluminum-free baking powder

Egg substitute for 2 large eggs

⅔ cup unbleached cane sugar

⅓ cup light brown sugar, firmly packed

⅓ cup canola or vegetable oil

1½ tsp. pure vanilla extract

1 cup (about 2) mashed bananas

½ cup vegan semisweet chocolate chips

1. Preheat the oven to 350°F. Line 12 to 16 muffin cups with paper cupcake liners.

2. Into a medium bowl, sift together all-purpose flour, ground cinnamon, salt, baking soda, and aluminum-free baking powder, or blend with a wire whisk.

3. In a large bowl, and using an electric mixer fitted with a paddle attachment on medium speed, mix egg substitute, unbleached cane sugar, and light brown sugar for 1 or 2 minutes or until blended. Add canola oil, vanilla extract, and mashed bananas, and mix for 1 or 2 minutes to combine, scraping down the bowl as needed with a rubber spatula.

4. Reduce speed to low, add ½ of dry ingredients, and mix to combine. Add remaining dry ingredients and vegan chocolate chips, and mix for 1 minute, scraping down the bowl, until batter is well blended.

5. Pour batter into the prepared cupcake tins, filling each cup about ¾ full. Bake cupcakes for 23 to 28 minutes or until tops spring back when lightly touched and a toothpick inserted into the center comes out clean.

6. Cool cupcakes for 10 minutes in the pans. Remove to a wire rack, and cool completely before frosting.

7. Frost with your choice of frosting (try Buttercream Frosting or Cream Cheese Frosting, recipes in Chapter 21), or double-wrap in plastic, and freeze.

> **BAKER'S BONUS**
>
> Instead of making full-size cupcakes, bake up a batch of mini cupcakes. Mini cupcake liners come in all colors and themes for any occasion. Reduce the oven temperature to 325°F, and bake for 12 to 18 minutes or until toothpick inserted into the center comes out clean. This recipe makes 30 to 36 bite-size cupcakes.

Confetti Cupcakes

Tender vanilla cupcakes studded with multi-colored sprinkles will bring a dash of fun to your party. They're the perfect cupcake for kids of any age!

Yield:	Prep time:	Bake time:	Serving size:
20 to 24 cupcakes	30 minutes	20 to 25 minutes	1 cupcake

2½ cups cake flour

1 TB. aluminum-free baking powder

½ tsp. salt

½ cup nonhydrogenated vegan margarine, softened

1½ cups unbleached cane sugar

Ener-G Egg Replacer or Bob's Red Mill All Natural Egg Replacer for 2 large eggs

1 tsp. pure vanilla or almond extract

1½ cups soy milk

7 TB. small colored organic vegan sprinkles

1. Preheat the oven to 350°F. Line 20 to 24 muffin cups with paper cupcake liners.

2. Into a large mixing bowl, sift together cake flour, aluminum-free baking powder, and salt, or blend with a wire whisk.

3. In a separate large bowl, and using an electric mixer fitted with a paddle attachment on medium speed, beat vegan margarine and unbleached cane sugar for 1 or 2 minutes or until light. Scrape down the sides of the bowl using a rubber spatula. Add egg substitute and vanilla extract, and beat again.

4. Reduce speed to low, and add ½ of dry ingredients, alternating with ½ soy milk, until well blended. Add remaining dry ingredients and soy milk, and mix for 1 minute or only until cake batter is nice and smooth with no lumps, scraping down the sides of the bowl as needed, and being careful not to overmix. Fold in 5 tablespoons sprinkles.

5. Pour batter into the prepared cupcake tins, filling each cup about ¾ full. Bake for 20 to 25 minutes or until tops spring back when lightly touched and a toothpick inserted into the center comes out clean.

6. Cool cupcakes for 10 minutes in the pans. Remove to a wire rack, and cool completely before frosting.

7. Frost with your choice of frosting (try Coconut Frosting, recipe in Chapter 21), and top with remaining 2 tablespoons sprinkles. Or double-wrap in plastic, and freeze.

DOUGH-NOT

Rainbow sprinkles make the cutest whimsical cupcakes, but they're also full of sugar. Most commercial brands are made with sugar, cornstarch, vegetable oil, and of course, food coloring. A number of companies carry vegan sprinkles made with organic evaporated cane juice, organic corn malt syrup, water, natural colors, and extracts of seeds, vegetables, or fruits. As always, check the label to be sure there are not any hidden dairy or egg products in them. Organic chocolate sprinkles contain natural ingredients, but commercial chocolate sprinkles most often contain whey and/or egg whites.

Very Vegan Frostings

In This Chapter

- Doing double layer cakes right
- "Buttery" beaten vegan frostings
- Delicious cooked frostings

Now that you've baked all the delicious cakes and cupcakes in the previous chapters, you'll need something sweet to decorate them with. The vegan frostings in this chapter range from the humble Buttercream Frosting, to the delicious and dark Chocolate Frosting, to the rich and flavorful Penuche Frosting (brown sugar frosting), to the tasty Maple Frosting.

Most of the recipes that follow are quick and easy to whip up and require no more than beating the ingredients in a mixing bowl. Some take a little more time with an extra step or two on the stovetop. Whatever frosting you decide on, be sure to lick the bowl!

Decorating Double Layer Cakes

Before diving headfirst into cake decorating, it's important to start at the beginning. It's an ugly thing to see cake crumbs sprinkled through snow-white frosting, especially if you worked long and hard on that delicious cake. Take some time to prepare the cake layers and frosting before grabbing your frosting spatula.

After cake layers are baked and completely cool, place them on a baking sheet lined with waxed paper and lightly dusted with unbleached cane sugar.

Freeze or chill cake layers for at least 2 to 4 hours or overnight before frosting. Meanwhile, prepare the frosting according to directions. Remove cake layers from the freezer one at a time, and, if necessary, trim off the top of the layers to allow for flat tops.

Smear 1 tablespoon frosting on a round, flat decorative serving platter, but any appropriate size dinner plate will do. Professional cake decorators use cardboard circles specially cut for assorted sizes cake layers. Place one round frozen cake layer on top of frosting, and press down lightly to "glue" the cake to the plate. Spread a thick coat of frosting over the bottom layer, and place the second layer on top, pressing down lightly. It's helpful to turn the layer ½ turn while pressing down to seal the frosting between the layers.

Begin by applying a "crumb coat" to the cake, which is essentially a thin, see-through layer of frosting to seal in the crumbs. Depending on how thick the frosting is, you may need to thin a small amount of it (about 1 cup) for your crumb coating. You can do this by adding a bit of corn syrup or water before spreading—be careful not to add too much because you don't want it too thin or runny.

Using an *off-set spatula*, start from the top and work your way toward the edges with a very thin layer. Don't pull the frosting toward you; rather, push it away from the cake with the spatula. Pulling the spatula can rip crumbs from the cake into your frosting. Continue down along the sides of the cake, smoothing with the spatula, and sealing it as you go. Either chill the cake at this point, or place in a cool location, and let the thin layer of frosting dry before continuing. It doesn't take too long to develop a "crust," usually between 15 and 20 minutes.

VEGAN VOCAB

An **off-set spatula** is handy to use to frost cakes. It's a metal spatula with a stiff metal blade bent at an angle near the handle. This shape allows access to get into tight spots that an ordinary frosting spatula couldn't reach without tearing up the frosting.

To avoid messy crumbs in your frosting, it's very important to use enough frosting so the off-set spatula never comes into contact with the cake layers. Spoon about 2 cups of the thicker frosting on top of the cake, and as in the crumb coat, start by working your way out from the middle, and gently frost the top and sides of the cake using an off-set spatula, being careful not to rip up any cake crumbs. Gently smooth the top and sides of the cake with the spatula, and seal the edges evenly.

If you're having trouble spreading the frosting, try dipping the spatula in warm water and wiping it dry between spreading. It should help smooth the frosting and prevent any crumbs from spoiling your creation.

Decorate the top with frosting. Depending on the flavor of the cake, you can also decorate with chopped nuts, chocolate drizzle, toasted coconut, vegan candies, vegan chocolate chips, plastic novelties, etc. The sky's the limit when it comes to decorating cakes, so let your imagination run wild!

Buttercream Frosting

This classic white vanilla frosting, a perfect base for decorating with natural food coloring or cake colors, is just right for icing fancy celebration layer cakes and the cutest cupcakes.

Yield:	Prep time:	Serving size:
4 to 4½ cups	10 to 15 minutes	Varies

½ cup solid shortening (preferably nonhydrogenated natural shortening)

½ cup nonhydrogenated vegan margarine, at room temperature

2 TB. vegan marshmallow crème (optional)

¾ tsp. pure vanilla extract

4 cups *vegan confectioners' sugar,* plus more as needed

1 TB. soy milk or water, or as needed

1. In a large bowl, and using an electric mixer fitted with a paddle attachment on high speed, beat shortening, vegan margarine, vegan marshmallow crème, and vanilla extract for 1 minute or until well combined.

2. Add 2 cups vegan confectioners' sugar, and beat for 1 minute or until light and fluffy, scraping the bowl as needed with a rubber spatula. Add remaining 2 cups confectioners' sugar, and beat for 1 or 2 minutes or until frosting is nice and smooth with no lumps.

3. Add soy milk a little at a time until frosting is of spreading consistency. Add more liquid if necessary. If frosting is too thin, add a little more confectioners' sugar as needed, and beat again. Frosting should be smooth with no lumps.

Variation: For **Vanilla Bean Buttercream Frosting**, scrape out the inside of a vanilla bean pod, and add it along with the vanilla extract for some intense vanilla flavor!

VEGAN VOCAB

Vegan confectioners' sugar is a sugar made from either beet or cane sugar (not refined with bone char–based charcoal) that's processed with a starch, such as cornstarch, to prevent caking.

Cream Cheese Frosting

This frosting is smooth and "cream cheese"-y, and tastes just as good as the real thing, but with no dairy.

Yield:	Prep time:	Serving size:
3½ cups	15 to 20 minutes	Varies

1 (8-oz.) pkg. vegan cream cheese, softened

½ cup nonhydrogenated vegan margarine, softened

4 cups vegan confectioners' sugar, plus more as needed

1 tsp. pure vanilla extract

1 TB. water, or as needed

1. In a large bowl, and using an electric mixer fitted with a paddle attachment on high speed, beat vegan cream cheese and softened vegan margarine for 1 minute or until well combined.

2. Add 2 cups vegan confectioners' sugar, and beat for 1 minute or until light and fluffy, scraping the bowl as needed with a rubber spatula. Add vanilla extract and remaining 2 cups confectioners' sugar, and beat for 1 or 2 minutes or until frosting is nice and smooth with no lumps.

3. Add water a little at a time until frosting is of spreading consistency. If frosting is too thin, add a little more confectioners' sugar as needed, and beat again. Frosting should be smooth with no lumps.

Variation: For **Cinnamon Cream Cheese Frosting,** add ½ to ¾ teaspoon ground cinnamon along with the vanilla extract.

BATTER UP!

Vegan cream cheese is a snow-white imitation cream cheese made of partially hydrogenated soybean oil, guar gum, and sugar. Tofutti brand has no dairy, cholesterol, lactose, or butterfat in it, making it perfect for those recipes where cream cheese is called for.

Maple Frosting

This delicious nondairy frosting is made with pure maple syrup, vegan cream cheese, and maple extract. Just add chopped walnuts, and make believe you're leaf-peeping in New England.

Yield:	Prep time:	Serving size:
3½ cups	15 to 20 minutes	Varies

½ cup nonhydrogenated vegan margarine, softened

¾ cup vegan cream cheese

⅓ cup pure maple syrup, dark amber or Grade B

4 cups vegan confectioners' sugar, plus more as needed

½ tsp. pure maple extract

1 TB. water, or as needed

1. In a large bowl, and using an electric mixer fitted with a paddle attachment on high speed, beat vegan margarine, vegan cream cheese, and maple syrup for 1 minute or until well combined.

2. Add 2 cups vegan confectioners' sugar, and beat for 1 minute or until light and fluffy, scraping the bowl as needed with a rubber spatula. Add maple extract and remaining 2 cups confectioners' sugar, and beat for 1 or 2 minutes or until frosting is nice and smooth with no lumps.

3. Add water a little at a time until frosting is of spreading consistency. If frosting is too thin, add a little more confectioners' sugar as needed, and beat again. Frosting should be smooth with no lumps.

Variation: For **Maple Walnut Frosting,** add ½ teaspoon black walnut extract along with the maple extract. You can even add ½ to ¾ cup finely chopped walnuts to frosting before spreading on cakes and cupcakes.

BATTER UP!

The frosting recipes in this chapter have a range of measurements when it comes to vegan confectioners' sugar. Fluctuations in humidity and temperature are common in different locations. That's why you'll see "more as needed" in the ingredient list. You may have to adjust the amount of confectioners' sugar, and/or the liquid (soy milk and water) during the final stages of beating the frosting. If needed, start out with 1 tablespoon sugar at a time, or a few drops of milk or water. A little goes a long way when it comes to adding extra liquid to a batch of frosting.

Peanut Butter Frosting

This deliciously fluffy peanut butter frosting is made with smooth peanut butter.

Yield:	Prep time:	Serving size:
3½ cups	10 to 15 minutes	Varies

½ cup nonhydrogenated vegan
margarine, softened

1 cup smooth peanut butter

1 tsp. pure vanilla extract

Pinch salt

3 cups vegan confectioners' sugar,
plus more as needed

3 TB. soy milk, or as needed

1. In a large bowl, and using an electric mixer fitted with a paddle attachment on high speed, beat vegan margarine and smooth peanut butter until creamy. Add vanilla extract and salt, and beat for 1 minute.

2. Add 1½ cups vegan confectioners' sugar, and beat for 1 minute or until light and fluffy, scraping the bowl as needed with a rubber spatula. Add remaining 1½ cups confectioners' sugar, and beat for 1 or 2 minutes or until frosting is nice and smooth with no lumps.

3. Add soy milk a little at a time until frosting is of spreading consistency. If frosting is too thin, add a little more confectioners' sugar as needed, and beat again. Frosting should be smooth with no lumps.

Variation: For **Peanut Butter Cup Frosting,** add 1 cup vegan peanut butter cups, chopped small.

BATTER UP!

If your all-natural peanut butter has an oily puddle on top, simply stir it back into the peanut butter before using, especially if you're using it in baked goods. Most times this method works fine, but in this Peanut Butter Frosting recipe, the all-natural peanut butter combined with the additional vegan margarine makes for a very "greasy" frosting with an oily mouthfeel. If you want to use all-natural peanut butter for this recipe, drain off as much of the oil as you can, and use only the driest portion of the peanut butter.

Chocolate Frosting

Rich, dark chocolate frosting, made with cocoa and brown sugar, goes on just about anything.

Yield:	Prep time:	Serving size:
4½ cups	15 to 25 minutes	Varies

½ cup nonhydrogenated vegan margarine

1 cup light brown sugar, firmly packed

4 TB. dark cocoa powder

4 TB. soy milk

3 cups vegan confectioners' sugar, plus more as needed

1 tsp. pure vanilla extract

1 or 2 TB. water, or as needed

1. In a large saucepan over medium heat, melt vegan margarine. Add light brown sugar, and bring to a boil, stirring often. Reduce heat to low, add dark cocoa powder, and continue to boil for 2 minutes, stirring constantly.

2. Stir in soy milk very slowly, being careful not to splatter. Increase heat to medium, and bring to a boil, stirring continually. Remove from heat, and cool to room temperature.

3. In a large bowl, and using an electric mixer fitted with a paddle attachment on high speed, beat cocoa mixture with ½ of vegan confectioners' sugar for 1 minute. Add vanilla extract and remaining confectioners' sugar, and beat for 2 or 3 minutes or until nice and smooth with no lumps, scraping the bowl as needed with a rubber spatula.

4. Add water a little at a time until frosting is of spreading consistency. If frosting is too thin, add a little more confectioners' sugar as needed, and beat again. Frosting should be smooth with no lumps.

Variation: For **Mocha Frosting,** add 1 tablespoon instant coffee crystals to the melted vegan margarine and continue with recipe.

BATTER UP!

Brownies, chocolate cake, peanut butter cupcakes, graham crackers, …. What else can you think of to top with this chocolaty frosting?

Coconut Frosting

This snowy-white extra-fluffy frosting is flavored with pure coconut extract and vegan marshmallow crème.

Yield:	Prep time:	Serving size:
4½ cups	10 to 15 minutes	Varies

½ cup solid shortening (preferably nonhydrogenated natural shortening)

½ cup nonhydrogenated vegan margarine

¼ cup *vegan marshmallow crème*

3½ cups vegan confectioners' sugar, plus more as needed

1 tsp. pure coconut extract

1 or 2 TB. water, or as needed

1. In a large bowl, and using an electric mixer fitted with a paddle attachment on high speed, beat shortening, vegan margarine, and vegan marshmallow crème for 1 minute or until fluffy.

2. Add ½ of vegan confectioners' sugar, and beat for 1 minute or until light and fluffy, scraping the bowl as needed with a rubber spatula. Add coconut extract and remaining confectioners' sugar, and beat for 1 or 2 minutes or until frosting is nice and smooth with no lumps.

3. Add water a little at a time until frosting is of spreading consistency. If frosting is too thin, add a little more confectioners' sugar as needed, and beat again. Frosting should be smooth with no lumps.

Variation: For **Toasted Coconut Frosting,** add 1 cup toasted, sweetened coconut with the confectioners' sugar.

VEGAN VOCAB

Vegan marshmallow crème is gluten free and kosher. This fluffy, sweet, and smooth product is made with brown rice syrup, soy protein, and natural gums and flavors. It can be used in most recipes that call for marshmallow crème.

Penuche Frosting

Also known as caramel icing, this frosting tastes so buttery, you'll swear it was made with real dairy butter. It's the perfect topping for spice cake, carrot cake, gingerbread cupcakes, or chocolate fudge brownies.

Yield:	Prep time:	Serving size:
5½ cups	15 to 25 minutes	Varies

½ cup nonhydrogenated vegan margarine	4 cups vegan confectioners' sugar, plus more as needed
1 cup light brown sugar, firmly packed	1 tsp. pure vanilla extract
⅓ cup soy milk	2 or 3 TB. water, or as needed

1. In a large saucepan over medium heat, melt vegan margarine. Add light brown sugar, and bring to a boil, stirring often. Reduce heat to low, and continue to simmer for 3 minutes, stirring constantly.

2. Stir in soy milk very slowly, being careful not to splatter. Increase heat to medium, and bring to a boil, stirring continually. Immediately remove from heat, and cool to lukewarm.

3. In the same saucepan, and using an electric hand mixer fitted with a paddle attachment on high speed, beat cooked brown sugar and vegan margarine with 2 cups vegan confectioners' sugar for 1 minute. Add vanilla extract and remaining 2 cups confectioners' sugar, and beat for 2 or 3 minutes or until nice and smooth with no lumps, scraping the bowl as needed with a rubber spatula.

4. Add water a little at a time until frosting is of spreading consistency. If frosting is too thin, add a little more confectioners' sugar as needed, and beat again. Frosting should be smooth with no lumps.

DOUGH-NOT

Be careful when boiling vegan margarine and brown sugar. The hot mixture may foam up and boil when you add the soy milk, so be very careful not to let it splatter. Use an extra-large saucepan to prevent accidents.

Carob Frosting

This creamy frosting has a slightly nutty flavor that goes well with the "buttery" taste of vegan margarine and pure vanilla extract.

Yield:	Prep time:	Serving size:
4⅔ cups	10 to 15 minutes	Varies

½ cup nonhydrogenated vegan margarine

½ cup vegan marshmallow crème, or vegan cream cheese

⅔ cup carob powder

3 cups vegan confectioners' sugar, plus more as needed

1½ tsp. pure vanilla extract

3 or 4 TB. soy milk, or as needed

1. In a large bowl, and using an electric mixer fitted with a paddle attachment on high speed, beat vegan margarine and vegan marshmallow crème for 1 minute or until fluffy.

2. Add carob powder and ½ of confectioners' sugar, and beat for 1 minute or until light and fluffy, scraping the bowl as needed with a rubber spatula. Add vanilla extract and remaining confectioners' sugar, and beat for 1 or 2 minutes or until frosting is nice and smooth with no lumps.

3. Add soy milk a little at a time until frosting is of spreading consistency. If frosting is too thin, add a little more confectioners' sugar as needed, and beat again. Frosting should be smooth with no lumps.

Variation: For **Mexican Carob Frosting,** add ½ teaspoon ground cinnamon with the carob.

BATTER UP!

Carob is a good alternative if you can't have chocolate. Its flavor is very much like the "real thing"!

Toppings and Fillings

In This Chapter

- Tempting icings and drizzles
- Sweet and fruity fillings
- Fabulous finishing touches

I saved the best for the last! This chapter includes all the sweet finishing touches you can use to turn your vegan dishes into culinary masterpieces!

From sweet icings to luscious fillings, you're sure to have a ball trying out these recipes. They're very easy to prepare, but your cakes, tarts, and cobblers just wouldn't be the same without them.

Simple Syrup

Most commonly used in iced drinks and lemonade, Simple Syrup also has a place in the baking world. Brushing it over dry and overbaked cake adds moistness and brings the cake back to life!

Yield:	Prep time:
2 cups	5 minutes

1 cup water   1 cup unbleached cane sugar

1. In a medium saucepan over medium heat, bring water and sugar to a boil. Boil until sugar is completely dissolved.

2. Remove from heat, and cool completely before storing. Refrigerate covered, for up to 1 week.

Variation: Spike this simple syrup with a little Kahlúa, Grand Marnier, or Amaretto, and drizzle it over your favorite cake or pastry.

DOUGH-NOT

Don't let the syrup boil too long or it will thicken too much. Be careful handling the hot syrup, too. The temperature has reached the boiling point and will burn your skin if it splatters.

Chocolate Ganache Icing

Just two ingredients—vegan semisweet chocolate and soy milk—make the most wonderful silky chocolate ganache that's perfect for decorating cakes and cupcakes, spreading on brownies, or drizzling over pastries and cheesecakes.

Yield:	Prep time:
3 cups	5 minutes

2 cups vegan semisweet chocolate chips   1 cup soy milk

1. Place vegan chocolate chips in a medium, heat-proof bowl.

2. In a medium saucepan over medium heat, bring soy milk to a boil. Turn off heat immediately, and pour over vegan chocolate chips, stirring until mixed. Blend with a wire whisk for 2 to 4 minutes or until chocolate chips have melted and ganache is thick and smooth.

3. Let cool before drizzling over pastries. Cool completely before covering with a lid or plastic wrap, and refrigerate for up to 1 week.

Variation: For **White Chocolate Ganache,** use vegan white chocolate chips instead.

BAKER'S BONUS

The easiest way to apply drizzle or thin ganache is with clean fingers. Dip your fingers into the drizzle and wiggle your fingers over the baked goods. This is messy, sure, but it's effective. Another easy—and cleaner—way to apply drizzle is to pour it into a zipper-lock bag, cut off a tiny corner of the bag with scissors, and gently squeeze the drizzle out of the bag onto the baked goods.

Lemon Icing

This icing is sweet and tart all at the same time! Vegan confectioners' sugar and fresh lemon juice are all you need to top off your cakes and pastries with a wonderfully lemony flavor.

Yield:	Prep time:
1 cup	5 minutes

1 cup vegan confectioners' sugar

2 TB. fresh lemon juice

1. In a small bowl, mix vegan confectioners' sugar with fresh lemon juice, and stir until smooth.

2. Use right away, or cover the bowl and refrigerate for later use.

BATTER UP!

This recipe also works well with fresh lime or orange juice. Be sure to strain the seeds from the juice before using.

Raspberry Coulis

Sweet raspberry blended with a touch of fresh squeezed lemon juice, this thick syrup will liven up cakes and cheesecakes, and add a splash of color to anything it decorates.

Yield:	Prep time:
1 cup	5 minutes

2 cups fresh or frozen raspberries, thawed if frozen

½ cup unbleached cane sugar
1 TB. fresh lemon juice

1. In a blender, add raspberries and unbleached cane sugar, and blend on high speed for 1 minute or until smooth. Add lemon juice, and blend for 10 to 20 more seconds.

2. Press *coulis* through a fine mesh strainer using the back of a rubber spatula to squeeze and press juice through seeds. Discard seeds. Cover and refrigerate for up to 3 days.

VEGAN VOCAB

Coulis (pronounced *koo-LEE*) is French, derived from Latin, meaning "strained liquid." A coulis can be made from fruit, meat, or vegetables, usually seasoned or flavored, but for our baking application, it is made from fruit. This coulis is a thick sauce made from puréed and strained raspberries. It is most often used over desserts, ice cream, or as a garnish. Drizzle the coulis over desserts, pool it on a plate next to the dessert, or have the dessert swim in a puddle of coulis for a dramatic presentation.

Whipped Topping

This whipped topping is so tasty, it's hard to believe it's vegan. Nondairy whipped topping gets its texture from soft tofu and its sweet taste from agave syrup and pure vanilla extract.

Yield:	Prep time:
1¼ cups	5 minutes

1 cup soft tofu, drained and blotted dry

3 TB. canola oil

¼ cup vegan confectioners' sugar

2 TB. agave or brown rice syrup

½ tsp. fresh lemon juice

1 tsp. pure vanilla extract

1. In a blender, add soft tofu, canola oil, vegan confectioners' sugar, agave syrup, lemon juice, and vanilla extract, and blend on high speed for 3 or 4 minutes or until smooth and creamy, scraping down the sides of the blender as needed with a rubber spatula.

2. Refrigerate for 4 hours or overnight to set up before using. Cover, and keep refrigerated for up to 3 days.

BATTER UP!

Before you begin to juice a lemon, roll it on the countertop back and forth firmly under your palm. This helps break up some of the fibers and allows the juice to flow easily. You can also microwave the lemon before cutting for 5 to 10 seconds on medium power. Then cut the lemon in half horizontally, cup it in one hand, and firmly squeeze until enough juice is extracted.

Confectioners' Sugar Drizzle

Another easy recipe, this drizzle is made with vegan confectioners' sugar and soy milk (or water). Use it on pastries, coffee cakes, muffins, and more!

Yield:	Prep time:
1 cup	5 minutes

1 cup sifted vegan confectioners' sugar

2 TB. soy milk or water, plus more as needed

1 tsp. pure vanilla extract

1. In a small bowl, combine vegan confectioners' sugar, soy milk, and vanilla extract, and stir until smooth. Adjust liquid according to the consistency desired.

2. Use right away, or cover the bowl for later use. It's not necessary to refrigerate drizzle.

Variations: For **Almond Drizzle,** substitute pure almond extract for the vanilla extract. For **Rum Drizzle,** substitute rum, or rum extract for the vanilla extract.

BATTER UP!

Sometimes called Powdered Sugar Drizzle, this Confectioners' Sugar Drizzle has so many uses. A thin drizzle is perfect for the top of coffee cakes. Thicker drizzle is a good consistency for Danish pastries and muffins. Even thicker, and it would probably be called icing, and would be good for … well, so many things!

Apple Pie Filling

This homemade apple pie filling is mildly spicy with just the right amount of cinnamon and nutmeg for pies, turnovers, or filling Danish pastries.

Yield:	Prep time:
6 cups	30 minutes

1 cup Florida Crystals or
    unbleached cane sugar

¼ cup cornstarch

½ tsp. ground cinnamon

¼ tsp. salt

⅛ tsp. ground nutmeg

2½ cups water

6 cups (about 6 large) baking
    apples, cored, peeled, and
    sliced

1. In a large saucepan over medium heat, combine Florida Crystals, cornstarch, ground cinnamon, salt, and ground nutmeg. Add water, and stir well. Bring to a *boil*, and cook for 4 to 6 minutes or until liquid is clear and sugar is dissolved.

2. Add apples, and bring to a boil again. Reduce heat to low, cover, and cook for 8 to 10 minutes or until apples are tender.

3. Remove from heat, and cool completely before using in recipes. Cover with plastic wrap, or covered container, and refrigerate for up to 5 days. If a small amount of juice separates, pour it off before using.

Variation: For **Apple Raisin Pie Filling,** add 1 cup seedless raisins with the apples, and cook as directed.

BATTER UP!

To **boil** is to heat a liquid to a point where water is forced to turn into steam, causing the liquid to bubble.

Blueberry or Raspberry Pie Filling

This basic fruity pie filling is perfect for pies, turnovers, or strudels.

Yield:	Prep time:
6½ cups	30 minutes

1 cup unbleached cane sugar

¼ cup cornstarch, arrowroot powder, or ground tapioca powder

½ tsp. ground cinnamon

4 cups fresh or frozen blueberries or raspberries

1 cup water

2 TB. lemon juice

¼ tsp. pure vanilla or almond extract (optional)

1. In a medium saucepan over medium heat, combine unbleached cane sugar, cornstarch, and ground cinnamon with a wooden spoon or wire whisk. Stir in 2 cups blueberries or raspberries with water, and bring to a boil, stirring constantly until mixture is thick.

2. Add lemon juice and vanilla extract (if using), and boil mixture for 1 or 2 minutes.

3. Remove from heat, and add remaining 2 cups blueberries or raspberries. Cool completely before filling pie shells, turnovers, etc. Cover and refrigerate up to 5 days, or until ready to use.

Variation: For 5½ cups **Cherry Pie Filling,** omit the cinnamon, substitute 3½ cups fresh or frozen pitted cherries for the blueberries or raspberries, and use ⅓ cup ground tapioca powder or arrowroot powder instead of the cornstarch. When you add the cherries, add them all at once. Cherries need more cook time.

DOUGH-NOT

Some pie makers use a thickener called Clear-Jel in their fruit pies. This modified food starch is great for firming up fruit pies and fillings, but it's processed in a facility that also packages nonvegan products containing eggs and milk. If that isn't an issue to you, it would be a good alternative thickener.

Chocolate Mousse Filling

Soft, silky, and smooth, this chocolate "mousse" filling, made thick and sweet with agave syrup, vegan chocolate chips, and silken tofu, is perfect for filling between cake layers. Or eating straight from the bowl!

Yield:	Prep time:
3½ cups	15 to 20 minutes

1¾ cups vegan semisweet chocolate chips or 1 (10-oz.) vegan chocolate bar, chopped

1 (12-oz.) pkg. soft silken tofu, drained

¼ cup warm soy, rice, or almond milk (optional for thinner Chocolate Mousse)

3 TB. agave or brown rice syrup

1 tsp. pure vanilla extract, or ½ tsp. almond extract

⅛ tsp. ground cinnamon (optional)

1. In a medium microwave-safe bowl, microwave chocolate on medium power for 1 or 2 minutes, stirring every 15 seconds or so, or until melted. Alternately, you can melt chocolate in a bowl over hot water. Be sure no water comes into contact with chocolate, or it will seize up. Let cool slightly.

2. In a blender, combine soft silken tofu, warm soy milk (if using), agave syrup, vanilla extract, and ground cinnamon (if using). Blend on high speed for 1 or 2 minutes or until nice and smooth. Scrape blender with a rubber spatula as needed.

3. Slowly add melted vegan chocolate to tofu mixture, and blend on high for 1 to 3 minutes or until well blended, with no lumps, scraping down the sides of the blender as needed with a rubber spatula.

4. Remove to a medium bowl, and chill for 2 or 3 hours or until firm. Keep refrigerated for up to 5 days.

Variations: This Chocolate Mousse is very thick and can easily be scooped and made into chocolate truffles. If you desire a softer, more puddinglike mousse, add the ¼ cup warm soy milk to the tofu when blending. You can lighten this mousse by folding in 1 cup Whipped Topping (recipe earlier in this chapter). Or layer Chocolate Mousse with Whipped Topping in parfait glasses and sprinkle with chocolate shavings.

BAKER'S BONUS

Vegan chocolate shavings and curls are a lovely way to decorate vegan desserts. All you need is a vegan chocolate bar and a vegetable peeler with a metal blade. For short, brittle chocolate shavings, hold a cool chocolate bar with one side wrapped in a paper towel in one hand. Shred the chocolate bar by pushing the vegetable peeler away from you. The lighter your touch, the shorter and smaller shavings you'll produce. For chocolate curls, microwave a vegan chocolate bar for 5 seconds. Wrap a paper towel around one end of the bar to hold, and firmly pull the peeler toward you to create curls. The more pressure you exert, the thicker and longer the curls.

Glossary

agar-agar Also known as agar or kanten, agar-agar is an odorless and tasteless seaweed derivative used as a vegan alternative to animal-based gelatin.

agave nectar Also known as agave syrup, agave nectar is a liquid sweetener derived from the Mexican agave cactus. It has a light, delicate flavor sweeter than honey. Agave is often used as a vegan alternative to honey in cooking. It also has a much lower glycemic index and glycemic load than table sugar (sucrose).

all-purpose flour Flour that contains only the inner part of the wheat grain. It's usable for all purposes, from cakes to gravies. It has equal protein and starch content, as opposed to cake flour, which has more starch for a more tender product, or bread flour, which has more protein (glutenin) for tougher elasticity.

allspice Named for its flavor echoes of several spices (cinnamon, cloves, nutmeg), allspice is used in many desserts and in rich marinades and stews.

almonds Mild, sweet, and crunchy nuts that combine nicely with creamy and sweet foods.

arrowroot A starch that comes from the tubers of the arrowroot plant. Virtually tasteless, arrowroot is a snow-white powder used as a thickener much like cornstarch but without the pasty mouthfeel. It thickens at a lower temperature than cornstarch, and it doesn't weaken with acidic ingredients.

bake To cook in a dry oven. Dry-heat cooking often results in a crisping of the exterior of the food being cooked. Moist-heat cooking, through methods such as steaming, poaching, etc., brings a much different, moist quality to the food.

baking powder A dry leavening agent used in baking. It usually contains alkali. Baking powder is sodium bicarbonate (baking soda) with the addition of an acidic salt, which causes activation when moistened and heated. Traditionally recipes needed baking soda and an acidic ingredient (like vinegar or molasses) to get the carbon dioxide to erupt.

baking soda Bicarbonate of soda, it must be combined with an acid to activate. Activation results in the gas carbon dioxide, which leavens baked goods.

beat To quickly mix substances.

beet sugar Sugar made from sugar beets and processed much like cane sugar. Unlike cane sugar, it's never bleached with bone char.

blackstrap molasses A dark, thick, bittersweet syrup that results from the production of sugar. It contains several B vitamins, calcium, magnesium, potassium, iron, copper, and manganese. All molasses is a product of sugar refinement.

blend To completely mix something, usually with a blender or food processor, more slowly than beating.

blind-baking Also known as prebaking, blind-baking is the method of partially or fully baking an empty crust specifically for pies and tarts filled with refrigerated fillings and pudding or cream fillings, and for pie crusts that need a little more baking time than the filling needs. Partially blind-baking also helps prevent the crust from becoming soggy when baking custardlike pies.

Bob's Red Mill All Natural Egg Replacer Unlike Ener-G Egg Replacer, this egg substitute contains wheat gluten, so it's *not* suitable for gluten-free diets.

boil To heat a liquid to a point where water is forced to turn into steam, causing the liquid to bubble. To boil something is to insert it into boiling water. A rapid boil (212°F at sea level) produces a lot of bubbles on the surface of the liquid.

breadcrumbs Tiny pieces of crumbled dry bread, often used for topping or coating.

cacao nibs The small, broken pieces of shelled, raw cacao beans used to produce chocolate. They're dark brown with a slightly bittersweet, coffeelike flavor.

cake flour A high-starch, soft, and fine flour used primarily for cakes. Cake flour has high starch–low protein content, which produces a tender crumb. It can be used instead of pastry flour.

caraway A distinctive spicy seed used for bread, cheese, and cabbage dishes. It's known to reduce stomach upset, which is why it's often paired with, for example, sauerkraut.

cardamom An intense, sweet-smelling spice, common to Indian cooking, used in baking and coffee.

carob   A tropical tree that produces long pods. The dried, baked, and powdered flesh of the pods (carob powder) is used in baking, and the fresh and dried pods are used for a variety of recipes. The flavor is sweet and reminiscent of chocolate.

chop   To cut into pieces, usually qualified by an adverb such as "coarsely chopped," or by a size measurement such as "chopped into $\frac{1}{2}$-inch pieces." "Finely chopped" is much closer to minced.

cider vinegar   Vinegar produced from apple cider, popular in North America. Cider vinegar mixed with baking soda creates a chemical reaction that helps baked goods rise. This alternative is a good leavening substitute for eggs because it creates the gas carbon dioxide.

cinnamon   A rich, aromatic spice from the bark of a tree, commonly used in baking or desserts. It can also be used for delicious and interesting entrées.

clove   A sweet, strong, almost wintergreen-flavor spice used in baking.

cornmeal   Cornmeal comes in fine, medium, and coarse grind and yellow, white, and blue colors. Steel-cut yellow cornmeal is ground with almost all the husk and germ removed. Stone-ground cornmeal is a bit nuttier. White cornmeal is most often used in Southern cooking for cornbread. Blue cornmeal is a little more rare.

cream of tartar   A by-product of winemaking, the potassium acid salt of tartaric acid, a carboxylic acid, it is needed to create carbon dioxide with baking soda to leaven. A white, odorless, acidic powder used for many culinary and other household purposes, it prevents sugar syrups from crystallizing.

crumb   A tender crumb is something to be desired when baking cakes, muffins, and bread. *Crumb* refers to the internal structure of the baked good. When saying something has a tender crumb, it generally means the item has an even texture, not crumbly or ragged.

custard   A cooked mixture of eggs and milk popular as a base for desserts. Although not a true custard, "mock" custard can be made using soft silken tofu without the eggs.

cut in   A method of incorporating a fat, such as nonhydrogenated vegan margarine, into dry ingredients by breaking it into small pieces. With heat, moisture is released from the fat, creating a flaky texture.

dash   A few drops, usually of a liquid, released by a quick shake of, for example, a bottle of hot sauce.

dollop   A spoonful of something creamy and thick, like vegan sour cream or vegan whipped topping.

double boiler   A set of two pots designed to nest together, one inside the other, and provide consistent, moist heat for foods that need delicate treatment. The bottom pot holds water (not quite touching the bottom of the top pot); the top pot holds the ingredient you want to heat.

dredge   To cover a piece of food with a dry substance such as flour or cornmeal.

drizzle   To lightly sprinkle drops of a liquid over food, often as the finishing touch to a dish.

Earth Balance vegan margarine   A nonhydrogenated expeller-pressed natural oil blend (soybean, palm fruit, canola, and olive oils), with soy protein, soy lecithin, and lactic acid derived from sugar beets. It's 100 percent vegan and can be used interchangeably in most recipes that call for butter or margarine.

Ener-G Egg Replacer   A product made with potato starch, tapioca flour, and leavening agents that can be substituted for eggs in many vegan baked goods.

flaxseed   Flaxseeds come in brown or golden, or you can purchase already ground flaxseed meal. The whole seeds can be used raw or toasted for a nutty flavor. Ground flaxseed acts as a binder, taking the place of eggs in certain recipes, while adding a good deal of fiber, too.

Florida Crystals   Made from pure sugar cane, organic Florida Crystals have no additives and can be used in most recipes that call for granulated sugar.

flour   Grains ground into a meal. Wheat is perhaps the most common flour. Flour is also made from oats, rye, buckwheat, soybeans, etc. *See also* all-purpose flour; cake flour; whole-wheat flour.

focaccia   Similar to pizza, focaccia is a flat, oven-baked bread usually seasoned with olive oil and herbs and sometimes topped with onions, vegetables, cheese, and salt. Before baking, it's often "docked" by pressing oiled fingers into the dough to create "dimples." Then more olive oil is brushed on and settles in the dimples. Focaccia can be eaten as is or used to make sandwiches.

fold   To combine a dense and light mixture with a circular action from the middle of the bowl.

fructose   Sugar naturally found in fruit, slightly sweeter than granulated sugar.

ginger Available in fresh root or dried, ground form, ginger adds a pungent, sweet, and spicy quality to a dish.

glucose The simplest natural sugar.

graham flour A type of wheat flour used in making graham crackers. It's available in health food stores and most large supermarkets. If you can't find it, substitute all-purpose flour and whole-wheat flour in equal parts.

granulated sugar Most commercial brands of granulated cane sugar are processed using bone char from cattle. Animal bone char is used in the refining process as a whitening filter. Look for organic sugar at the health food store, and read the label to be sure no animal ingredients are used in the processing.

grate To shave into tiny pieces using a sharp rasp or grater.

grease and flour To prepare the baking pan with some sort of fat and flour to produce a nonstick surface. In most cases, we use either nonhydrogenated vegan margarine or a vegan solid shortening such as Crisco and a bit of flour you're using in the recipe.

grind To reduce a large, hard substance, often a seasoning such as peppercorns, to the consistency of sand.

hazelnuts (also filberts) A sweet nut popular in desserts and, to a lesser degree, savory dishes.

knead To work dough to make it pliable so it holds gas bubbles as it bakes. Kneading is fundamental in the process of making yeast breads. Kneading activates the gluten proteins that create elasticity in doughs.

kosher salt A coarse-grained salt made without any additives or iodine.

maple syrup A sweetener made from the sap of sugar maple or black maple trees. Maple syrup comes in different grades. Dark amber or Grade B maple syrup is most often used in baked goods and desserts. Both these grades have a stronger maple flavor than the Fancy Grade A maple syrup used for pancakes.

meld To allow flavors to blend and spread over time. Melding is often why recipes call for overnight refrigeration and is also why some dishes taste better as leftovers.

mold A decorative, shaped metal pan in which contents set up and take the shape of the pan.

nutmeg A sweet, fragrant, musky spice used primarily in baking.

nutritional yeast   An inactive yeast with a nutty, cheeselike flavor. It contains a wide assortment of minerals and B vitamins and can provide a reliable dietary source of B_{12}.

oat bran   The outer husk of the oat grain. It's loaded with fiber and has a rich, nutty flavor.

off-set spatula   A handy tool to use in frosting cakes. This metal spatula has a stiff metal blade bent at an angle near the handle. This shape allows access to get into tight spots an ordinary frosting spatula couldn't reach without tearing up the frosting.

olive oil   A fragrant liquid produced by crushing or pressing olives. Extra-virgin olive oil—the most flavorful and highest quality—is produced from the first pressing of a batch of olives; oil is also produced from later pressings.

pastry blender   A U-shape tool consisting of several wires with a handle. It's used to cut fat into dry ingredients.

pecans   Rich, buttery nuts, native to North America, that have a high unsaturated fat content.

phyllo   Paper-thin sheets of pastry dough, sold in several varieties made from wheat or spelt flours, used to prepare many sweet and savory Mediterranean and Middle Eastern dishes.

pinch   An unscientific measurement term, the amount of an ingredient—typically a dry, granular substance such as an herb or seasoning—you can hold between your finger and thumb.

poppy seeds   Tiny, slate-blue poppy seeds and poppy seed oil come from the opium poppy plant. They have very little flavor until toasted, when they yield a slightly nutty flavor. These are most often used in pastries.

preheat   To turn on an oven, broiler, or other cooking appliance in advance of cooking so the temperature will be at the desired level when the assembled dish is ready for cooking.

prick   To make small holes in the surface of a food so it won't rise or blister. This is usually done with the tines of a fork.

pulse   To pulse in a food processor means to push the power button on and off multiple times in a row, stopping for 1 or 2 seconds between processing.

score   To make shallow cuts in the surface of a food.

sesame oil   An oil, made from pressing sesame seeds, that's tasteless if clear, and aromatic and flavorful if toasted and brown.

soy margarine   A vegan alternative to dairy butter, this fat is made of partially hydrogenated soy oil and can be substituted in most recipes calling for margarine or butter.

springform pan   A two-piece pan with a removable bottom and sides that spring open with a hinge and latch. The sides are closed and latched when baking and opened after the cake is cool enough to release without it breaking or oozing out.

Sucanat   A brand of sugar made by dehydrating and granulating sugar cane. It has a slightly coarse texture, a dark brown color, and a high concentration of molasses.

tapioca   A starch extracted from the cassava root used as a thickener in puddings, pies, and jellies. Use either whole pearls or quick-cooking tapioca. Quick-cooking or minute tapioca works well in binding pies. Usually, no other preparation is needed. Tapioca is sold in the baking section of most supermarkets.

tofu   A cheeselike substance made from soybeans and soy milk.

turbinado sugar   A sugar made with pure raw sugar cane juice and often labeled as raw cane sugar. It has a golden caramel color; light molasses flavor; and coarse, crystalline texture.

vanilla bean pods   Natural vanilla beans, also known as pods, are a flavoring derived from orchids. Vanilla beans come in long, thin, dried, brown pods that contain thousands of tiny seeds that can be scraped out and used in baking recipes.

vegan buttermilk   Traditional dairy buttermilk is a fermented dairy product that gets its tartness by either artificially adding lactic acid bacteria to cow's milk or from naturally occurring bacteria. Cultured buttermilk is generally pasteurized and homogenized for safety reasons, but it's also a thicker product than traditional buttermilk, which makes it appealing to most bakers. Vegan buttermilk produced with plant-based milk (soy milk) is slightly different from its animal-based counterpart. The end results should be the same in most recipes that call for dairy buttermilk.

vegan confectioners' sugar   Sugar made from either beet or cane sugar (not refined with bone char–based charcoal) that's processed with a starch, such as cornstarch, to prevent caking.

vegan cream cheese   A snow-white imitation cream cheese made with partially hydrogenated soybean oil, guar gum, and sugar. Tofutti brand contains no dairy, cholesterol, lactose, or butterfat.

vegan marshmallow crème   Gluten-free and kosher, this fluffy, sweet, and smooth product is made with brown rice syrup, soy protein, and natural gums and flavors. It can be used in most recipes that call for marshmallow fluff.

vegan sour cream   A unique blend of tofu, lemon juice, oil, vinegar, and salt that, when blended together, makes a product very similar to regular dairy yogurt. It can be used in most recipes that call for sour cream with good results.

vent holes   Small cuts made in the top crust of a double-crusted pie to allow steam to escape from the hot, bubbling filling. They can be as simple as straight knife cuts or scissor snips, or decorative cuts made with tiny cookie cutter shapes.

vital wheat gluten   Also known as instant gluten flour, vital wheat gluten is a powdered form of dehydrated pure wheat gluten (protein) used in the production of seitan.

walnuts   A rich, slightly woody flavored nut.

whisk   To rapidly mix, introducing air to the mixture.

whole-wheat flour   Wheat flour that contains the entire grain.

yeast   Tiny fungi that, when mixed with water, sugar, flour, and heat, release carbon dioxide bubbles, which, in turn, cause the bread to rise.

zest   Small slivers of peel, usually from a citrus fruit such as lemon, lime, or orange.

zester   A kitchen tool used to scrape zest off a fruit. A small grater also works well.

Resources

Maybe you still have some questions about vegan baking, or perhaps veganism itself. You've come to the right place! In this appendix, I've pulled together a whole resource center so you can dig deeper into vegan issues, leisurely browse through some of my favorite vegan cookbooks, or find a new vegan blog or website. Take a look through the links while you're here. There's plenty of vegan love to go around!

Vegan Cookbooks

Balcavage, Dynise. *The Urban Vegan: 250 Simple, Sumptuous Recipes from Street Cart Favorites to Haute Cuisine.* Guilford, CT: Three Forks, 2009.

Gordon, Elizabeth. *Allergy-Free Desserts: Gluten-Free, Dairy-Free, Egg-Free, Soy-Free and Nut-Free Delights.* Hoboken, NJ: Wiley, 2010.

Holechek, Kris. *The 100 Best Vegan Baking Recipes: Amazing Cookies, Cakes, Muffins, Pies, Brownies and Breads.* Berkeley, CA: Ulysses Press, 2009.

Kaminsky, Hannah. *My Sweet Vegan: Passionate About Dessert.* Henderson, NV: Fleming Ink, 2007.

Katzinger, Jennifer. *Flying Apron's Gluten-Free and Vegan Baking Book.* Seattle, WA: Sasquatch Books, 2009.

McCarty, Meredith. *Sweet and Natural: More Than 120 Sugar-Free and Dairy-Free Desserts.* New York, NY: St. Martin's Press, 2001.

McKenna, Erin. *BabyCakes: Vegan, (Mostly) Gluten-Free, and (Mostly) Sugar-Free Recipes from New York's Most Talked-About Bakery.* New York, NY: Clarkson Potter, 2009.

Moskowitz, Isa Chandra, and Terry Hope Romero. *Vegan Cookies Invade Your Cookie Jar: 100 Dairy-Free Recipes for Everyone's Favorite Treats.* Cambridge, MA: Da Capo Lifelong Books, 2009.

———. *Vegan Cupcakes Take Over the World: 75 Dairy-Free Recipes for Cupcakes That Rule.* Cambridge, MA: Da Capo Press, 2006.

———. *Vegan with a Vengeance: Over 150 Delicious, Cheap, Animal-Free Recipes That Rock.* Cambridge, MA: Da Capo Press, 2005.

———. *Veganomicon: The Ultimate Vegan Cookbook.* Cambridge, MA: Da Capo Press, 2007.

Noyes, Tamasin. *American Vegan Kitchen.* Woodstock, VA: Vegan Heritage Press, 2010.

Patrick-Goudreau, Colleen. *The Joy of Vegan Baking: The Compassionate Cooks' Traditional Treats and Sinful Sweets.* Beverly, MA: Fair Winds Press, 2007.

Robertson, Robin. *1,000 Vegan Recipes.* Hoboken, NJ: Wiley, 2005.

Valencik, Sharon. *Sweet Utopia: Simply Stunning Vegan Desserts.* Summertown, TN: Book Publishing Company, 2009.

Villamagna, M.S.J. Dana. *The Complete Idiot's Guide to Vegan Eating for Kids.* Indianapolis, IN: Alpha Books, 2010.

Vegan Health and Nutrition Books

Bennett, Beverly Lynn, and Ray Sammartano. *The Complete Idiot's Guide to Vegan Living.* Indianapolis, IN: Alpha Books, 2005.

Davis, Brenda, and Vesanto Melina. *Becoming Vegan: The Complete Guide to Adopting a Healthy Plant-Based Diet.* Summertown, TN: Book Publishing Company, 2000.

Diamond, Harvey, and Marilyn Diamond. *Fit for Life.* New York, NY: Warner Books, 1985.

Marcus, Erik. *The Ultimate Vegan Guide: Compassionate Living Without Sacrifice.* Santa Cruz, CA: CreateSpace, 2008.

Saunders, Kerrie. *The Vegan Diet as Chronic Disease Prevention: Evidence Supporting the New Four Food Groups.* Brooklyn, NY: Lantern Books, 2003.

Silverstone, Alicia. *The Kind Diet: A Simple Guide to Feeling Great, Losing Weight, and Saving the Planet.* Emmaus, PA: Rodale Books, 2009.

Taylor, Sarah. *Vegan in 30 Days: Get Healthy. Save the World.* Gig Harbor, WA: Taylor Presentations, Inc., 2008.

Tuttle, Will. *World Peace Diet: Eating for Spiritual Health and Social Harmony.* Brooklyn, NY: Lantern Books, 2005.

Books on Vegan Issues

Baur, Gene. *Farm Sanctuary: Changing Hearts and Minds About Animals and Food.* New York, NY: Touchstone, 2008.

Joy, Melanie, Ph.D. *Why We Love Dogs, Eat Pigs, and Wear Cows: An Introduction to Carnism.* Newburyport, MA: Conari Press, 2009.

Marcus, Erik. *Vegan: The New Ethics of Eating.* Ithaca, NY: McBooks Press, 2000.

Masson, Jeffrey Moussaieff. *The Face on Your Plate: The Truth About Food.* New York, NY: W. W. Norton and Company, 2010.

Robbins, John. *The Food Revolution: How Your Diet Can Help Save Your Life and Our World.* Newburyport, MA: Conari Press, 2001.

———. *Diet for a New America.* Tiburon, CA: HJ Kramer, 1998.

Schlosser, Eric. *Fast Food Nation: The Dark Side of the All-American Meal.* New York, NY: Harper Perennial, 2005.

Torres, Bob, and Jenna Torres. *Vegan Freak: Being Vegan in a Non-Vegan World.* Oakland, CA: PM Press, 2010.

Vegan Nutrition Websites

American Vegan
www.americanvegan.org

Go Veg
www.goveg.com

Go Vegan
www.govegan.net

Vegan.com
www.vegan.com

Vegan Action
www.vegan.org

The Vegan Society
www.vegansociety.com

The Vegan Store
www.veganstore.com

Favorite Vegan Blogs

FatFree Vegan Kitchen
blog.fatfreevegan.com

Vegalicious Recipes
www.vegalicious.org

Healthy. Happy. Life.
kblog.lunchboxbunch.com

Vegan Baking.net
www.veganbaking.net

The Joy of Vegan Baking
www.joyofveganbaking.com

The Vegan Chef
www.veganchef.com

Namely Marly
www.namelymarly.com

Vegan Planet
veganplanet.blogspot.com

Post Punk Kitchen
www.theppk.com

VeganYumYum
veganyumyum.com

Random Hag
www.randomgirl.com

VegFamily
www.vegfamily.com

Index